Selected as a *Foreign Affa*

"Even for jaded Civil War readers who think they have explored the war from every conceivable angle, this is fresh material compellingly explored.... Mr. Smith is onto something original and important, and his relentless intensity, rigorous attention to detail and dazzling vocabulary make for a beguiling, if occasionally numbing, read." —*Wall Street Journal*

"Smith braids his interest in the senses and Civil War history into a burnished gem of a book that bracingly defamiliarizes intensively worked terrain.... Graceful, insightful, and forceful in its brevity, this book should earn a place as a touchstone of contemporary Civil War historiography."—*Journal of American History*

"Many Americans experienced their Civil War as a cacophony of exploding shells, the sight of burning buildings, the stench of rotting corpses, the taste of spoiled rations in the armies or mule meat in starving cities under siege, and the touch of unwashed bodies crowded in small spaces. A pioneer in the field of 'sensory history,' Mark Smith re-creates these unpleasant experiences as closely as possible through the medium of the printed word."—James M. McPherson

" 'The real war will never get in the books.' This may be the most famous sentence ever written about the Civil War.... Even before its official start in 2011, the Civil War sesquicentennial has brought many attempts to prove [Walt] Whitman wrong.... [P]erhaps most striking is the surge of books that belong to what might be called the school of gore—exemplified most recently by Mark M. Smith's *The Smell of Battle, the Taste of Siege: A Sensory History of the Civil War*—books that almost seem to savor the range of ways in which living bodies were converted into corpses by fire or disease, in mud or in bed, quickly enough to block awareness of death's arrival, or slowly enough to taunt the dying with false promises of reprieve."—*The New York Review of Books*

"...[T]his book is a vital first step in making sense of the Civil War's sensate past. It will sharpen historians' sensibilities of how combatants processed 'the smells of battle, the tastes of sieges, the traumatic pain of injury, the sights of engagement, and the sounds of strife, loss, and victory.' It will encourage historians to subject other events to similar analysis—'to turn up the volume, to make the whiffs smell, the caresses touch.' "—*Chronicle Review*

"Eminently readable.... *The Smell of Battle* is an unconventional history of the Civil War, written with special attention to olfaction, touch, taste, sight, and hearing. It joins other recent histories of the war—Drew Gilpin Faust's *This Republic of Suffering: Death and the American Civil War*; Michael C. C. Adams' *Living Hell: The Dark Side of the Civil War*—in trying to represent the war's massive levels of death and disruption so that 21st-century readers will really *feel* the history, deep in their bones.... Sensory history, *The Smell of Battle* makes clear, is more than just an exercise in providing colorful detail.... A book like Smith's, which tries to put reports of sights, sounds, and tastes in context, is a powerful argument for the importance of reading original historical sources while trying to understand the social mores of the time."—*Slate*

"Historians often ask readers to imagine the intense sights, sounds, and smells of battle. Smith goes one step further and explores how such sensory assaults affect the conduct of war itself.... Smith gets into these gritty details by narrating some of the most important encounters of the American Civil War: the noise of the shelling of Fort Sumter; the confusion caused by the proliferation of different uniforms and badges at the First Battle of Bull Run; the stench of death at Gettysburg, which lingered from July to October; the hunger caused by the siege of Vicksburg; and the claustrophobic conditions faced by the crew of a crude Confederate submarine."—*Foreign Affairs*

"*The Smell of Battle, the Taste of Siege* is an incredible book, one not only to read but also to be felt. Using diaries and letters, it provides us with a look at what it must have been like to be there—how it sounded, smelled, tasted and felt. Well-written and moving at times, it provides readers with an aspect of the war that has been neglected by historians."—*Bowling Green Daily News*

"Turning his historical eye (and ear and nose...) to the sensory experience of war provides Smith the opportunity to write more evocatively than most historians, to bring to life the individualized experience of war—the howl of the cannons, the smell of burning horses, the taste of mule meat—in ways other histories cannot."—*Failure Magazine*

The Smell of Battle, the Taste of Siege

A Sensory History of the Civil War

Mark M. Smith

OXFORD
UNIVERSITY PRESS

OXFORD
UNIVERSITY PRESS

Oxford University Press is a department of the University of Oxford.
It furthers the University's objective of excellence in research, scholarship,
and education by publishing worldwide.

Oxford   New York

Auckland   Cape Town   Dar es Salaam   Hong Kong   Karachi
Kuala Lumpur   Madrid   Melbourne   Mexico City   Nairobi
New Delhi   Shanghai   Taipei   Toronto

With offices in

Argentina   Austria   Brazil   Chile   Czech Republic   France   Greece
Guatemala   Hungary   Italy   Japan   Poland   Portugal   Singapore
South Korea   Switzerland   Thailand   Turkey   Ukraine   Vietnam

Oxford is a registered trademark of Oxford University Press
in the UK and certain other countries.

Published in the United States of America by
Oxford University Press
198 Madison Avenue, New York, NY 10016

Library of Congress Cataloging-in-Publication Data
Smith, Mark M. (Mark Michael), 1968–
The smell of battle, the taste of siege : a sensory history of the Civil War / Mark M. Smith.
pages cm
Includes bibliographical references and index.
ISBN 978–0–19–975998–9 (hardcover); 978–0–19–065852–6 (paperback)
1. United States—History—Civil War, 1861–1865—Social aspects.   2. United States—
History—Civil War, 1861–1865—Psychological aspects.   3. Senses and sensation—
United States—History—19th century.   4. United States—History—Civil War,
1861–1865—Personal narratives.   I. Title.
E468.9.S654 2015
973.7'1—dc23
2014012114

For Connor

The Civil War is our only "felt" history—history lived in the national imagination. This is not to say that the War is always, and by all men, felt in the same way . . . . It is an overwhelming and vital image of human, and national, experience.

ROBERT PENN WARREN,
The Legacy of the Civil War (1961)

CONTENTS

List of Figures and Maps | xi

Introduction | 1

Chapter One: The Sounds of Secession | 9

Chapter Two: Eyeing First Bull Run | 39

Chapter Three: Cornelia Hancock's Sense of Smell | 66

Chapter Four: The Hollowing of Vicksburg | 84

Chapter Five: The *Hunley*'s Impact | 115

Epilogue: Experiencing Total War | 134

ACKNOWLEDGMENTS | 147
NOTE ON SOURCES | 150
NOTES | 153
INDEX | 189

LIST OF FIGURES AND MAPS

Figures

1.1. The Sounds of Secession, Charleston, 1860   20
1.2. The Sounds of Politics, Charleston, 1860   22
1.3. The Sounds of War   35
2.1. Seeing Death at First Bull Run?   64
2.2. First Battle of Bull Run   65
3.1. Cornelia Hancock   68
3.2. Gettysburg, Pa. Confederate dead gathered for burial at the edge of the Rose Woods, July 5, 1863   76
3.3. Dead Horses of Bigelow's (Ninth Massachusetts) Battery, 1863   82
4.1. The Siege of Vicksburg   93
4.2. Vicksburg Riddled   99
5.1. Schematic of the *H. L. Hunley* submarine   118
5.2. Interior view of the *H. L. Hunley* showing crankshaft and bench   121
5.3. The First Cotton Gin   129
6.1. Columbia, South Carolina, after Sherman   143
6.2. Charleston, South Carolina, at War's End   145
6.3. The Sounds of Freedom   146

Maps

1.1. Charleston Harbor, 1861   12
2.1. Seeing from Above: First Bull Run   41
4.1. Vicksburg   85

Introduction

How Did People Experience the American Civil War?
Eight years before South Carolina seceded from the Union in 1860, the wildly popular periodical *Harper's New Monthly Magazine* ran a piece that would go some way toward answering this question. The 1852 essay summarized contemporary knowledge and understanding of the five senses. Central to the piece was the idea that they not only required cultivation and careful tending but also were themselves helpful proxies for what it meant to be civilized and noble. The senses were "our perpetual bodyguards, surrounding us unceasingly," and Americans had to understand how to properly use and care for their sense receptors—their eyes, ears, noses, tongues, and skins. They also had to learn to appreciate these "powerful agents in life" as reliable cultivators of refinement, standing, and character that, as such, should not become polluted. The "eye should not be injured by resting on a vulgar confusion of colors, or clumsy, ill-proportioned forms; the ear should not be falsified by discordant sounds and harsh, unloving voices; the nose should not be a receptacle for impure odors; each sense should be preserved in its purity." A great deal was at stake, the essay's author implied: impure sensory experience, experience that did not cultivate the senses, that jarred, strained, and overloaded them, could weaken the character of man and, by extension, that of the nation.[1]

A certain confidence underpinned the piece, based as it was on an assumption that Americans of the 1850s had gone some way toward mastering their sensory environments. Social protocols, laws, and advances in technology lent late antebellum America an aura of sensory stability. In the larger towns and cities especially, noise ordinances, social pressure, and architecture supposedly contained noise and noisemakers. Personal hygiene had increasingly deodorized the air, and rudimentary sewage systems had started to channel stench underground. Touching—who got to touch whom, how, and where—was socially prescribed and regulated. Aesthetic taste had been braided with gustatory taste, which, in turn, was increasingly controllable, courtesy of the market revolution that delivered better quality food to discerning palates. And the idea that seeing was believing—thanks to technologies of vision such as photography and print—was all but received wisdom.

Such conceits would be exposed in a few years' time. The looming war, unimaginable by most, would injure and pollute eyes, subjecting them to new, confusing sights; expose ears to sounds discordant and inhuman; bombard noses with odors rank, fetid, and impure; treat skin with a new, brutal contempt; and initiate radical changes in taste. The sensory experience of the American Civil War reminded Americans, North and South, that their putative mastery of the senses was, in fact, hollow. This war, one veined with meaningful talk about the nobility of the Union, the morality of Emancipation, and the nonnegotiable need to preserve American civilization, was also a war whose sensory experience overwhelmed refined sensibilities and effaced the very notion of civility.[2]

As with all things to do with the Civil War, the question of what it meant to experience it has been asked and answered many times and in many different ways. Every year, thousands of people attempt to reexperience the war by re-enacting it. Central to their efforts is an attempt to re-create what it was like. In their quest to experience the authentic Civil War, many go to incredible lengths. They adopt period garb, accurate in every detail, down to stitching and buttons; prior to re-enacting, say, the Battle of Gettysburg, many refuse to wash, believing they can thereby smell more like the troops who did battle those sweltering July days in 1863; still others eat only replications of what the soldiers at the time would have chewed and swallowed. They also endure the numbing chafe of boots and uniforms on skin and listen hard for the shrill sounds of muskets, rifles, and gut-churning, booming cannon.[3]

There are problems with re-enactments, of course. They can con the participants into believing that they are experiencing the sensations the same way and with the same meaning contemporaries attached to them. Plainly, that cannot be the case. The meaning people attached to certain sensory experiences in, say, 1863 cannot be understood with the same or even similar meaning today. What sounded loud or smelled rancid or tasted foul in the 1860s is different and even irretrievable, not least because history has happened between then and now. Events and developments have changed our sensory habits, the ways we hear, smell, and taste—sense generally—and the meaning we attach to those sensations. Our refrigerated, food-processed age has changed our judgment of taste, for example: what we might consider stale and unpalatable now was likely deemed edible and appropriate in the prerefrigerated past; what we think of as sweet-tasting now would have been wholly alien to a tongue in medieval Europe when there was no sugar (only honey). The same is true of the other senses. The meaning of touching—who could touch whom and how—has also changed, not least because that terrible war nobly ended slavery, the power of ruthless tactile force gradually being replaced by the invisible, touchless hand of the market. What is loud, quiet, and noisy now was qualitatively and quantitatively different in a preautomobile, prejet, preelectronic age. And so on.[4]

The most ardent re-enactors also assume that they are able to reproduce the sounds, taste, sights, touches, and smells of the past with fidelity. For example, acoustic shadows—sounds that seemed to come from one direction but really originated elsewhere on the battlefield—were important in deciding the outcome of several

Civil War battles and skirmishes.[5] But they were purely a product of their moment, hostage to their own, unique, historical time, dependent on weather, topography, and the position of listening ears. Acoustic shadows cannot be re-created; without them, it is impossible to re-enact engagements where they were important.

More than that, only certain aspects of the war are ever re-enacted. There is a reason re-enactors do not attempt to recapture the air-gulping desperation of Civil War sailors drowning in doomed submarines or attempt to reexperience the lice-ridden, stomach-churning ordeals of Civil War prisoners. There is good reason they use blanks and not real bullets and never bayonet-charge one another to the point of slitting skin. When accidents happen on Civil War re-enactment battlefields—when people get injured—they are whisked away in ambulances, not left to fester, reek, and writhe on the battlefield.

Whatever the shortcomings of re-enactment—and there are many—there is nonetheless something laudable in trying to understand the experiences of the Civil War through attention to the senses. The problem with re-enactment is not that it attempts to reexperience the past by paying special attention to how people sensed the war. This, in fact, is the benefit of the whole exercise. Rather, the problem has to do with the perhaps unwitting warping of history that re-enactment entails. The desire to re-enact tells us more about our desire to consume—to experience—the past than it does about what people at the time thought about their experience, how they—not we—understood the smells of battle, the tastes of sieges, the traumatic pain of injury, the sights of engagement, and the sounds of strife, loss, and victory.

Re-enactors are not the only ones who have paid attention to the sensory experiences of the Civil War. Historians and writers—Shelby Foote, Bruce Catton, and Bell Irvin Wiley, among others—use the poetics of the senses to great effect. They evoke the immediacy, depth, feeling, and texture of battle experience and soldiering life. They capture and convey this not only because their command of the evidence is so masterful but also because they know how to use sensory evidence. Their narratives are riddled with sounds, whiffs, stenches, the feel of violence as well as the tender caresses.[6] This is because they are, primarily, writers rather than academics.

It is not that these writers have not noted the relevance of, say, smell, sound, and touch to the experience of war; they clearly have. But they have not always done so in either a sustained fashion or an especially historicized one. Put another way, when such writers as Foote and Catton tell us that various battlefields reeked, we enjoy the poetry of the description but are left with unanswered questions that perhaps only a historian of the senses—or "sensory historian"—can answer: what did *reek* mean in the context of 1863? Whose nose was doing the smelling? Is there a larger meaning, one independent of that particular place and time? These questions, and the effort to historicize the senses, animate this book.

It is increasingly apparent that virtually any period from the past can be understood in a more textured fashion by trying to uncover (not recover) the sensory experience of people at the time. Books abound on any number of topics—the history of sound in colonial America, of touch in early modern England, of sight in Victorian London—but relatively little sensory history has been written of wars generally or of this war in particular.[7] Any war offers especially fertile ground and is worthy of its own sensory history. Yet the Civil War generated and circulated new and especially intense sensory experiences. Part of this had to do with the scale of the event: four long years involving more than 3 million soldiers and countless civilians, resulting in the deaths of roughly 750,000 troops. The sheer concentration of soldiers and the technology of warfare took a toll on an unprecedented scale. So, too, sounds, smells, sights, tastes, and touches were overwhelming in scope and intensity.

Yet four years of fighting deadened some to the experience of war, and sounds, for example, once so new in 1861 became depressingly normal, simply part of the fabric of the American soundscape by 1865. Like the other sensory experiences, they became part of the texture of American life. Whatever else this war was about—liberty and freedom, Union and state sovereignty—it was also a war that rearranged the sensory experiences of the participants—soldiers, civilians, women, slaves, sailors—in profound ways. The nation that had prided itself on its civilized control of the senses lost that control.[8]

We know this because the evidence pointing to sensory experience during the war is ubiquitous. We find it everywhere—clearly detectable in diaries, letters, official reports, and newspapers. People left evidence of one sort or another, revealing not only what senses were at play during the war but also how they experienced them. The evidence is so commonplace that it often sits in secondary sources, too, ready to be read and extracted for different effect.

New sources were not necessary to write this book; old sources offered new ways to locate sensory evidence. Even the most written-about events revealed just how important the senses were to mediating experience and even, in some instances, shaping the outcome. In fact, I have been quite deliberate in selecting some of the best known events of the war to show just how central the senses were to them. Choosing them highlights how careful attention to the senses can help us better experience the familiar.

Any number of moments during the war could be subject to similar analysis, and I hope that this book will encourage this.[9] It aims to foreground what has often been back-grounded, to turn up the volume, to make the whiffs smell, the caresses touch. Most history is based on what was observed, reflecting Enlightenment beliefs about sight and truth. Too, the proliferation of supposedly objective visual technologies like photographs, telescopes, and print itself, has sometimes resulted in a preference for the reliability of "eye" witnesses and not "ear" or "nose" witnesses. I show that the nonvisual senses were also important in shaping the experience of war in and of themselves—and not simply during moments when soldiers couldn't see because smoke, geography, or other factors clouded vision. Rather, the nonvisual senses played their own roles in shaping experience, sometimes in concert with vision, sometime independently of it.[10]

The experience of this war—told through the voices of soldiers, sailors, women, and slaves—was inherently a sensory one, giving us more than an eyewitness account. Attention to these voices tells us how all of the senses were not only engaged throughout those four dreadful years but also took on particular importance. They reveal how certain events assumed principal sensory signatures—how, for example, the Battle of Gettysburg was, of course, very much about sights but also about sound, touch, and especially smell; how and why the siege at Vicksburg moved from being very much an auditory affair (given the ferocious shelling the city took) to becoming a story about taste and the denigration of palate.

It is important not to be reductive. I do not pretend that the firing on Fort Sumter was simply and exclusively an auditory affair or that the experience of Confederate submariners on the *H. L. Hunley* was just a tactile experience or that First Bull Run was only a visual moment. All of the senses were animated in all of these events. War is hell on them; the violence of it engraves sensory memory in ways other experiences cannot approach, memory so powerful it can be relived, over and over again. Indeed, as far as the senses are concerned, all war is total war, pushing them to their limits and beyond, dulling and then overwhelming and then dulling them again. Distinctions become muddied, nerves fray, and the sense of self shatters. Whether the Civil War was a total war is a frequent topic of debate. At the very least, we can say that it exposed Americans to experiences that had been until then beyond their ability to comprehend and, if they survived them, all but drained them of feeling.

Rather than capture all of those feelings—the sensory totality of war—I propose in this book to isolate the particular senses, devoting one chapter to each of them and their essential role in one event, and premised upon the argument that focusing on one sense might offer a new way of understanding how that event was experienced by those present.

War offers a logic for the very notion of sensory history. Although each of the chapters emphasizes one sense over the others, it is not meant to be artificially exclusionary, for the senses themselves are not. They blend and interact. Nonetheless, I have attempted to find evidence from each event, showing how one sense came to dominate and to overwhelm the others, while also informing them all.

Chapter One

The Sounds of Secession

Evening, December 26, 1860. Charleston, South Carolina. In 1860, the Holy City—as it is sometimes called, given the number of its churches and the Mecca-like significance it held in the hearts of so many Southerners—was a quieter place, without today's constant low rumble of cars, the irritating drone of planes. It was darker then, too. It would be many years before the advent of electric streetlights. Even the then-recently installed but relatively feeble gaslights still allowed the stars to dance, splashing dollops of light on the men gathered below, talking softly among themselves.[1]

Those men were federal troops stationed at Fort Moultrie, standing on Sullivan's Island, a scythelike arm of land arcing into Charleston's harbor. There was no wind, and the crispness of the night—forty-four degrees at 9 P.M.—was in keeping with the clear, beautiful day. The rolling waters of the harbor could both mask sound with their incessant chopping and, in calmer moments, carry it great distances, so that listeners gathered something was happening but had trouble identifying precisely what. The waves also reflected light. No wonder the men were unusually alert.[2]

One of the soldiers was especially pensive, his high, furrowed brow mimicking the rippled water. In his mid-fifties, five feet nine inches tall, he was thickset and "soldierly," with thinning "iron-grey" hair, dark, intelligent eyes, and skin roughened by war in foreign lands. A prominent nose led his face; his voice was rich and sonorous. He had an air of dignity and conviction. Unlike many who would direct the fighting in the Civil War, he was a man of experience. Those intelligent eyes had seen fighting; that strong voice had urged others into battle, sometimes to their death, other times to glory. He had fought against the Florida Indians, served with Abraham Lincoln in the Black Hawk War in 1832, and suffered a nasty wound in the Mexican War. He was once called "a man of undaunted courage." He was also a Southerner in the odd position of being in charge of a federal fort in South Carolina's harbor.[3]

Major Robert Anderson's plan that December night was as audacious as its effect would be dramatic. Its success depended on fooling the ears and the eyes of listening and watching sentinels and on just a little bit of luck. Should he succeed, the United States would be set on a path of destruction, its eventual scale taxing the imagination of even the most fanciful minds. We cannot reliably say that the major's actions the night of December 26, 1860, caused the Civil War. Such a claim simplifies what is messy and contingent. Anderson acted in a context not of his making; he inherited the decisions of others. But his actions that night set into motion a series of events that led to a very bloody war. Had the major not acted, it would have started someplace, somewhere, and very probably in Charleston, South Carolina. It was just too emotionally charged an environment for the spark not to be struck here. Yet it would not have unfolded as it did, had the major not decided to abandon his base at Fort Moultrie and occupy, without explicit orders, the larger, more powerful fort guarding the harbor, Fort Sumter. In doing so, according to the *Charleston Courier*, he "achieved the unenviable distinction of opening civil war."[4]

Water was the challenge. There wasn't much of it between Moultrie and Sumter—barely a mile, in fact. But on that night the swelling crests, imported without tariff from the mighty Atlantic Ocean, were clearly accented by moonlight. So much was visible. And so much could be heard. Human voices, rattling oars, the cut of the boat—all traveled over the water. Ears were everywhere: on land, at sea, on a Confederate patrol boat plying the waters between the forts. Anyone daring to move over that spit of water was vulnerable and exposed. Still, there was no wishing it away, and the water lay between the major and his destination: an impressive granite construction, walls sixty feet high in places, lodged in the mouth of Charleston's harbor (map 1.1).

Getting his men across that choppy stretch of water without being seen or heard required stealth not usually associated with soldiers at the time, who moved in formation with music or shouting. What was required was the stealth of a slave.

For well over a century, Charleston had been evolving into one of the most beautiful yet highly regulated cities in North America. By 1860, it was the largest city in South Carolina and, arguably, the cultural capital of the South (hence, of course, the Holy City). It was also slave country. With a population of just over 70,000, Charleston County's 2,880 slaveholders owned about 37,000 slaves (18,000 men, 19,000 women). The city was also home to a robust free black population (slightly in excess of 3,000) and a steadily increasing population of white Irish and German migrant workers. Although in some ways industrialized in the manner of a Northern city—it boasted forty-six manufacturing establishments in 1860, as well as daily railroad service to Columbia, the state capital—it was, at base, thoroughly Southern.

Slavery dominated not only its economy and society but also its very culture. By the closing decades of the antebellum period, Charleston bore the imprint of the planters, many of whom had residences within the city in addition to their estates scattered around the Lowcountry. Industry was subservient to the slaveholders' aesthetic, which centered on consumption, unapologetic aristocratic pretensions, and a sense of civilization rooted in privilege and hierarchy. The fabulous wealth generated by the "peculiar institution" seeped into the very fabric of the city, helping fund, in full or in part, breathtakingly impressive Federal- and classical-revival-style homes, replete with walled gardens and wrought-iron fences. The churches, public buildings, and hotels were often quite as

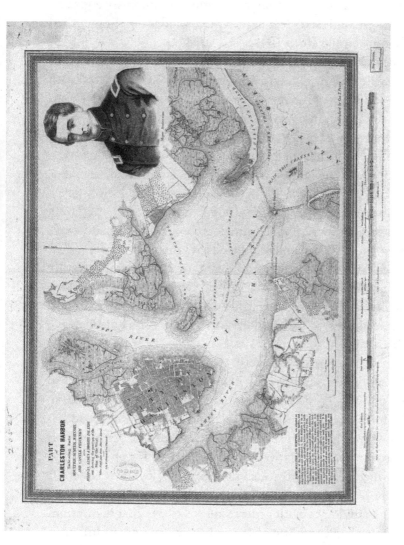

MAP 1.1. *Charleston Harbor, 1861.*

Part of Charleston Harbor, embracing forts Moultrie, Sumter, Johnson, and Castle Pinckney, also Sullivan, James, and Morris islands and showing the position of the Star of the West, when fired into from Morris Island (Philadelphia: Duval & Son, 1861), Call Number G3912.C4 1861.P4, Library of Congress Geography and Map Division, Washington, D.C.

impressive. The main thoroughfares, especially Meeting, were wide, lined with palmettos and magnolias and, thanks to the city's unofficial, airborne sanitation department—in 1852 British visitor William Surtees described dozens of buzzards that swooped down from building tops to "devour any scrap of meat that was tossed away"—relatively clean. The promenade—known then, as now, as the Battery—skirted the harbor's edge and came in for particular praise by visitors and residents alike as a place to walk and, as two sisters visiting the city in 1860 put it, "inhale the pure and cool breezes" that wafted in from the Atlantic. The city's skyline was punctuated by towering church spires, each piercing the air with authority and commanding genuflection from the people looking up from below.[5]

Slavery built this city, and the culture that built slavery defined how people behaved. Like the architects who insisted on precise, balanced, symmetrical classical proportions, the city's ruling population—all men—insisted that their authority be echoed—quite literally—in their city and society at large. It all came down to one word: order. For these men, some of whom ranked among the most influential on the North American continent, slavery was not just desirable; it was essential to the preservation of hierarchy. By 1860, their need for order was in their minds nothing less than absolute, because the very foundation of slavery demanded order; every social relation—between husbands and wives, fathers and sons, masters and slaves—was based on command and on obedience. The world around was crumbling: rapid industrialization, urbanization, the extension of the vote, increasing immigration, and the rise of wage labor—all so pronounced in recent years in nonslaveholding, Northern states—threatened their existence. What if some of those destabilizing qualities fingered their way southward? What if the enslaved saw and heard these Northern iterations of freedom? What if the North managed to gain political ascendancy over the Southern states? What if . . . ? Chills lodged in the spines of the Southern aristocracy.[6]

Slavery was, noted the *Southern Episcopalian* in 1859, "a necessary element towards the composition of a high and stable civilization." Dissension would not be tolerated. Talk about freedom, resist bondage in any way, and the men in power promised to gag and punish you. And they did.[7]

These men in power also wrote order into every crevice of their daily lives. At dances, "the ladies were planted firmly along the walls, in the coldest formality, while the gentlemen . . . stood in close column near the door," as one European visitor to the city observed. Outside, space and movement were similarly regulated. One Englishman saw slaves "walking in the road instead of on the pavement, . . . touching their hats to every white passer-by."[8]

How the city and its inhabitants sounded echoed this order. Slaveholders understood that, as a later *Harpers* article, published in 1856, framed it, "the hearing ear and the seeing eye, the Lord hath made even both of them"; that sounds "form an empire of their own, whose children rule over our feelings and master our thoughts"; that what was heard was indicative of peace, love, danger; that sounds located people and events; that who made which sounds and when revealed their standing, their character, and told of their nobility or betrayed their vice; that the sounds and silences around them marked their degree of civilization or their slip into barbarism.[9] As such, they were attentive listeners, monitoring their society as much through the ear as through the eye.

Of course, cities, given their tendency to concentrate people, were inherently louder than plantations, and many slaveholders recoiled at the "crowd and noise of city life," believing the "hum of men and cities . . . puerile and childish," as the South Carolina novelist William Gilmore Simms put it in 1829. Charleston was no exception. Aspects of how the city sounded were seasonal and particular to the city: February's horse racing brought excited multitudes to the city, filling it with celebratory and raised voices; "the turn-out of the Fire Companies on any gala day" was a loud affair, replete with banners and bands. Beyond that, the slaveholders recognized that Charleston was always going to be boisterous. Cities, especially port cities, were essential to Southern economic life, providing access to the outside world, to which they shipped cotton and from which they imported manufactured goods.[10]

All the slaveholders could do was to try to regulate the sounds. Sometimes they led by example, priding themselves on their own silence, their own calibrated voices, sober and calm. Raucous behavior, noise, undisciplined shouts—all indicated transgressions and affronts to order. The pastoral ideal of harmony, which planters fancied they could hear, literally, in the singing voices of the slaves, in the absence of strife, and in the gentle hum of plantation industriousness, had its urban counterpart in Charleston. "No sound ungrateful to the ear breaks upon the charm of quietness," mused one city listener in 1839, "except the musical chime of the distant bells as they signal the passing hours."[11]

It had been this way for years. Noisy public displays and gatherings on Sundays and special holidays by anyone—white or black—invited arrest by the city guard. The Holy City was supposed to be without strife and tumult. Instead, the sounds of churches, especially the sonorous bells of St. Philip's and St. Michael's, not only boomed out God's time, calling parishioners to worship, but also opened and closed the city's markets. This was deemed entirely suitable. Church and state met in the sound of those bells. They chimed civilization, resoundingly imposing order on Charleston's streets and people.[12]

We should not misunderstand these men: they did embrace limited industrial endeavors, as long as that industry was in tune with slavery; they did adopt some modern elements into their society, tolerating a modest extension of the franchise, the use of clocks and bells to regulate labor, and the hum and bustle of commercial activity. As long as these elements proved supportive of the status quo, the slaveholders embraced them. What they strove ardently to avoid was recklessness, the unhinging of social relations bound by those bound.[13]

And slavery meant controlling slaves. "Charleston keeps in pay a company of police soldiers, who during the night occupy several posts," observed one visitor in the 1820s. "At nine o'clock in the evening, a bell is sounded; and after this no negro can venture without a written permission from his master." For those who broke the rules, there were fines for the master and lashes for the slave. For the most part, it seemed to work. A Scottish visitor to Charleston was surprised to see slaves vanish from the streets at night. If the streets of Charleston were darker and less visible at night, at least they were now quieter, fitting for a society that prided itself on order and highlighting any disruption.[14]

Beyond white Charlestonians' more abstract claims about order, a very real fear underwrote regulations. Put simply, white slaveholders were petrified of servile revolt. History guided them. At least since the mid-eighteenth century, slaves had plotted to insurrect and sometimes succeeded, the results bloody, brutal, and chilling for Lowcountry whites and blacks alike. The Stono Insurrection in 1739, in which more than sixty slaves had tried to battle their way to claim freedom in Spanish Florida, had left twenty whites and more than forty slaves dead. Denmark Vesey's plot in 1822, designed to kill slaveholders and free the city's slaves (or so white authorities claimed), ended with more than thirty hangings. The region's slaveholders had become sensitive to any wrinkle in the social fabric that just might encourage slaves to rebel.

Nighttime was therefore especially worrying. The dark, never truly conquered with streetlights, camouflaged movement, and this fear accounted for the police presence and nightly curfews. Charleston's Margaret Izard Manigault fretted a great deal about insurrection, always fearful of "les villains Noirs." She was haunted by "horrible ideas," especially "at night when nothing interrupts them." Her consternation is loud and clear: "I almost envy those who have already died peaceably in their beds." The fear was felt by visitors, too. Fanny Kemble, the well-known English actress, dwelt on the evening hours especially. She understood that "a most ominous tolling of bells and beating of drums" meant the city guard was clearing the streets of slaves in an effort to minimize the chances of revolt; she plainly preferred to live in a less skittish, nerve-wracking society where she could "sleep without the apprehension of my servants' cutting my throat in bed." As much as she adored the city's architecture, the gardens, the foliage, all so "pleasing to the eye," this was a place all about "dread," veined by a pressing "insecurity," a deep "apprehension." The price to pay for failing to control slaves was almost too horrific for white minds to countenance.[15]

In their insistence on preserving a social order, white Charlestonians paid a psychological price, one measured in fear and jitters. And the slaves themselves, perfectly sensible of what their masters were doing, only upped the ante. You want quiet? Then quiet, deafening quiet, shiver-inducing quiet is what you shall have, reasoned the enslaved. Over the years, they learned the art of stealth, not just to revolt—although quiet, noiseless movement was necessary for that—but also to run away or, more commonly, to carve out degrees of independence in a world that constantly tried to contain them. On the plantations, slaves had learned how to practice their religion beyond the earshot of listening masters—by praying into pots, by understanding sound-absorbing materials, by speaking quietly in their makeshift "hush arbors." At other times, they literally put their ears to the ground, listening for intruders' steps. Those who tried to escape did so by using their ears and eyes, listening for clues in the countryside: was that the sound of waves? Voices? The wind? Avoid those branches—they will crack—and be careful to listen to the sounds of voices, dogs, and horses as you make your way. In the towns, similar practices applied, but urban slaves had a bit more leeway. The gentle buzz of urban activity could mask their sounds, allowing them to move, talk, and exchange with less risk of detection, even at night.

The slaveholders had succeeded too well, or rather, their slaves had taken their insistence on quiet so literally that they had turned it into a weapon. Slaves knew how to move "as silently as a cat" and struck the fear of God into masters. "If they want to kill us," wrote Mary Boykin Chesnut, "they can do it when they please, they are as noiseless as panthers."[16] What the slaveholders secured through the imposition of a predictable, regular soundscape they bought in the currency of frayed nerves and restless nights.

The sculpted world of Charleston's soundscape underwent a profound change beginning in early November 1860. The relatively muted sounds of the city—at least compared with the much louder, cacophonous, and nosier metropolises in the North—exploded. If we could listen to the city between the autumn of 1860 and the late spring of 1861, it would resemble a mounting crescendo, the volume increasingly turned up until eardrums almost shattered. After April 1861, the city's soundscape would never be the same.

That auditory revolution started with the election of Abraham Lincoln on November 6, 1860. A day before, fearing the worst, South Carolina's governor, arch-secessionist William Henry Gist, preemptively recommended the formation of a ten-thousand-strong standing army. News of Lincoln's election reached Charleston on the seventh. Disunionists "ran through the streets shouting 'Hurrah for Lincoln!'" Wealthy plantation owner and political activist Edmund Ruffin "made a fiery secession speech to an immense audience" in the state capital, Columbia. Measured by orations, voices, chatter, and shouts, it was the most sound-filled day in the state's history. By November 9, the state swarmed with militia.[17]

Although never men of understatement, South Carolina's politicians now filled public venues—churches, halls, streets—with vocal, loud, boisterous, strident talk, at a decibel level not heard in generations. Revolutions—even in conservative causes—are rarely quiet affairs; they give an opening to the voices that either want to be heard or claim exclusive right to drown out all others.[18] Echoes of nullification from thirty years ago reverberated loudly. Lincoln's election and all that it seemed to foretell—Southern dependence, the rapid evaporation of order, the dismantling of slavery—gave unprecedented vent to white voices. The frustrations of the past few years, decades even, punched into the public realm like heavy verbal shot landing everywhere.

Hints of the reaction could be detected earlier in the year. In fact, 1860 was very much a year "unusual in the opportunities offered to the political orator." In addition to the usual reviews of militia companies, Fourth of July celebrations, and ceremonies marking the evacuation of Charleston during the Revolutionary War, the spring of 1860 saw a meeting in the city of the state Democratic convention, followed by the national Democratic convention meeting. October was dominated by elections to the state legislature, as well as ratification mass meetings. Oratory, sloganeering, mass rallies, brass bands, and "noise in general" underwrote this hectic political year.[19] As early as July, toasts protesting the federal government were not uncommon in the city and inspired even more talk of secession. By early November, this relatively ceremonious talk degenerated into "violent speeches to the mob," backgrounded by the sounds of military drills.[20]

With Lincoln's election, even once silent Unionists now shouted openly for independent action by the state of South Carolina. But listeners wanted more. Meetings to discuss secession degenerated into little more than "noisy demonstrations." "The populace were becoming excited," wrote US Army officer Abner Doubleday, and it was palpable to the ear[21] (figure 1.1). In keeping with this increased volume, garish images previously unseen by Charleston residents started to appear: blue cockades in hats and flags, "except the National colors, were everywhere." The clamor spread, inspiring even Northerners and tradespeople to post signs in support of secession.[22]

The noise spilled beyond Charleston, deluging the land and architecture with the force of hurricane-driven waters. First, the waves surged across the harbor from the city. By early November, crowds of locals were frequent visitors to Fort Moultrie, sometimes

FIGURE 1.1. *The Sounds of Secession, Charleston, 1860.*

Wood engraving, "The government arsenal in Charleston, S.C., guarded by detachments of the Washington Light Infantry/from a sketch by our special artist," *Frank Leslie's Illustrated Newspaper*, December 1, 1860, p. 25. Reproduction Number: LC-USZ62-132571 (b&w film copy neg.), Library of Congress Prints and Photographs Division Washington, D.C.

marching around it in full view of the federal troops, who were doing their best to ready the vulnerable fortifications in case tensions escalated further.[23] How different it had been but a few months earlier, when Charleston's elite had bustled around Fort Moultrie, using the parapet as a promenade, with the fort's federal band serenading them.[24]

But no longer. Across the harbor, the waves of sound cascaded into buildings. The meeting of the Secession Convention in Columbia was a bust, and delegates reassembled on December 18 in Charleston instead to deliberate. Nestled right next to St. Philip's church and its sonorous bells, they gathered in Institute

Hall—now called Secession Hall—at four o'clock in the afternoon. "Crowds of excited people thronged the streets and open squares of the city, and filled the passage and stairways of the hall." The session there lasted but one hour, time enough for the members to agree to prepare an address to the South.[25]

The hubbub from the streets was too much. "To enable the speakers to be better heard" above the din, they left Institute Hall and adjourned to St. Andrew's Hall, principally to discuss, in relative quiet, the question of what was state and what was federal property in South Carolina. Members of South Carolina's Secession Convention met there on December 19, doors closed, speeches and reports kept to a minimum. The contrast between the commotion of the streets and the deliberations inside was stark. In the hall, slack-mouthed excitement gave way to grave silence as delegates came to terms with the gravity of their decisions. The measured tones had been set earlier, on November 7, during Judge A. G. Magrath's speech announcing his resignation and support of secession, which was met with silence, "without the display of emotion . . . without any demand for hasty action."[26]

By December 20, however, that kind of sober civility was increasingly challenged: Charleston's streets now hummed nervously with anticipation, expectant knots of men gathering on corners, filling the squares hours before the convention's scheduled starting time of noon (figure 1.2). Rumor, ever louder, spread: the committee was ready to pass the Ordinance of Secession that day. As noon approached, milling groups coagulated, forming small crowds that, in turn, gained in size, thronging the streets and narrow alleyways outside St. Andrew's Hall and throughout the city. With large areas of the city's main roads paved, the sounds of feet and voices resounded off the hard surfaces, pinballing down and around the streets. The mood inside the hall remained determinedly somber. "Ordinary business" of the convention "was quietly disposed of." This was a historic moment in their city's history, their state's history—their country's history—and one to be approached with calm deliberation. "Quietly the Convention

FIGURE 1.2. *The Sounds of Politics, Charleston, 1860.*

Frank Leslie's Illustrated Newspaper, wood engraving, "Great mass meeting to endorse the call of the Legislature of South Carolina for a state convention to discuss the question of secession from the Union, held at Institute Hall, Charleston, S.C., on Monday, Nov. 12, 1860." Reproduction Number: LC-USZ62-48464, Library of Congress Prints and Photographs Division Washington, D.C.

had met and had been opened with prayer to God. There was no excitement. There was no visible sign that the Commonwealth of South Carolina was about to take a step more momentous for weal or woe than had yet been known in her history."[27]

As the chairman of the committee, Chancellor Inglis of Chesterfield, rose to report the secession ordinance, an "immediate silence pervaded the whole assemblage as every eye turned to the speaker." Garrulousness seemed rude, unfitting; the "fewest and simplest words" were all that were necessary for reporting on the committee's ordinance. It was read aloud, each word given its full weight.[28]

And then it started, the sound of political voices, growing from a murmur to a shout, and that would culminate, months later, in explosions and booms. At 1:30 P.M., 169 voices, unanimous, said yea. The Union had been cut off; secession was now full-throated, spilling out of the assembly into the streets, as the convention made its way back to Institute Hall, where they would meet with the governor, Francis W. Pickens, and both legislative branches. Moving in procession, the assembly was greeted by noisy, cheering crowds.[29]

Where St. Andrew's Hall had been hushed, the scene in Institute Hall was boisterous. The news simply could not be contained, inside or out. Outside, men roared, women's scarves snapped in the wind, and hats were raised high above heads. Inside, excited men and women packed the galleries; the crowded hall hummed, resounding with applause as the leaders of secession signed the ordinance.[30]

Sentence was pronounced by the president of the Secession Convention, D. F. Jamison of Barnwell: "The Ordinance of Secession has been signed and ratified, and I proclaim the State of South Carolina an independent Commonwealth." A "storm of cheers" from the audience "shook the very building, reverberating, long continued." The noise "rose to Heaven, and ceased only with the loss of breath," wrote Samuel Wylie Crawford, a US Army surgeon who witnessed the entire scene. Individuals merged into a whole, seemingly one. Men and women rushed outside, grabbing and shredding bits of palmetto trees for mementos as the news spread throughout the city. Conventional sounds, the hum of business, the typical sounds of Charleston's streets, were suspended, as shops closed and crowds thronged. Crawford described sounds colliding, creating odd aural marriages: "the peals of the church bells mingling with salvos of artillery from the citadel. Old men ran shouting down the street." Copies of the ordinance, printed in "less than fifteen minutes after its passage," were passed hand to hand, generating even more shouts and cheers, which, in turn, drowned out the music of various military bands. Throats were loosened by the event, as were social norms, the ordinarily calm chieftains of "quiet plantation[s]" standing "side by side" with "poor white[s]," as Crawford put it. Voices were raised in unison. Bonfires added their flickering light to humbler street gaslights, church bells clanged, and "rockets were incessantly sent into the air," the sounds of celebration echoing long into the night.[31]

For Union soldiers still in the vicinity, these cheers and political melodies were nothing more than the noise of secession madness.[32] And talking back was, in many cases, not an option for those in disagreement. Listening ears were unforgiving, as "a poor seamstress" from New York, sent to jail in Charleston for stating that she did not believe in slavery, found out. Even influential politicians who did not raise their voices in support were doubted. Loyalty had to be univocal; anything else was suspect.[33]

All this seemingly ceaseless chuntering about secession and slavery afforded one group of people in Charleston unique opportunities. A mark of slavery had long been speaking only when spoken to. Now, in the winter of 1860, knowing how to listen, how to keep your head down and ears open, proved more important than ever. "The negroes overhead a great deal that was said by their masters, and in consequence became excited and troublesome," recalled Abner Doubleday, who was a captain in the US Army stationed at Fort Moultrie beginning in the summer of 1860. Slaves listened and, sotto voce, spread the word: "the news flew like wild-fire among them that 'Massa Linkum' was coming to set them all free." For now, though, they knew to remain quiet. They had learned that skill only too well.[34]

In the immediate vicinity of Charleston were three fortified slabs of federal property: Castle Pinckney (a small masonry fort, perched on Shute's Folly, an island a mile off Charleston), the more substantial Fort Moultrie on Sullivan's Island, and the increasingly imposing Fort Sumter, still in the process of being completed, in Charleston Harbor. South Carolinians believed these forts should be claimed by their new state. Washington thought they were the property of the US government and subject to federal authority. The debate had been ongoing for most of the autumn of 1860 and, now, with secession formalized, matters reached a breaking point. How the issue would be resolved, if it was going to be resolved, had a great deal to do with the actions of Major Robert Anderson. He had been eyeing and listening to events in the city, even as he pondered the desirability of moving to Fort Sumter from Fort Moultrie.

At first blush, Sumter seemed an unlikely prize. Pentagonal, with a parapet rising sixty feet out of the water, Fort Sumter, lodged, as Crawford described it, "tight in the jaws of the channel, in its narrowest part," sat unfinished in December 1860, only the sound of 120 workmen animating the walls. As a work of engineering, it was impressive. Built on a stone foundation a mile from shore, the dark brick walls were intended for three tiers of guns, 140 pieces of armament in all. Viewed from afar or up close, it had the feel, wrote Doublebday, of a "deep, dark, damp, gloomy-looking place, enclosed in high walls, where the sunlight rarely penetrated." It was a difficult fort to invade, having few weaknesses when finished and properly manned. It was not a fort to be taken lightly.[35]

For anyone inside the fort, though, the engineering must have seemed both a blessing and a curse. "Gloomy, prison-like," Doubleday called it. Sumter was an uninviting place and had an air of sadness about it. It also had a morose history, for in 1859 it had been used to quarter "some negroes that had been brought over from Africa in a slaver" captured by the US Navy. The Africans were replaced by a family—an ordnance sergeant, his wife, and their two little children. The soldier succumbed to a vicious bout of yellow fever once they had moved to the fort. Realizing her husband was on the brink of death, the sergeant's wife raised and lowered the flag multiple times in an effort to signal for help. None came. Desperate, she wrote a note describing her plight, gave the note to her children, and placed them in a small boat, praying that the tide and chance would scoot them to shore and alert a doctor. It was an act born of pure desperation. Miraculously, the boat reached Mount Pleasant, the children were safe, and a doctor managed to struggle to the fort. He arrived too late. The sergeant died.[36]

But it was not Sumter's history Major Anderson cared about. It was its future. Anderson was no fool. Three years prior to assuming command of Moultrie in the autumn of 1860, he had been promoted to major and was now the senior major of his regiment, the First Artillery. Lieutenant-General Winfield Scott knew him— Anderson had served under Scott in the war with Mexico—and liked the man. Born near Louisville, Kentucky, Anderson was a Southerner even in his sympathies, but his refined, calibrated sense of honor and "strong religious nature"—as Crawford put it—made him steadfast in the federal cause. He was a Union man, pure and simple. These qualities led General Scott to appoint Anderson to the command of Fort Moultrie on November 15, 1860, not an enviable slot in light of unfolding events.[37]

The major had little faith in Moultrie's security, which was too susceptible to sharpshooters and too easily cowed by the ever-strengthening Fort Sumter. Anderson rightly attempted to persuade the War Department that holding and reinforcing Fort Moultrie held little worth, especially in light of the fact that Sumter would soon have guns mounted and magazines full of powder and ammunition. By December 1, 1860, Anderson was convinced that not only should Castle Pinckney be garrisoned but also that the fort being finished in Charleston Harbor should be as well. The secretary of war denied his formal request on both counts, despite Anderson's insistence that Sumter "so perfectly commands the harbor and this fort."[38]

Increasingly, Anderson's command, consisting of seven officers, seventy-five enlisted men, two noncommissioned staff, and seventeen noncommissioned officers, felt pressed by the growing "excitability"—a favorite term at the time used to describe

Charlestonians and those who daily visited Fort Moultrie, which was, after all, separated by a simple street from "Citizen's houses." As Christmas approached, able-bodied men in Charleston were enrolling and forming military companies, the sounds of their drilling audible day and night, all counterpointed by "speeches of the most inflammatory character," as Crawford described them. They seemed, he feared, increasingly poised to try to take Fort Moultrie and, as the day of the convention drew near, threats were "loudly proclaimed."[39]

Chances are, Anderson had already decided to abandon Moultrie and secure Sumter before the December 19 convention was scheduled to meet. Certainly, he seemed to have the support of Major Don Carlos Buell of the Adjutant-General's Department, who, in his "Memorandum of verbal instructions to Major Anderson," told Anderson to "carefully avoid every act which would needlessly tend to provoke aggression" and advised him not "to take up any position which could be construed into the assumption of a hostile attitude." Yet the memorandum concluded: "The smallness of your force, will not permit you, perhaps, to occupy more than one of the three forts, but an attack on or an attempt to take possession of any one of them will be regarded as an act of hostility, and you may then put your command into either of them which you may deem most proper, to increase its power of resistance."[40]

Anderson was, as we have seen, a man of strong resolve, although understandably anxious as Charleston became more "excitable" and, from his perspective, combative. Crowds were now large, voices evermore raised, the place simply louder, and the effect unsettling. And Anderson was fearful of what would happen should Fort Sumter be taken by the Charlestonians. From the perspective of Union troops at Moultrie, the tactical disadvantage of having Sumter seized—and "its powerful armament upon us"— was disconcerting. Moultrie would be exposed on two sides and impossible to defend without significant loss of life. The major feared, quite reasonably, that he had insufficient forces to capture Sumter and also that that he would be driven from Moultrie. He felt he should act. Buell told the Kentuckian: "my personal advice is, that you do not allow the opportunity to escape you."[41]

Although the major's tongue was tied by Washington (he kept insisting to his officers that he had no right to vacate Moultrie or take Sumter without orders), his actions suggested that he was, as Doubleday ventured, "now merely awaiting a favorable opportunity." He continued to work on the defenses of Fort Moultrie; said very little, except to his trusted officers (and even some of those knew almost nothing of the details); and prepared a feinting gesture of chartering three schooners and a handful of barges for, ostensibly, the exclusive purpose of transporting some of the soldiers' families—not just women but potentially noisy children, too—from Moultrie to some dilapidated federal buildings at Fort Johnson, located at the opposite side of the harbor.[42] But when, exactly, he would make his move was unknown, perhaps even to the major himself.

Evening, December 26, 1860. The sun was beginning to dip as Captain Abner Doubleday, artillery captain at Moultrie who would later see service at Chancellorsville, Antietam, and Gettysburg, walked up the steps to Moultrie's parapet. Anderson stood in the middle of a group of officers. The mood was somber, the officers "silent." Anderson told Doubleday, quietly: "I have determined to evacuate this post immediately, for the purpose of occupying Fort Sumter." The gravity of the decision was not lost on the men. Doubleday was given just twenty minutes to form his company and prepare for departure. He needed only ten of them to form and inspect his company; the other ten he used to tell his wife, the last female at Moultrie, to leave as soon as possible.[43]

The move from Moultrie to Sumter was a stealthy operation. It was, simply, all about keeping quiet. Private John Thompson of the First United States Artillery wrote to his father in Ireland, just after sundown, "We were formed in heavy marching order, and quietly marched out of Moultrie." Ears alert, actively listening, Thompson and Doubleday's vanguard "passed out of the main gates" to the fort and "silently made our way for about a quarter of a mile to a spot where the boats were hidden behind an irregular pile of rocks."[44]

Fortune smiled: the quiet group was neither heard nor seen. Behind the rocks crouched the crewmen who would try to ferry Doubleday's company to Sumter. "In a low tone they pointed out to me the boats intended for my company." His equipment-laden men clambered in as noiselessly as they could and set out on the rippling water. Between them and Sumter a rebel steamer, the *General Clinch*, on the lookout for any unusual activity, plied the harbor, bisecting the waters between the two forts. Landlubbers, the soldiers did not row well, and the going was sluggish. There was every chance eyes peering from the steamer would spot them. The steamer approached the slow-moving boat. The sun was down, "and the twilight had deepened." Despite the moonlight, the night was "very dark." The men also engaged in visual trickery, hiding shiny buttons and metal—including military insignia—on their muskets by means of their coats. A hundred yards off, the steamer stopped, paddle wheels silent. The men were spotted. But the gambit paid off. To their "great relief," the steamer pressed on after a "slight scrutiny." They were probably mistaken as workmen.[45]

And so the boat and Doubleday's company made it to Fort Sumter fifteen, perhaps twenty, minutes later. No audible celebration was allowed. They secured the fort and detained the workmen who were still there, and the other boats followed, troops and materiel and the major, all avoiding the guard boat. The workmen were eventually returned to the shore, and Fort Sumter was now in the hands of federal troops.[46]

The stealth of the night of December 26 quickly gave way to nervous, bustling noise on the morning of December 27. Realizing what had happened, "messengers were at once dispatched to all parts of the city, to ring the door-bells and arouse the people." That

Anderson had managed to spike Moultrie's guns the night before, rendering them useless, only added to the alarm and aggravation of the Carolina forces now in charge of Moultrie and its restoration as a fighting fort. On Sumter, Anderson raised the flag amid prayers, the playing of the "Star-Spangled Banner," and cheers from his troops. Days later, confidence, perhaps foolish hope, abounded. "Now," wrote one soldier from Sumter, "we can say *We are ready.*" In "spite of all their bluster," he continued, referring to the noisy preparations in Charleston, "I am almost sure they never will fire a shot at us." The officers trained their spyglasses to monitor what might happen next.[47]

The weeks and months that followed were something of a rehearsal for what looked increasingly like war. Nothing was inevitable, of course. A great many conversations were taking place between South Carolina and the Buchanan administration in Washington and between Governor Pickens and Major Anderson, often in an attempt to dilute tensions. But what South Carolina wanted—the return of the Sumter—Anderson would not give.

In many respects, the way the war would affect people—its tenor and feel—was previewed in the months leading up to the actual firing on Fort Sumter. Charleston was on edge, often in a state of "uproar and excitement," and nervous about being bombarded. The sounds of industry, of preparation for war, were common, "workshops in the city . . . going night and day," as one witness put it, with work on Sumter and Moultrie—now in the hands of Charlestonians—often feverish and loud. It was a refrain that would be heard again and again during the next four years as various Southern cities, towns, and hamlets prepared for federal invasion and worked to arm Confederate troops and sailors. Sounds largely alien to the civilian soundscape all became increasingly familiar, an acoustic prelude for the years to come. Martial sounds became part of everyday life. Children, according to one report, "evidently thought every well-regulated family kept a drummer and fifer on hand, to sound the calls." Being exposed early on to martial sounds had the effect of toughening Charlestonians. A couple of years later, when Union forces bombarded the city, those who flinched most were those who had not been exposed to real fire. "As a rule, the morale effect of shells, particularly on green men, is far greater than their destructive power," remembered one observer, believing "the morale effect be proportioned to the size of the shell."[48]

The wartime deprivations that would become common were also first glimpsed in the months between Anderson's daring capture of Sumter in December 1860 and the eventual Confederate bombardment four months later. For a time, what Confederates would experience in Vicksburg, Mississippi, in 1863—impoverished diets and little communication with the outside world—were also experienced by Sumter's federal troops when South Carolina's governor stopped their mail and supplies, reducing their diet to pork, beans, and hardtack; for a month—January 1861—they got no food at all from the city. For a time, they had no soap, sugar, or even candles. By April 11, soldiers were down to one biscuit a day each for their allowance. They now chewed spun yard instead of tobacco.[49]

The need for vigilance, heightened during the war, also began here. From Charleston and Moultrie, Confederates watched intently for signs and clues, scrutinizing Sumter and the federal troops. For their part, Anderson's men kept a constant lookout. At times, their "glasses in vain swept the horizon." Sometimes, their eyes read the distance for hints of what was happening on land and at sea; other times, they felt blind, even though they could see. Night was especially nerve-wracking. Confederate boats, painted black, were almost invisible as they patrolled the waters. The federal soldiers feared that the enemy would "choose a dark night to drop down noiselessly with the tide" and land a party on the rocks. The major paced.[50]

The decision to fire on Fort Sumter began with news. Brigadier General P. G. T. Beauregard, commander of Confederate forces in Charleston, told Colonel James Chesnut, Colonel James

A. Chisholm, and Captain Stephen Dill Lee to offer Major Anderson the opportunity to surrender the fort. Anderson refused. Beauregard told President Jefferson Davis. This news, in turn, "passed from tongue to tongue, and soon the whole city was in possession of the startling intelligence," as one reporter put it.[51]

Hundreds gathered on the Battery, looking out on the bay. It was eight o'clock at night when they started to stare across the rolling waters, "straining their eyes over the dark expanse," waiting to confirm that something, anything, was at long last happening. But waiting was numbing business, testing even the most patient. Old signals suggested the time was not quite right. One newspaper reported: "The clock told the hour of eleven, and still they gazed and listened," like anxious theatergoers waiting for the curtain to open. Finally, at midnight, tired of watching, many plodded their way home.[52]

Those who stayed on the Battery saw otherwise. Four and a half hours after the bulk of the spectators had left the Battery, P. G. T. Beauregard, presented with Anderson's refusal to surrender, had consequently decided to open fire. "The last expiring spark of affection" between the remaining women and children on the Charleston shore and the men huddled in Fort Sumter had evaporated and, said a Charleston paper, now "must be quenched in blood."[53]

At 4:30 A.M., on April 12, 1861, as gray streaks of morning struggled to subdue the waning night, the signal came. The diehards on the Battery saw before they heard, courtesy of physics. As lightning precedes thunder, so "the great volcanic crater" they called Fort Sumter "was illuminated with a line of twinkling lights; the clustering shells illuminated the sky above it," wrote one anxious reporter. The men inside Sumter saw and heard the same: "at 4.30 A.M. a flash as of distant lightning in the direction of Mount Pleasant, followed by the dull roar of mortar." But they were on the receiving end of "the shell as it mounted the stars . . . then descended with ever-increasing velocity, until it landed inside the fort and burst. It was a capital shot." It was just the beginning: "Then the batteries opened on all sides, and shot and shell went screaming over Sumter as if an army of devils were swooping around it."[54]

The next sounds were of the balls clattering, "thick as hail," on the fort's sides. And then the roar of cannon erupted, a wall of sound carrying on it the colossal "bursting of bombs" and the "roaring of ordnance," according to one witness. What had begun with Anderson's whispered move months earlier from Moultrie to Sumter was culminating now in a level of sheer sound few people in the city or in the fort had ever heard.[55]

It was all-enveloping, all-penetrating. "The firing of the mortar woke the echoes from every nook and corner of the harbor," wrote Captain Stephen Dill Lee, one of the envoys Beauregard had sent to Anderson to ask him to surrender the fort. Although coming from the Battery and directed to the fort, people felt as though it were directly on them. The effect was dramatic. Even in the heady atmosphere of April 1861, the loudness came as a concussive surprise. Within minutes, thousands emptied their homes, adding to a thickening crowd anxious to see the meaning of what they heard. "[U]nused as their ears were to the appalling sounds, or the vivid flashes from the batteries, they stood for hours fascinated with horror," noted Lee. The crowd—ladies and gentlemen alike—was unprecedented in size. The suddenness of the eruption began to take on a syncopated feel, guns "steadily alternating," the batteries spitting their arsenal at "the grim fortress rising so defiantly out of the sea."[56]

As night fell on April 11, the eve of battle, sandbags that had shielded from Anderson's view the forty-two-pounders on Cummings Point on Morris Island, barely 1,200 yards of water away from Sumter, were quickly removed. Lanterns were lit to illuminate the point, allowing gunners to sight and train their machines of destruction toward Sumter. Time passed. Impatience mounted among the Confederates on the point. Still no signal to fire on Fort Sumter. Just after eight o'clock, according to one correspondent, "the tattoo resounded over the dark sand hills," and soldiers were directed to their quarters. No firing just yet by these point men.[57]

Drizzle accompanied the coming and the passing of midnight, and the Cummings Point gunners slept on until they heard "the distant boom of a shell" at 4:30 A.M. This was their cue. They scurried to their posts and opened fire on Sumter. To their eyes and ears, the "dull detonation" of the shells exploding over Sumter, the incessant flashing, and what one reporter described as the "dense brown cloud of crumbling brick and mortar" of the fort's ramparts were nothing short of "picturesque."[58] As sunlight grew, the day took on a subliminal air, especially for those a little removed from the action. Just outside the city on James Island, Confederate Brigadier General Johnson Hagood saw slaves working, "the air was vocal with birds," all "contrasting strangely with . . . the roar and reverberation of the distant bombardment."[59]

And so Cummings Point kept pounding and lobbing, shell after heavy shell, and, like their counterparts in Charleston, the gunners there remarked on the silence of Sumter, wondering whether the major would reply. A few minutes after seven o'clock, the query was answered. Anderson began firing shell from his heavy casemates directly at Cummings Point. In addition to the obvious danger, it was the sounds, the noises of the bombardment erupting from Sumter, that impressed ears at Cummings Point. Now it was the Confederates' turn to hear the terrible sounds of war. Balls bounced thunderously off the heavy iron-cased sheeting fitted around the guns and then "splashed" into the surrounding marsh. Whizzing shot, "hissing shot . . . leaving wreck and ruin in their path," in the words of one newspaper man, wracked nerves at Cummings Point, causing heads to dip intuitively, reflexively. Sensibly. And those that hit the Confederate iron battery created "the noise of concussion" to men inside[60] (figure 1.3).

The Confederates at Cummings Point responded in kind, upping the volume and returning fire. If the shots failed to hit the Yankees inside their granite bowl, the shock wave from exploding

FIGURE 1.3. *The Sounds of War.*

Fort Sumter, April 1861. Currier and Ives engraving, circa 1861, "Bombardment of Fort Sumter, Charleston Harbor: 12th & 13th of April, 1861." Reproduction number LC-USZC2-1990 (color film copy slide), Library of Congress Prints and Photographs Division, Washington, D.C.

shells would certainly disorient them. A steady booming tattooing the harbor, the sounds blanketing water, rock, and land, imposed a dome of noise over the entire area. And so it kept on and on and on, the Union soldiers inside Sumter pummeled by shot and shell and the constant noise. "The enemy," wrote one of the troops inside the granite chamber, "kept up a slow but steady fire on us during the entire night, to prevent our getting any rest." Some troops did manage to sleep; doubtless many others did not.[61] Nerves were shot.

The next day, no spyglass was needed to determine the effect the firing had had on Sumter. From Cummings Point, one could see clearly how balls had pitted the southern and eastern facades of the fort. Chimneys and roofs were perforated; parapets fragmented, toppling into the water; and the fire that could be seen so plainly from Charleston took on a vivid red quality to the men peering over Cummings Point batteries. But there would be no respite. Cummings Point redoubled the shelling of the hapless fort.[62]

Anderson did not return fire. Some onlookers concluded the battering had worked, that Anderson and his men had been pummeled into submission. This was what silence meant to the ears of slave owners. As smoke cleared, the Stars and Stripes still floated proudly. Again, the firing, the batteries continuing, according to a Charleston newspaper, "at regular intervals to belch iron vengeance." "Still no answer." And then a response, what a reporter described as two "hissing" balls from Sumter bouncing off Fort Moultrie's bricks. Then silence, "no sound," again.[63]

As it turned out, this was the silence of necessary delay, and between six and seven o'clock Anderson answered, lobbing thunderous shells toward Fort Moultrie and Confederate batteries. Not to respond would have been slavish—but respond Anderson and his men did, firing in earnest determination.

War was engaging all the senses. "The atmosphere was charged with the smell of villainous saltpetre," wrote a correspondent, marveling at the amount of smoke, the heavy clouds, and the seemingly perpetual "jarring boom" that "rolled at regular intervals on the anxious ear." Charleston's harbor seemed "surrounded with miniature volcanoes belching forth fire and smoke."[64]

But sound dominated. Barely fourteen hours after the first shot was fired, the sounds of war were beginning to take on a metronymic quality, overlaying a new soundtrack on the city. Starting around seven o'clock, "the guns boomed, throughout the night of Friday, at regular intervals of twenty minutes," marking the close of the first day's bombardment. Darkness heightened the sound, as did the direction of the wind. "The guns were heard distinctly, the wind blowing in shore." While the shells punctuated the night sky, the darkness hid the damage. As dawn approached, the firing lessened, its rhythm replaced by "random shots from outlying batteries" and very little firing from Sumter, a marked change from Anderson's "long, fierce, and rapid" shooting throughout the night. A westerly wind explained why: smoke cleared, revealing a robust fire in the fort, threatening the magazines and keeping them from firing except at "distant intervals."[65]

The Confederates saw their chance and fired with even greater ferocity, every battery pouring "in its ceaseless round of shot and shell." This was grand if lethal theater, replete with stirring sights and thrilling sounds. "As in the opening, so in the closing scene": from the Battery, Confederates lobbed shell after shell, making a spectacular show for the "view of thousands crowded upon the wharves and housetops," all "amid the booming of ordnance." The effect was disastrous for Sumter. The fort was cauldron-like, its thick walls capturing sound, careening it in its closed environment, bashing ears, until the noise ricocheted out, carried back to Charleston over water. The shells that exploded in or directly above the fort must have been concussive.

Suddenly, the fort was rocked by a massive explosion, followed by silence. This time, it was indeed the silence of surrender, one announced by the shout of spectators in Charleston. Anderson had little choice: his men were "fast suffocating" from the fire, his cause hopeless. "All firing had . . . ceased," and the federal flag was lowered on Fort Sumter.[66]

Charleston's entire bay, on land and on sea, was filled with voices, resounding, resonating, knit together into one aural tapestry. These were "deafening shouts," followed by thunderous celebratory firing from the batteries, voice and cannon clearly audible at the fort, filling the "entire circuit" of the bay. Now, they all knew, victory was complete.[67]

Inside Fort Sumter was a terrible scene. Walls now warren-like, courtesy of shot, stood blackened, still smoking in places. The men were in similar shape. Sleepless for so many hours, they looked haggard.[68] Ammunition was scarce, and the fire, eating up a fifth of the fort, had been whipped by wind, smothering the troops in dense, choking smoke. To Abner Doubleday, suffocation seemed imminent as men "lay down close to the ground, with handker-chiefs over their mouths," gasping for air. Damage to the fort was significant, "the sound of masonry falling in every direction."[69]

Major Anderson, equally fatigued, was despondent but defiant. At the very least he had endeavored to do his duty as an officer, and "he had not taken the life of a fellow being." He congratulated, in all sincerity, Major Stevens, whose iron battery had pounded the fort so relentlessly, for a job well done. As his "command marched out to the tune of 'Yankee Doodle' and the booming of a salute," he wept hard. And so he left the fort, gentle sobs lingering amid the ruins. The fighting concluded, for now, for this briefest of moments, the fort, the bay, and the city—rock, water, land—were once again quiet, mere prelude to what would become the loudest four years on American soil. The war would sound like hell before it was all over.[70]

Chapter Two

Eyeing First Bull Run

Early July, 1861. Fairfax Station, Virginia. Maps—lined, marked, annotated, flat, gridded—lay strewn before the men, all brigade commanders of the Confederate States of America. They studied and scrutinized these maps, which were aerial views of Northern Virginia. There seemed something so certain about the lines, so very reliable, almost predictive, about the neatly arranged columns and squares. One of the men seemed especially confident. He was the room's senior officer, General P. G. T. Beauregard, a sharp-nosed, angular man of Creole heritage, with a strong, square jaw. Only his thin, flossy beard and mousy hair softened his otherwise geometric features. His eyes—bright and active—were locked on the maps, absorbing details.

A lot rode on the Louisianan's steady gaze. Charged with protecting Richmond from what he believed would be a full-bodied onslaught from Union General Irvin McDowell, Beauregard wanted his commanders—names that would become famous: Bonham, Cocke, Ewell, Evans, D. R. Jones, Longstreet, Early—to fall back to the south of the modest stream called Bull Run and outflank McDowell's advancing forces. This, he hoped, would fell the federals, saving the Confederacy's capital.

He was so confident about what he was looking at that it gave him a bit of swagger. And why not? He was an accomplished soldier. He was still glowing from Sumter, having commanded the defenses in Charleston, ears still ringing with the sounds and bombast of victory. A few days earlier, on May 31, Robert E. Lee entrusted him

with command of the Alexandria line, the critical string standing between Washington and Richmond. Beauregard was also
a product of planter aristocracy, which lent him a self-possessed,
weighty authority. But there was something very specific about his
self-assurance, perhaps having to do with the type of soldier he was
and had trained to be. Beauregard was a topographical engineer
and had, off and on, been designing, planning, and diagramming
plans for forts and works since his 1838 graduation from West
Point, where he had taken classes with Major Robert Anderson,
the man he had just defeated in Charleston. Beauregard was accustomed to planning, a "Napoleon in Gray," who relied upon seeing an architectural plan enacted, a man who, while occasionally
apprehensive, nevertheless was a product of an era that encouraged
men of power to believe in what they planned and to be convinced
that what they sketched and committed to paper had a very good
chance of becoming reality.

And so here he was, in July 1861, pointing to where his brigades
would go, whom they would stop, and the points on the map where
it would all happen. His confidence was contagious. "The routes by
which all these movements were to be made," remembered Jubal
Early, "were pointed out and designated on maps previously prepared." Beauregard was capricious and terribly petulant, but, above
all, he believed in the power of his plan. Its "columns" of troops, its
interior "lines," its wholly "concerted" nature made him believe in
it, even if it relied entirely too much on unproven suppositions of
what the federals might do.[1]

Beauregard, then, was a commander who relied a great deal on
his eyes to gauge and judge. After being formally appointed by Lee
to manage affairs and prepare Camp Pickens, near Bull Run, the
engineer in him came out. He saw clearly that Bull Run was a better
place to stop a federal advance than Camp Pickens, which he considered too easily seen and too transparent. On horseback, wearing
his "old blue uniform coat," which he had had since his days in the

US Army, he surveyed the land until he was confident he had found the best spots to place his batteries and earthworks (map 2.1).[2]

Beauregard's reports of First Bull Run are filled with talk of "within the lines of Bull Run" and "topographical features," such words as *traverse* and *intersect* and *column* and *precision*, descriptions

MAP 2.1. *Seeing from Above: First Bull Run.*

War Department, Office of the Chief of Engineers, "Map of the Battle Fields of Manassas and the Surrounding Region," Record Group 77, Records of the Office of the Chief of Engineers, Series Civil Works Map File, compiled 1800–1947, National Archives Identifier 305595, Local Identifier 77-CWMF-G136.

of ground that "was commanded at all points" by height, sharp eyes on the lookout for "bayonets, gleaming above the tree-tops, alone indicat[ing] their presence and force." The other senses—notably sound, listening to the sound of musketry—were relevant mainly for locating troops who were concealed by brush. Victory, in turn, was measured in the disruption of enemy lines and achieved through gridlike discipline. Beauregard knew success when he saw it: "heavy masses in the distance were plainly seen to break and scatter, in wild confusion and utter rout, strewing the ground with cast-away guns, hats, blankets and knapsacks." Appended to his report was, of course, a detailed "map of the field of battle."[3]

Union General Irvin McDowell was, like Beauregard, a bad listener. He had a difficult time latching onto other people's words. But he was adept at sightlines, and his main hobbies were architecture and landscape gardening. Neither would serve him well in this battle, and his social ineptness did nothing to inspire loyalty among his officers. Worse, his belief in the veracity of sight would prove a profound handicap.[4]

Like his Confederate counterpart, McDowell was a map man. On June 29, he presented to the president, members of the cabinet, and the Union military's top brass his plan of attack. The precision of his outline—columns directed exactly, thousands of men pointed toward particular terrain—was undermined by the simple fact that McDowell still as yet had no accurate roadmap of Northern Virginia. But he pressed on, his faith in the diagramming he had worked on so patiently inspiring him, lending him the confidence he needed to take the fight to the Confederates and, he hoped, take the Union army to Richmond. It was this faith that led McDowell to move on July 16, when his multicolored battalions, many wearing the garb of their local militia and not the deep blue of the US military, headed toward Manassas.[5]

The idea that seeing was believing was nowhere more revered than in the officer corps on both sides of the Civil War. These were men who trusted their eyes, and understandably so. They had been taught, over and over, that the ability to see the battle-field, to visually imagine where troops were and would be, gave them the perspective essential for victory. Antoine Henri Jomini, whose translated writings occupied a very prominent place at the US Military Academy at West Point, espoused a heavily quantified, scientific, prescriptive, and thoroughly Enlightenment approach to warfare that influenced both Confederate and Union officers early on in the war. Jomini considered the visual advantage of hav-ing the high ground important, though not necessarily determina-tive; maps and diagrammatic representations of troop movements, on the other hand, were essential—the general who made heavy use of them, he wrote, "will seldom be in doubt, in real campaigns, what he ought to do." Indeed, "acquiring a rapid and accurate *coup d'œil*" could thwart even "sudden and expected movements" by the enemy. It was the beholder's ability to capture in one look the scene before his eyes—the coup d'œil, or "quick look"—that was more critical than any other sensory input. Reconnoiter ("to recognize") could be aural, true—locations were revealed sometimes through sound and listening—but the best officers trusted the eye to locate and guide.[6] Constructing battle lines, ordering columns, framing engagements—all this appealed to officers whose civilian skills and interests shaped how they viewed the military situation: Beauregard the topographer and engineer, McDowell the architect, Stonewall Jackson the professor of mathematics. Even Lincoln was a surveyor. The pattern was clear. These were observant men.[7]

Little wonder that technologies of sight lined the battlefield at Manassas. The inaugural battle witnessed the war's first use of a military surveillance balloon, an attempt to capture an aerial understanding of positions and tactics. Beauregard, forever on the lookout for, well, lookouts, had Captain E. Porter Alexander deploy a system of signaling the captain had devised while in the US Army. Soldiers stationed at four specially built towers used a system of flags to communicate. Although not all four towers were in a direct line of sight, messages could be passed from one to another down the line during the day and, by dint of torches, also at night.[8]

These watchers were also being watched. Unlike the officers, those observing them would not descend to the field and experience the sights of battle up-close. They were eyewitness journalists.

On July 21, 1861, as the battle started, the witnesses gathered on this "bright and beautiful" day. Four Southern newspapermen trudged up a hill above Mitchell's Ford, a place "almost entirely bare of trees, and sufficiently high to afford an unobstructed view of the opposite heights." It was height they wanted, offering them a bird's-eye picture of what was happening on the plains of Manassas below. These were also individuals who subscribed to the belief that seeing was believing; they were used to digesting information visually and letting events unfold. From here, they thought they would be able to trace movements, describe the essence of the moment, and accurately relay this monumental story to their readers.[9]

For these reporters, Bull Run was best witnessed as a panorama, one granting unprecedented perspective of the "armies of the North and South," fighting with "that desperate courage which Americans can only show." One of the reporters, for the *Charleston Mercury*, noted that there were few other spectators, explaining that all civilians had to "retire beyond a distance of four miles from the battle." Reporters were given permission to remain "to witness a scene not often enacted." And what was enacted was "a scene of terrific grandeur and sublimity," imprinted on his memory and captured in print. Seeing First Bull Run from this vantage point— a little under two miles from "the enemy battery"—was not unlike attending a play. It was visually consumable, without the sickening smells and sounds of battle. The nearest the reporters came to experiencing the war was hearing "the peculiar whiz and hissing of the balls" fired in their direction, against which "the aid of our glass" was limited. It was safe. "The whole scene is before us—a grand moving diorama," enthused the *Mercury*'s reporter.[10]

And it was exciting because it all seemed so authentic. The reporters' enthusiasm at witnessing this first major engagement of the war—and for all they knew, for all anyone knew, it was to be the only battle—blinded them. Arriving at the northwest fortifications of Manassas Junction, they discovered they had left "entirely unprepared either in the way of the commissariat or with glasses to view the distant field." Colonel William G. Bonner came to the rescue, bringing them a "powerful opera glass." The glasses opened up the battle, the men now being "permitted to see."[11] They took it all in. All "around us were eminences on which were posted small but anxious knots of spectators, forming the most magnificent panorama I ever beheld."[12]

These reporters and military officers were, according to the early-nineteenth-century natural historian Lorenz Oken, the "eye men" of their age. Oken elaborated a hierarchy of the senses indexed explicitly to race, giving pride of place to sight and sound and relegating the proximate senses of smell, taste, and touch to the bottom. For Oken, the refined man of reason and intellect was the "eye-man," a European. Just below him, also "civilized," was the Asian "ear-man." The Native American "nose-man" came next, followed by the Australian "tongue-man." At the bottom, associated with the primal and least intellectual of the senses—touch— was the African, the "skin-man." By contrast, the "eye-men" were the professional classes of America's late antebellum period, and if they had a shared credo, it was simply that seeing was, indeed, believing.[13]

Oken was not alone in his beliefs. Just six years before Bull Run, *Harper's* magazine—in an article similar to the ones that appeared in 1852 and 1856 on all the senses—summarized what seeing meant to people in the mid-nineteenth century, at least those in the West. The eye was "high and noble," with important truth-telling duties. The eye "receives the finest impressions from the outer world" and "measures the boundless limits of space," and one glance is enough to calibrate the "space around us in all directions." Seeing provided

perspective and offered the mind an appropriate lens. The eye har-
vested knowledge, gathered information, and came nearer to truth
than any of the other senses.[14]

And yet, awareness remained that one could not place utter
faith in sight. The "power of the eye is itself not unbounded," the
Harper's article warned, and "even the experienced eye is liable
to be sadly deceived in regions where the usual objects are wanting that serve us as standards for a comparison." Eyes, then, had
to learn to see. And certain circumstances made sight vulnerable. "Even the more acute eye of men whose life may depend on
their accurate sight measures distance but by experience." Here,
the writer was thinking of the soldier. "The riflemen of our army
also learn very soon that at certain distances the buttons of their
enemies' uniform are no more seen; then the pompon, and at last
the epaulets on the officers' shoulders." At a distance, the eye could
not be trusted to detect such details and needed more information.
A coup d'œil wouldn't cover it.[15]

Plunging down from the ridges, from the lofty heights occupied
by the reporters and onto the fields of battle—leaving the safety
of maps—we confront something very different, a space fully
engaging all of the senses. What witnesses of the battlefield wanted
was something that the nature of battle—and the specific nature
of this particular battle—could not give them: certainty in what
they saw. Their request was naive—for battle muddled the senses
generally—but not entirely unreasonable. Was it too much to ask
to be able to tell friend from foe?

As it turned out, it was. Had those fighting it been able to distinguish, the battle would have turned out differently. Men who died
might well have lived; men who survived might well have never
limped, or winced, or struggled; and a Union army that ended up
running back to Washington to face the slog of war for four more
years might well have sauntered into the Confederate capital, turning the tide of the war and rewriting American history.

The experience of battle—including the march to the site of engagement—was disorienting. Shots and smoke competed to distract and confuse the eye and bombard the senses, leaving men dazed and numb. Experienced officers knew all of this, of course. For some, actual field experience was key to managing the sensory overload of battle. Inexperienced officers, tutted Captain Thomas Pitts, were men who had "never seen the flash of musketry or heard roaring of cannon."[16] Old hands brought ears accustomed to the field and were able to pick out what was important. Brigadier General Daniel Tyler, the Union officer who later was highly critical of McDowell's performance at Bull Run, observed: "I could hear the trains coming in from the direction of Winchester, and my railroad experience convinced me these railroad trains were heavily loaded, judging from the exhausts of the locomotive." What Tyler heard was Johnson reinforcing Beauregard at Manassas, a critical piece of intelligence.[17]

Officers understood that warfare was dangerously confusing for troops, especially green ones. Trying to train soldiers' eyes to look carefully, to keep their sights focused, was challenging. For many, on both sides, the march toward battle was a novel experience, full of distractions. Troops sometimes sang as they marched; ate a wide variety of foods, some of them quite awful; slept outside beneath skies "studded with the sentinel stars"; and rose to tattoos, notes filling air and ear.[18] Often giddy, their nerves were on edge.

The battlefield itself made a mockery of the generals' maps. The heat, "a white ball of fire overhead" while soldiers were waiting to engage the enemy, took its toll. Eyes were filled with sweat, and bodies slouched, warping supposedly straight lines. According to Alexander Hunter, who served with Lee, "Jackets were cast aside, and the line, so well dressed before, was now about as straight as a corkscrew." Men given the task of observation lapsed: "The lookouts were no longer lookouts" but instead stared dreamily into lands of fear and hope.[19]

Like all battles, Bull Run was a combination of sensory over-load and sensory irritation. In the heat, soldiers thirsted for fresh water as their mouths filled with the dust generated by thousands of marching feet, choking their throats and rattling their lungs. Tongues begged for water. Hoof-shaped pools of mud-water proved tempting, and men siphoned from them when they could.[20] Skin was bruised and scraped by trees, bushes, and thorns. And when skin was torn, exposing flesh to the air, flies laid eggs. Then the maggots came, nibbling, eating, infecting. Quite literally, war got under their skin.[21] Hunger, not that peckish sort of hunger but real gnawing, longing for something more than hardtack and salt pork, was a serious problem, especially during battle when caloric expenditure was enormous. Famished troops could strip bushes of their berries in locust-like fashion. A "spell of Diareah" resulted.[22]

Then there were the sounds—raw and terrifying. For some men, it seemed historical. "There was the heaviest cannonading ever heard in Virginia, not even excepting the battles of the Revolution," offered one Michigan soldier, and he might well have been right.[23] This was a battle that would feature, for the first time, the rebel yell, as well as introduce men to the sound of "the slow and funeral booming of a distant cannon," and in which bodily movement was orchestrated in part by "the shrill music of the drum and fife."[24]

Being under intense fire was an unfamiliar experience, and men grasped for ways to convey what it was like. Listen, they urged in their letters home, listen. "The balls whistling around us like hail stones," wrote John C. Gregg of the Second Michigan. "I cannot compare them to anything else than a lot of Bumble Bees flying by only a great deal faster," he added. For men from rural areas, the comparison was a natural one. George Miller, of the Third Michigan, also invoked bees. For him, though, it was "the can-non shot" that "whirred over heads like a shower of bumble bees." And for others, it was simply the indirect feel of the bullets: "I got behind a large tree & every time I would stand up I would feel the wind of a ball in my face."[25]

Sounds jarred, running up against one another. One minute, everything was quiet, "the drowsy hum of the big blue bottles and the cawing of the crows" lending a pastoral sound to the scene. And then a "stunning and rattling volley"; "whir, whir, sh, sh, sh, bang-bang, the shells come," wrote a Union man.[26] Confederates' experiences were no different. Federal shell "was more like the neigh of an excited or frightened horse than anything I can compare it to," noted a Virginian: "a kind of 'whicker, whicker, whicker' sound as it swapped ends in the air."[27] Incredibly, even on the field of battle, with bullets whistling overhead, some soldiers went about ordinary business. Some ate and "took the opportunity of picking a few black berries that grew within arm reach of me while we were lying on the ground the bullets flying in every direction." Another read a letter "among the bursting bombs or the whistling of balls."[28]

Mostly, though, men held onto their senses for dear life. Dodging cannonballs, for example, was possible if seeing and hearing were carefully coordinated—along with a good deal of luck. "I used to think it foolishness to dodge a cannon ball but I think the other way now," mused a soldier of the Third Michigan, explaining: "you can hear a cannon ball quite a while before it gets to you and sometimes you can see them. I saw several that were coming pretty strate for us in time to dodge them . . . ." Even though "we did not like the sound of the things," ears trained eyes, and both trained bodies to react. Shells were a different matter: by the time soldiers heard them, it was too late. The shell was already over them—or through them. Other terrors abounded: "while the sound of big guns was more terrific, the real danger in battle was the whistling 'minnie,' which reached one without note or warning."[29]

Whether cannon, shell, or ball, the screaming and whizzing and the way the bullets kicked up puffs of dirt at their feet induced jitters even among the most experienced soldiers. Even William T. Sherman, leading the US Thirteenth Infantry regiment, ducked at the sound, despite having advised his men that doing so was pointless. Bodies reacted to sound involuntarily.[30]

Sound served to locate enemy and friend, gave men time to duck, allowed men to push their bodies forward, and impelled them to push their bodies backward, "guided by the roar of the cannon and the volleys of musketry." Sound was sensation, and the augury of worse: "the increased roar of the guns warned us that we might soon feel as well as hear."[31] It also served to inspire, ready the gut, stiffen the spine. The Confederates had their rebel yell. "Yankee Doodle" roused federals to press up forbidding hills in the face of fierce shooting.[32]

Of all the senses, though, sight, and the certainty associated with seeing, was the main casualty in this battle. Eyes at Bull Run were often blinded because of dust and smoke, forcing men to rely on other senses, not always accurately. Was that water from a punctured canteen running down my arm, wondered a soldier, or blood? Instinct warned blood, but it was only sun-warmed water. What was that "chocolate hue, spreading irregularly like a map" in the dry grass? Battle taught men it was dried blood.[33]

Dust caked on perspiring faces, masking skin and altering appearances. Familiar features were cloaked.[34] That same dust altered visibility, sometimes "so thick," moaned a First Marylander, "that it was impossible to see more than a few feet ahead of one." Officers up ahead disappeared, hidden by dust; colors became murky (blue? gray?); flags were pixilated.[35]

Even without the dust, the enemy wasn't always visible, especially when "sheltered by the woods"—of which there were some around Manassas—and soldiers "had to take aim from the flashes of the discharges." The sheer confusion of battle made it difficult to distinguish friend from foe.[36] During the battle, bushes bristled with rebels, although hard looking did not reveal a single one. They were "like so many 'ingins,'" indistinguishable from the land around them.[37] At times, men shot blind. "The enemy can't see us and we can't see them being covered by trees," complained a federal.[38] These men had grown up in a world where seeing was certainty and were ill equipped to fight in a battle in which their sentinel sense had lost its power. The real tragedy, though, was not that these men's eyes were less reliable now; rather, it was that they staunchly maintained their belief in seeing.

Old soldiers knew better. Those who had seen action had also learned to un-see; they understood that battle conditions altered how things looked. Captain James Chester of the US Army, although writing of his experience of Fort Sumter, offered lessons of broad import for the war generally: "Few artillerymen, without actual experience, have any idea of the difficulty of aiming a gun during a bombardment. They may be able to hit a target in ordinary practice with absolute certainty, and yet be unable to deliver a single satisfactory shot in a bombardment. The error from smoke is difficult to deal with, because it is a variable, depending upon the density of the smoke clouds which envelop your own and your adversary's batteries . . . . But for night firing or when the enemy is enveloped in smoke—as he is sure to be in any artillery duel,—the eye cannot be depended upon. Visual aiming in a bombardment is a delusion and a snare."[39] Cataracts were inherent to war.

But persuading green troops—as well as green officers, for they were many in this battle—was difficult. Visual habits were hard to break. In letters home, soldiers relied on perspective in an effort to convey the visual panorama. A Confederate officer invited his family to take in the view from "Camp Beauregard," "perched on the top of our earth entrenchment" that his men were busying shoveling. He described, "The angular tents of the privates in groups, with here and there the round pointed Sibley tents of the officers." Words were not enough: "I cannot do justice with my pen." He thought a sketch—lines, angular, pointed, horizontal and vertical, intersecting—the best, most "accurate" way to capture the truth of the place.[40]

And who can blame men for wanting to see clearly, for the stakes were impossibly high, and assessing danger was key. "I am trying to do my duty," wrote one Confederate to his sister in the days leading up to Bull Run, "& be sure that I understand it too well ever to make an unnecessary or rash risk of the life which belongs to my family."[41]

Given this, soldiers were understandably not fond of being made to form in "open field," more visible and vulnerable as it made them.[42] They tried, whenever they could, to gain the high ground, like their officers, mounting gateposts to view "the panoramas spread out before them."[43]

Because officers and men held sight in such high esteem and relied on vision to plan and execute, they found attempts to deceive the eye little better than blasphemy. Visual deception was a tactic employed but condemned as cowardly, verging on unmanly. Colonel J. B. Kershaw of the Second Palmetto wrote disgustedly that the "escape of so many of the Zouaves [New York] to our rear was accomplished by their lying down, feigning to be dead or wounded, when we charged over them, and then treacherously turning upon us, they murdered one of our men in cold blood after he had surrendered."[44] Beauregard considered deliberate ignoring of signs offensive, complaining that Union forces at Bull Run aimed for the wounded at a field hospital, "the special target of the enemy rifle guns, notwithstanding it was surmounted by the usual yellow hospital flag."[45]

Yet many officers understood perfectly well the tactical desirability of not being seen, of seeking out hollows, trees, and ridges and camouflaging troops for hours, leaving "no evidence of our nearness to the enemy except the occasional firing of musketry by our skirmishers in the road."[46] Tactics often relied on hiding from sight. "Skirmishers uncovered rebel batteries," wrote one reporter, who talked of "masked batteries." These invisible enclaves became something of a bugaboo for Union soldiers, inspiring fear of the unseen. To "our imagination," a soldier from the Seventy-Ninth Highlanders confessed sheepishly, "every strip of woods contained a body of 'secesh' infantry, and every hillock a concealed battery." Another claimed, implausibly, that his regiment had stumbled upon "a masked battery" with "some 20,000 men hid in the scrub."

For men accustomed to surveying and assessing, blinding of this sort was understandably unnerving, inviting phantoms and specters in their minds' eyes.[47] Batteries could be so well masked that troops could stumble upon them suddenly. The skirmishes that followed could be brutal and vicious.[48]

Terrain, too, served to dilute the power of sight. Trees and brush hid Confederates from New York troops; by the same token, men of the Second Michigan learned, during the battle, how "to lye flat on the ground to be more out of sight."[49] Troops on the move sometimes stooped low, attempting to fool spyglasses by taking their bodies out of sight and causing the enemy to underestimate their true numbers.[50]

The troops who fought at the first major battle of the Civil War believed they would know at whom to fire. Whatever visual confusion they encountered on the battlefield, however much their other senses came into play, all soldiers held this expectation. Indeed, quite understandably, the expectation was so assumed that any alternative seemed absurd. Soldiers fired at the enemy, and the enemy could always be identified by their uniforms.

For many soldiers, the decision as to whether to squeeze the trigger was governed by color identification. Under stressful, confusing, deafening circumstances, the sight of "blue coats" or the gray-clad dictated reaction or, at least, was supposed to do so. The enemy was supposed to be distinguished by a color; that was all that was supposed to matter. Factor in what Confederate soldier John O. Cassler termed "buck fever"—the nervousness of the first-time hunter and the visceral desire to fire—and color became even more important.[51] It separated friend from foe. "Company colors," even "the same buttons," were signs of belonging, of shared history, of anticipated shared sacrifice. Colors imparted identity.[52] So they went into battle with the expectation that they would know their enemies from their friends.

But of course, it was not that clear-cut. Smoke, dust, and topography rendered even bright and odd colors murky.[53]

A lack of standardization, a thrown-together quality, was one signature of the buildup to Bull Run. The war had outpaced leaders, the imperative to mobilize resources lagging behind other considerations. From the very beginning, a sense of visual uncertainty haunted the men who would do the fighting. Confederate soldiers from different states and indeed from different regiments wore different uniforms. Many of the soldiers were ill equipped and quite literally ragtag. Despite private efforts to supply Confederate troops from Maryland, for example, with gray uniforms—supposedly the color chosen for Confederate soldiers, at least according to General Orders No. 9, issued on June 6—Confederate soldiers hardly looked the same. It seems that the June 6 orders were either ignored or issued too late to be fully implemented. Louisiana soldiers often provided their own uniforms, and the First Louisiana Battalion, sporting French Zouave style—blue and white trousers, brown jackets, and a red tassel atop their caps—looked like nothing else in either the Confederate or Union armies. So, too, with the brilliant green outfits of the Sixth Alabama. And soldiers from a number of regiments on both sides sported paraphernalia—such as brass buttons—used by the US Army. Uniforms were so variegated in part because regiments were highly local affairs, formed often from battalions of local militia.[54]

Commanders knew these facts and did their best to rectify matters. Beauregard in particular worried about visual uniformity before Bull Run and had gone to some lengths to minimize what he feared might be a source of deadly confusion. He recommended that every Confederate put on a badge, or even a sliver of red cloth.[55] McDowell was similarly worried. As his men marched toward Bull Run, he insisted that they not only display the national colors but also place miniature flags on their cannon. With some of his men dressed in gray and knowing that some Confederates wore blue, McDowell had identified a potential problem—one the US Army would try to rectify immediately after the battle by

requiring Union forces to wear "sky-blue" and "dark blue" cloth—
and advised everyone to be careful about whom they had in their
sights.[56] Both generals knew the stakes were high; neither understood just how high. Whether these measures would work would
be known soon enough.

For many in the Union army, July 21, the day of battle, began
in eye-squinting darkness. The men who were fumbling around in
the dark at 2 A.M. had trouble forming a line, let alone finding the
road. They "had to *feel* our way" through the dense woods, with
ears attentive to the voice of whoever was next to them. They had
no earthly way of knowing what lay in store for them as they groped
their way toward Bull Run.[57]

High up in one of the signaling towers, a Confederate observer
scanned the horizon with his glasses. Toward the left of his
Confederate line, he saw a glimmer, the milky dawn sunlight
reflecting on something. It was a brass cannon, nestled among
marching armed infantry. Beauregard knew that glimmer was the
beginning of the federal advance.[58]

By 8:45 A.M., the sun was long up, and already it was hot. Federal
troops under General Ambrose Burnside crossed Bull Run, paus-
ing to drink from the stream.[59] Sherman's 3,400 men soon followed. Immediately, they started to ascend the bluff and quickly
were visually disoriented. Sherman was well aware that sight might
become unreliable. Conspicuously, he displayed "our colors" and
"succeed[ed] in attracting the attention of our friends." But he was
wary: "This regiment [the New York Sixty-Ninth] is uniformed in
gray cloth, almost identical with that of the great bulk of the secession army."[60]

This business of the uniforms was going to be a problem.
Colonel J. B. Kershaw of South Carolina found that even as he was
arranging troops for an advance, a Union surgeon named Stone,
mistaking them for his friends, asked why they were retreating. "He
was informed of his mistake, and sent to the rear as prisoner."[61] The

uniform confusion was great enough to litter the battlefield with urgent interrogatives. Who are you? "What troops are those?"[62]

Looking beyond the disorientation created by colors required care. Confederate Alexander Hunter recalled charging the First Massachusetts infantry. The federals "were dressed in gray like ourselves," and confusion reigned for a while: "friend and foe were mixed up together, and you would have to keep a sharp lookout to prevent yourself from being shot by your own men." For his part, Hunter managed to avoid firing on his friends by studying the uniforms of the Massachusetts men as carefully as the circumstances allowed. Yes, they wore gray, too, "only their jackets were of a peculiar cut." Sartorial details mattered.[63]

Luck, pure luck, could also make a difference. General William Smith of the Forty-Ninth Virginia stuttered, uncertain whether to allow his men to fire at the swarm of soldiers in front of them. "That is the enemy," came a voice, questioning, "shall we fire?" Smith couldn't be certain. Ours? Theirs? "Don't be in a hurry," he shouted, "don't fire upon friends." But how could they know? Then came an intervention: "At the instant a puff of wind spread out the Federal flag, and I added, 'There is no mistake: give them h___l boys!"[64] Even still, so addled were men that even a fortuitous and timely breeze could cause more rather than less confusion. An officer in blue ran behind the Second Wisconsin, "all dressed in the dilapidated gray with which we left our state," shouting that they were firing on friends. Large flags could not be deciphered without breezes to unfurl them; even when flags were seen, so doubtful were some soldiers that they began to suspect deliberate ruses.[65]

Early skirmishes showed just how deadly serious the uniform color problem was becoming and hinted at how catastrophic it could be during a full-scale engagement. Men of the First Michigan, wearing blue, almost fired on members of the First Massachusetts, dressed in gray. They "had already leveled their pieces to take aim, when Capt. Carruth ran in among them, inquiring, who are you here?" "Michigan men," came the answer. "Well, we are

Massachusetts men, don't fire!" It was a close escape. Others were not as lucky. Shortly thereafter, men of the First Massachusetts "encountered an unexpected embarrassment, from the fact that the rebels wore uniforms so nearly like ours in color that, a few hundred yards apart, it was impossible to tell who friends were, and who foes." "Lieut. William H. B. Smith discovered the enemy, as he supposed; but seeing how they were attired, and fearing to give the order to fire, lest he might shoot some of our own men, he ran forward." "Who *are* you?" shouted Smith, clambering through a small wood with his gray-clad federals. He directed his question to another group of gray-clad men. Friend? Foe? "Who are *you*?" came the reply. "Massachusetts men," shouted Smith. Seconds later, he was "dead upon the spot."[66]

Sherman's Sixty-Ninth New York regiment had two companies dressed in gray, and he was concerned that Hunter's forces to their left might understandably mistake them for rebels. They did, for a time, and "there was a universal cry that they were being fired upon by our own men." Walk slowly, Sherman counseled. Fate intervened, though, and worked to Sherman's advantage: he encountered General Barnard Bee's Fourth Alabama first, not Hunter's men, who were perched just off the Warrneton Turnpike, beyond Bee. Blue, gray, the colors were bleeding, dangerously. Bee's men paid the price; the New Yorkers were spotted and "were confidently regarded by us as friends." The Fourth Alabama then blundered: they signaled, thought they saw the regiment return it, and confidently unfurled their colors. The result was "murderous fire upon our ranks." The Fourth Alabama was now without any field officers. So many Confederates were mown down that even the normally cautious McDowell rejoiced: "Victory! Victory! The day is ours."[67]

McDowell urged his men onward to Henry House Hill, hot on the heels of the collapsing Confederates, who were puffing their way uphill. The hill was a critical slab of rock and soil, tactically and strategically a fulcrum. Capture it, and it was "On to

Richmond" for the Union—perhaps, just perhaps, beheading this rebellion before it had properly begun. By the same token, for the Confederates, it simply had to be held. Failure would open the new nation to Yankee despotism and quite possibly the end of slavery.[68]

The Confederate leaders—Nathan G. Evans, Bernard E. Bee, and Francis S. Bartow—their ranks disheveled, struggled up the hill. Wade Hampton III and his South Carolinians provided some relief, but it was not enough. Federals were advancing inexorably.

And then, off to the left, behind Henry House, appeared a Confederate man in blue: Stonewall Jackson.[69] Jackson arrived at that point by his own initiative—in fact, by ignoring orders. Instead of following Beauregard's directive to support Confederates between Ball's and Mitchell's Ford, he let his ears do the work and followed the sound of fighting until he was moving up the south slope of Henry Hill. Jackson was well prepared. Like Beauregard, he feared and understood the consequences of visual confusion. His men had to know who was friend and who was foe. The stakes were so large and the margin of error so slim that misdirected fire would be catastrophic. Jackson minimized the danger by turning to the crop of the South: hundreds of strips of white cotton fabric were tied around arms and hats to tell friend from foe. Yes, they might have had "the appearance of so many lunatics," as one Virginian winced, but the white gave them a better chance of being seen through the dust and smoke of battle and was a far superior way to tell friend from foe than another solution: shouting signs and using hand gestures. If you encountered an unknown soldier, you were to strike your left breast with your right hand and bellow, "Our Homes." ("We were given the watchword in a whisper, for fear the enemy, who was two miles off, might hear it," mused one Confederate cavalryman.) Strips of cotton were effective; shouts and hand signs less so, since they "gave the other fellow an opportunity to blow our brains out."[70]

Jackson's attention to the visual was not limited to battle preparations; his engagement on Henry House Hill was marked with
feints and ploys. As the federals streamed down Matthews Hill in
anticipation of roller-coastering up Henry House Hill, Jackson had
his men lie down just beyond the crest, their bodies on slate-specked
soil, limbs woven into the thin, wiry grass. Federals had trouble seeing them fully, or even ascertaining their precise numbers. Union
shot simply whisked over rebel heads. Keeping still was a challenge
for Jackson's men because they knew Bee's troops, lunging up the
hill, were taking heavy fire. But Jackson would not let them move.
There, hidden or barely visible, the men stayed, waiting, if not like
a stone wall then certainly like a hard-to-see line, ready to fire massive volleys the moment the enemy was upon them. As the federal
machine rolled its way across Young's Brach and up Henry House
Hill, Jackson's men lay quietly in the grass, seeing and unseen. They
had also taken sensible precautions: "We tore all the feathers out of
our hats, because we heard the Yanks had feathers in theirs, and we
might be fired on by mistake, as our company was the only one that
had black plumes in their hats."[71]

All the while, Brigadier General Joseph E. Johnston and
Beauregard were working hard to regroup their confetti-strewn
regiments and re-form on the hill. Their efforts were beginning
to pay off, with just shy of seven thousand men and thirteen guns
in their line. It just might be enough to stop the federal advance.
McDowell was pressing hard, though. He had William F. Barry, his
chief of artillery, move two batteries to the lower slopes on the hill,
which he began to heave up the incline. Barry was urged to go to
the very crest of the hill, a message he conveyed to Captain Charles
Griffin, who led Battery D of the Fifth US Artillery. Even as he
directed his fire at the crest, Griffin was nervous: "I had no support." Barry promised him support from the Eleventh New York—
the Zouaves, dressed in red.[72]

Jackson's men remained in their unseen position, crouching and
still. The Zouaves, as promised, ascended Henry House Hill. Blind

to what was beyond them, they saw nothing as they marched up that hill, each step emboldened by fear, trepidation, and hope. "Up, up, not a single enemy in sight," wrote one Zouave. Double quick time now. "Up, up till we gained the top and then . . . ." Jackson's line was there, their fingers trigger-itchy. Surely they could fire now. Yankees were almost upon them. The federals were so close that Jackson's men had their guns at a forty-five-degree angle. Finally, Jackson ordered them to fire. The result was slaughter. "We literally mowed them down."[73]

Visual confusion proved contagious. As the Zouaves were mown down, Jackson's left-flank regiment, the Virginia Thirty-Third, lingered in the woods, in the line of the advancing New York Fourteenth. Colonel Arthur C. Cummings of the Thirty-Third was uncertain of the identity of the New Yorkers, whose grayish uniforms had caused the confusion in the first instance, and Cummings was uncertain: friend or foe? No matter: the Thirty-Third had a signal to determine: right hand on forehead, palm out, with the word "Sumter." Cummings performed the mime and shouted the word. He thought he saw an approaching officer return the signal. Although Cummings "gave the signal," recalled one soldier in the fray, "it was returned by one of the officers, but how they got it was a mystery." Hold fire, Cummings told his men. "Cease fire, you are firing on friends," he admonished the trigger-happy. "Friends, hell." But the words were drowned out by a vicious volley from the New Yorkers. Cummings should have used cotton swatches.[74]

The Zouaves were down but not entirely out. They and reinforcements still had a chance to spill over the crest and head to Richmond. At that point, quite literally, the Confederate cavalry arrived under Jeb Stuart. Their arrival was smoke-filled, men on horses appearing out of the sulfur-heavy air like villains in a pantomime. Seeing the vibrant scarlet of what remained of the Zouaves was not a problem; identifying the meaning of the color was. Stuart knew that a Confederate regiment had a similar uniform.

He paused. Are those our men? His question was answered when he spotted the Zouave flag, and his men charged, "cutting right and left with their sabers" from horseback.[75]

Cummings and his blue-clad Virginia Thirty-Third were still in play, and luck was on their side. As Griffin and Barry watched Cummings's men emerge from the woods, Griffin swore blind they were Confederates; Barry was adamant: they were not. Aim and fire at them, Griffin ordered. Just in time, Barry intervened. No. They are wearing blue. They must be part of the Fourteenth New York, cried Barry, "don't fire there; those are your battery support." Griffin knew something Barry didn't: "they are confederates." Their blue uniforms did not fool him. But Barry would not have any of it. They were dressed in blue. They have to be ours. "I know they are your battery support," he insisted. Griffin buckled and watched tensely as Cummings's men in blue marched toward him. He could not stand being so exposed and again trained his guns. Barry repeated what was rapidly becoming his mantra: "I know it is the battery support."[76]

It is difficult to imagine what it must have been like to look up Henry House Hill at the troops above. For men who had to dig deep to find the courage to fight, to aim unwieldy rifles and muskets, to train a long metal barrel at another human being, to consider pulling that trigger and make sense of that act because it was the enemy in sight, the sudden realization that the man in sight was wearing the same colors and just might be friend and not foe must have been a terrifying thought. War allowed killing, but the possibility that they might have been firing at one of their own must have induced a gut-churning moment of indecision.

Barry and Griffin weren't the only federals arguing about what they actually saw. Joining the New York Eleventh, Colonel Willis Gorman of the First Minnesota also thought the Virginians were federals; Brigadier General Samuel P. Heintzelman, a little ahead of the Zouaves, agreed with Griffin: certainly, they were foe. But they had debated and stared too long. While the federals hedged,

Cummings ordered his blue Virginians to fire. The volley was devastating. Griffin: "That was almost the last of us, we were all cut down." Gone were fifty of his horses; gone were men, many shot from saddles; gone were almost all Griffin's cannoneers. The Virginians were relentless, inspired by the simple, reassuring knowledge that they were killing the enemy. They swarmed the Union soldiers, capturing cannon and caissons. The men in blue— the federal men in blue—scattered, running down the hill they had fought so hard to capture, frantic, hopes of victory replaced with raw, primal fears. This was the rout the Confederates had hoped for—the turning point that, at least for the moment, gave them as solid a footing on this sloping piece of Virginia earth as they could hope for.[77]

And then, mercifully, it all ended. One last attempt by federal forces to rush Henry House Hill failed. The end was fittingly disordered and chaotic, an accurate signature of the entire opening battle of the Civil War. By late afternoon, Union troops were rushing down the hill. Union Colonel Erasmus D. Keyes witnessed this "scene of confusion . . . which beggars description." Horses without riders, "pieces of artillery drawn by six horses without drivers, flying at their utmost speed and whacking against other vehicles," men throwing away their rifles, running backward, tumbling down that hill, rushing like a torrent, producing "a noise like a hurricane at sea." The fields were strewn with the remains of military kits—knapsacks, rifles, cannon—and items left behind by frightened spectators caught in the rushed withdrawal: buggies, a lady's slipper, a parasol, picnic hampers. Gone was any pretense at system or arrangement. Panic erased the last vestiges of visual order.[78]

Confederates knew they had won when the linearity was no more. The Union retreat was described by reporters, North and South, in ways that captured the visual disruption. In addition to knapsacks and weapons, bodies were "strewn," "heaped," and "scattered"; the injured were dazed and "wandering."[79] The prepared

columns of men and the careful orchestration before Bull Run were replaced with utter confusion, disorder, "awful appearances." Nothing was geometric after this battle, and both armies found themselves as ragtag in victory as in defeat.[80]

Darkness halted the Confederates from chasing after the retreating Union soldiers, retreat itself a disorganized affair. Gathering with his officers, McDowell, dozy and drained, opted to return all the way to Washington. Traveling blind at night seemed like a fitting end to Bull Run.[81]

The *Charleston Mercury* reported that for the fallen, at least the lucky fallen who died in the vicinity of comrades, "sympathizing hearts" and "soft, youthful hands" closed the eyes of the deceased. Blindness was peace (figure 2.1).[82]

The postmortem of this battle was, like all hindsight discussions, full of whats, ifs, and buts. There was, though, agreement on both sides that the uniforms and the visual confusion they caused accounted for much of the day's outcome. Confederate Lieutenant General Jubal Early put the matter of blame into appropriate perspective, quite literally. Early was criticized for mistaking the enemy and wrongly ordering Confederates to withhold fire. But Early thought he was entirely right to counsel caution. "At the time there was very little distinction between the dress of some of the Federal regiments and some of ours," he recalled, adding that on the day in question, the lack of wind left flags "drooping" so that federal staffs were "not to be distinguishable from the Confederate flag." He considered officers who refused to pause, to hold fire in the face of such evidence, reckless and caught up in the giddy orbit of the moment, failing "to preserve that clearness of judgment and calmness of the nerves which is so necessary to enable one to see things as they really are during an engagement." But Early well knew that no one, officers included, truly saw things as they really were at the brutal battle (figure 2.2).[83]

"It has been asserted," noted that reporter for the *Charleston Mercury*, "by numerous individuals engaged in the battle, that there

FIGURE 2.1. *Seeing Death at First Bull Run?*

"Confederate Dead on Matthews Hill, Bull Run?" Call Number 4168, no 42 [P&P], Library of Congress Prints and Photographs Division, Washington, D.C. These men were alive, their bodies staged by the photographer. Even photographic evidence betrayed the eye. See William A. Frassanito, *Antietam: The Photographic Legacy of America's Bloodiest Day* (New York: Charles Scribner's Sons, 1978), pp. 30–32.

was great confusion and slaughter among our own men, who mistook them for the enemy. This was less to be wondered at from the similarity of uniform."[84] No less a soldier than Sherman agreed. That dreadful afternoon was "an incessant clamor of tongues, one saying that they were not properly supported, another that they could not tell friend from foe."[85] The memory of uniform confusion lingered for years. In 1914, Samuel D. John evoked the tearing up of the Alabama Fourth courtesy of "a regiment in gray" that was "at first mistaken for Confederate reinforcements till they poured deadly fire into the ranks."[86]

In the coming days, on the battlefield itself, sight began to be eclipsed by another sense, one produced by the mangled bodies and bloating horses baking in the July sun. "The air was awful," noted one observer. It was "the most horrid of odors, especially when it arises from the living." And from the dead. Three days after the battle, bodies—of man and horse—lay unburied, creating a stench that "is insufferable and taints the air for miles around."[87] War was revealing its true colors.

BATTLE OF BULL RUN.

FIGURE 2.2. *First Battle of Bull Run.*

Lithograph by Kurz and Allison, 1889. Reproduction Number: LC-USZC4-1796 (color film copy transparency), Library of Congress Prints and Photographs Division, Washington, D.C.

Chapter Three

Cornelia Hancock's Sense of Smell

All of her features were striking: her hair—long, black, thick—was bisected on her small, delicate head by a severe part, conferring an air of authority on one so young. Her eyebrows were thick, and when arched, seemed to defiantly challenge the world. Her eyes, sorrowful but also tender, were unwavering. They bore no cynicism, and years of hard sights—having seen war, poverty, injustice, and dislocation—would not harden them. They remained full of wonder, of hope and determination.[1]

Mouth and jaw were perfectly in keeping with those eyes. Her lips were pencil-thin and resolute, suggesting tenacity; the edges of her mouth turned down, as if pulled by gravity. Her strong jaw, almost square, was too perhaps masculine for some tastes but suggested a determination to stand her ground. She is Cornelia Hancock of the tiny hamlet of Hancock's Bridge, in southern New Jersey. In 1863, she was all of twenty-three years old.[2]

Her nose merits more extensive comment. The glabella, the space between the eyes that was the bridge's top, was remarkable only for being slightly larger than usual; the nasion and the rhinion, which made up the bulk of the length of her nose, were quite sweeping but not overly; the nostrils were neither large nor small, only slightly flared; the columella normal-sized. The tip was buttonish, but this was not necessarily a bad thing. Women were not supposed to have expanded nostrils—suggestive of a wrathful nature—or "strongly marked" noses generally, "a sure sign of masculine temper," as *Harper's New Monthly Magazine* opined in 1856. By the standards of the day, Cornelia Hancock's nose was average.[3]

"Average" does not mean inconsequential. The nose was distinctly human, argued thinkers of the day. It led the face into the world, and according to that essay on smell in *Harper's*, was "an outward organ, bold, open, and striking"; animals had them, but their noses were mushed into faces, "mostly flat and close upon the jaws." The human nose, on the other hand, was noble because it performed so many functions: breathing, modulating the voice, presenting the character of the person, and, above all, smelling. Those with a "fine nose" and possessing a "keen scent" were of sound, refined judgment. The nose could distinguish easily between injurious and noxious smells and joyous, happy ones and, in this regard, was a sentinel against the objectionable and suspect. It could distinguish whether food was foul or safe, the body washed or unclean. It could detect character. In short, the nose was our "watchman."

But there was also something about the nose that rendered its unerring ability to smell a rat even more effective. Unlike the eye and mouth, which were "well defended"—eyes could blink and mouths could shut—the nose "can not close the gates." Smells are transgressive, punching their way inside, the only real defense being not to breathe at all. The nose and its sense of smell are always engaged, always in and of the world, constantly and instantly delivering unfiltered information to the brain. The sense of smell "is placed at the very entrance-gate where the air we breathe is constantly passing, and thus ever carries on its imperceptible waves [of] odorous atoms," read a nineteenth-century treatise on olfaction.

So profound and immediate is smell that language itself is only marginally up to the task to conveying its meaning, which is why, said the treatise, "we still speak of sharp and pungent smells, or we give them the name of flowers and animals by which they are produced." Although smell "is the poorest of all senses in point of languages" and "borrows a few names from other senses, mostly from the taste," it was still a noble sense not least because it could judge, in the blink of an eye, what was good and what was bad, what was true and what was false."[4]

So even Cornelia Hancock's ordinary-looking nose had the potential to reveal core truths (figure 3.1). And in the stifling summer of 1863, it got its chance, telling us something about the Civil War's greatest battle, something that no amount of seeing, hearing, touching, or tasting could achieve. And what it told us was so full of grim meaning that we can only look back at that battle and wonder why it didn't bring an end to war.

Gettysburg. We know so much about it that its component elements can be reeled off in staccato voice; the names, dates, places, and numbers are so familiar that they are embedded in American

FIGURE 3.1. *Cornelia Hancock.*

From the Collection of The New Jersey Historical Society, Newark, New Jersey (MG 1364, Photo Album 35).

consciousness. Three brutal days in July, the first through the third, 1863; Union forces under the direction of Major General George G. Meade; Confederate ones directed by General Robert E. Lee. Fifty thousand or so causalities, 28,000 of them Confederate—a third of Lee's army. A Union victory.[5]

The Confederate plan, a gutsy, audacious invasion for peace by Lee: fight on Northern soil, embolden the hand of Northern Peace Democrats, and relieve the federal pressure on Virginia. Had he succeeded, it might have worked: a defeated and increasingly anxious North might have agreed to peace, especially if the British, on the lookout for a Confederate victory, intervened. Had Lee succeeded, other dividends beckoned: a Confederate victory might have helped to allieviate pressure on beleaguered Vicksburg. The French might have recognized the Confederacy. These were Jefferson Davis's dreams and hopes.

July 1: Coming in from the north and west, Lee's entire army faced some of the Army of the Potomac. The Confederates enjoyed success, pushing federals back to Cemetery Hill and forming a line running south down Cemetery Ridge and east to Culp's Hill. Confederates claim Seminary Ridge and the town, Gettysburg.

Night brought reinforcements for both sides, including, for the federals, Meade himself and the bulk of the Army of the Potomac. Meade reinforced his line and extended it south by two miles, ending at Little Round Top.

Unaware of Meade's deployment south (he is sans cavalry then), Lee attempts an all-out assault. General James Longstreet and Lieutenant General A. P. Hill are instructed: strike the Union left flank at the Peach Orchard, Devil's Den, the Wheatfield, the Round Tops. Lieutenant General Richard S. Ewell attacked the Union right at Culp's and East Cemetery Hills. Evening revealed the result: Ewell has been mostly turned back; Little Round Top was still in Union hands.

July 3 was especially brutal. The Confederates lost Culp's Hill; General George Pickett's charge was murderously damaging to them, too; and the cavalry lunge by Major General J. E. B. Stuart failed. The next day, Lee began to withdraw. Fourteen miles of his own wounded men were left in his wake. An estimated three thousand died in battle; still others were ravaged by disease. Battle deaths dwarfed the population of Gettysburg, a town of 2,400 souls in 1860. The scale of death was unprecedented and never repeated in the country's history: more than 50,000 dead and wounded in total.

We know about Gettysburg: the movements, deployments, tactics, charges, defenses. We also accept the significance; this was a battle for a unified country, for nation, for liberty, for freedom. Four months later, President Lincoln would utter words about equality so "nobly advanced," sentiments now etched into stone.

But what was it like to experience Gettysburg, to be immersed in it? This is where Cornelia Hancock's nose comes in. A battle for modern civilization Gettysburg may have been, a battle in which some of the latest fighting technologies were deployed, but the result was a throwback to a different age.[6]

The men in blue—this time, those supposed to be in blue were—knew Lee was coming, and so they marched northward through Frederick County, Maryland, always keeping themselves between the 70,000-strong Confederate army—the Army of Northern Virginia making its way north through the Shenandoah and Cumberland Valleys—and their capital, Washington, D.C. Their sheer scale was impressive: 97,000 thousand Union men in seven corps. This was the mighty Army of the Potomac, with the recently appointed Meade at the helm.[7]

There were so many of them that you could hear them long before you saw them. Union nurse Charlotte McKay saw cavalry, stretching miles, "whose sabres always announce their approach before you hear the tramp of their horses." Then came the infantry a "few hours" later, a "long, dark line in motion," snaking through the countryside, "colors and battle-flags waving on the air," some of them shredded and torn. The massive, meandering, and bristling line "of flashing bayonets" slicing through rural Maryland was awe-inspiring. And then they were gone, on their way to glory and death, leaving in their wake a "painful . . . stillness," grim prelude to the cacophony that would ensue.[8]

Cornelia Hancock, over a hundred miles away in her sleepy village of Hancock's Bridge, New Jersey, itched to see something of the world. Perhaps she took after her father, something of a "nonconformist by nature," an individualist, a fisherman who prized his independence and who, according to Cornelia, took "as little interest as possible in other people's affairs." Or perhaps the young woman's need to do something outside of Hancock's Bridge, "to overcome the inertia" of rural life, came from her maternal grandmother, a woman for whom "no teakettle could pour fast enough." Cornelia had become even more fidgety as the war dragged on and "my only brother and every male relative and friend that we possessed" had gone off to fight. Alone in the house, bored, fearful that the "teakettle of life was pouring out very slowly," and tired of the "endless waiting," Cornelia resolved that, somehow or other, "I, too, would go and serve my country." Her conduit was Dr. Henry T. Child of Philadelphia, her brother-in-law and an active antislavery man. She confided in him her desire, and he, in turn, "promised to let me know of the first available opportunity."[9]

Cornelia Hancock's little New Jersey village was not unlike Gettysburg: both were resolutely rural in composition and tempo, places where the sounds of animals competed with the sounds of people and where both had little competition from the sounds of industry. Unlike Hancock's Bridge, though, Gettysburg's gentle rural hum, its Arcadian rhythm of slumber and work, was about to be violently disrupted, the village and its environs—and its people—changed.

Nothing offered a hint of the strife that was to descend. W. W. Potter, a medic attached to the Forty-Ninth New York, sat on a haystack near the town, staring up at the moon peeking from behind clouds. "The air was refreshing and the ripe harvest of the new-mown hay gave it a sweet and wholesome odor."[10] That scent, the smell of the countryside, the smell of rural America, the smell of places like Hancock's Bridge and Gettysburg: "Where lately peach-blooms scented all the air."[11]

Just before 9 A.M., July 1, an odd quiet prevailed in the town, a deathly stillness. Even the usually garrulous animals—hungry to be fed or milked—were mum. Everything "was quiet and not a soldier in sight; in fact the stillness was oppressive, and at this time of day when ordinarily the sounds from the farm are the loudest." Rumors of an attack were thick. Where were the rebels? Would they attack? If so, when?[12]

In answer to the question came the sound of cannon. The shell "seemed to fly over your heads," startling in its suddenness and loudness. And then, zombie-like, "thousands of men rose from the earth," populating the fields. The battle had begun.[13]

There was no stopping it. As more and more men arrived, they marched onto the fields and prepared to fight. This first day was one of frightening sights and deafening, unnatural sounds. The sight of Confederate "bayonets glistening in the sun" and the "deafening roar of musketry" invited horror in the hearts of civilians. The physical effects became apparent quickly. Within a short time, Gettysburg residents saw mutilation that defied belief: amputated and misshapen limbs; digits dangled; horse flesh gaped. Young women of fifteen, whose lives had been shielded from these things, saw men with eyes blown from their yawning sockets, soldiers limping, sometimes crawling from the field of battle.

For some "these horrible sights were too much . . . to bear." The dead were buried but feverishly in the shallowest of graves. There was no time to do anything but half a job, given the heat of the day baking and crisping the crumb-top graves. The wounded—too often, the imminent dead—in the fields migrated to the houses, sheds, churches, and barns of the little town, which were filled with appalling sights and awful groans. Those attending to the wounded were overwhelmed, literally struggling through the bodies and limbs, clothes smeared with the blood and guts of the dead and dying. The always-thin line between soldier and civilian was obliterated, their worlds commingling shamelessly.[14]

July 2. Dawn revealed the carnage of the night. Harrie Hamilton Bayley saw it from her farm just outside Gettysburg. "As far as I could see there were men, living and dead, and horses and guns and cannon, and confusion everywhere." Venturing into the body-strewn fields and meadows, she came upon dying men with horrific wounds clinging to life. Some cried out for water; others pleaded for help. One soldier begged for water simply so he might loosen the desiccated wadding plugging a nasty wound. The cloth he'd used "had become so dry with clotted blood" that it would not budge without moisture, the fibers braiding into his exposed flesh, forming a new layer of grit-riddled skin.[15]

The scale of fighting that day was tremendous: more than 30,000 Union soldiers and almost 25,000 Confederates battled, all "facing the cannon's lurid breath" and skin-tearing, bone-shattering shot. The noise was tremendous, so loud "that it was with great difficulty we could hear ourselves speak." It seemed as "though the heavens were sending forth peal upon peal of terrible thunder directly over our heads," shaking the very ground beneath nervous feet. At night, the firing continued, notably on Culp's Hill, where Confederates finally, around 10 P.M., overran parts of the Union line. Federals and rebels were now within shouting distance of one another.[16]

What could be heard couldn't always be seen. Here Lee had the disadvantage, although he seemed unaware of it. His scouts were unreliable, and he did not have the high ground. Despite his efforts, he failed to see the scale and size of key Union divisions, and, like many of the men at First Bull Run, his faith in what he saw betrayed him.[17]

It was also a day of violent smells, starting with the powerful, nostril-stinging odor of gunpowder and saltpeter. Ever since First Bull Run, "smelling the powder" had become shorthand among soldiers for fighting.[18] Men who malingered in field hospitals were told by physicians to join the battle, "have a chance to smell the invigorating fumes of burnt powder, and take your share and chance of the toil and danger of your comrades in the field, instead of bumming round here any longer."[19] Fighting men were men who experienced the smell of gunpowder, not men who kept a safe distance from the battle.[20]

Day Three was a steroidal version of Day Two. Battle sounds at dawn again. "May I never again be roused to the consciousness of a new born day by such fearful sounds," prayed one Gettysburg resident.[21] It would be an appallingly loud day, this third day, with a death toll to match. At about 1 P.M., an extraordinarily heavy cannonade began. A hundred and seventy Confederate guns along Seminary Ridge shot at 110 Union guns perched across Cemetery Ridge. The two-hour booming was astonishing that afternoon, "as if the heavens and earth were crashing together." Even from cellars under houses, this "terrific sound" of strife forced its way into ears. The "scream" of each shell was sickening, suggestive of "excruciating pain." Sounds "more terrible never greeted human ears."[22]

On this day, perhaps more than on any other day, the "air was filled with moanings and groanings," the fields so littered with dead and wounded men, with dead horses "swollen to almost twice their natural size," that those caring for the dying had to master a gruesome tiptoeing. The "moaning of wounded soldiers" could be heard the first day; "the patter of rifle balls" lodging into houses was audible on the second. But nothing quite prepared soldiers or civilians for the sheer scale of butchery that third day.[23] This was the day when 12,000 Confederates, led by Major General Pickett, stepped off Seminary Ridge and walked a mile through an open field to take Cemetery Ridge from the federals. Those who made it to the ridge fought bravely, courageously, hand-to-hand in many cases—but so many of them did not. Approximately 7,000 Americans died in that roughly one-hour interval. That's about 116 deaths per minute; almost two deaths every brutal second. Laid end to end, their bodies would have stretched over seven miles.[24]

The intensity and scale of the violence could be more than heard and seen; it could be smelled. For those running and gulping for air, there was no escaping the odor of processed saltpeter, a concoction of deadly, violent snuff. "The pungent smell of burnt gunpowder pervaded the evening air" for these men, the signature of hard battle, as much a clue to the day's violence as the "sighs and groans" and "gouts of blood."[25] When gunpowder mingled with dust and smoke, the effect was choking: "The air, thick with smoke and sulphurous vapor, almost suffocated the troops in support of the batteries." Sights, sounds, groans, splinters flying, "men flung to the ground, horses torn and shrieking." There was a haze so thick that men became subsumed by the "murk" consuming them, capturing and encapsulating the literally appalling violence.[26]

The smell can't be recreated. The epic battle would become immortalized by sight—the recently developed technology of photography. Even before the battle had ended, those in the business of visual recording, including Alexander Gardner and Timothy O'Sullivan, were at the scene (figure 3.2).

On July 4, that most hallowed day for Americans, that greatest of all battles ended. The bulk of the grand armies of North and South had left the fields of battle; Lee limped south; a few federal divisions went after him, but—to Lincoln's frustration—didn't engage him in his weakened state.

What they had left behind was a different kind of struggle. The carnage of Gettysburg was so great, on a scale so unprecedented, that the wounded and the dead and the dying remained there for many days afterward, fighting for survival. And the men—and the many women—who came to help them fought for them, too. They fought against diseases, they fought to keep men alive, and they fought to preserve their own sense of civilization. In the days immediately after Gettysburg, the scene offered something antithetical to America's sense of itself, something primeval. And perhaps most degenerative was the smell of decomposition—of men, horses, once-healthy limbs and organs. The deaths of the first day were, by

FIGURE 3.2. *Gettysburg, Pa. Confederate dead gathered for burial at the edge of the Rose Woods, July 5, 1863.*

Alexander Gardner. Reproduction Number: LC-DIG-cwpb-00882 (digital file from original neg. of left half), Library of Congress Prints and Photographs Division, Washington, D.C.

July 4, beginning to be counted in new ways. A North Carolina soldier commented: "No fighting to-day, but we are burying the dead. They have been lying on the field in the sun since the first day's fight; it being dusty and hot, the dead smell terribly."[27] The rains that fell so hard immediately after the battle did not discriminate between wounded federal and wounded Confederate. Makeshift hospitals, really nothing more than coagulations of tents in fields or, if lucky, an old barn, were primitive at best. The wounded lay "upon heaps of manure, reeking with rain," tormented by vermin brushing up against undressed wounds, "many longing for amputation as the happy long for food or drink," the despair palpable.[28] It was a brutal Independence Day. One soldier, J. L. Porter, "celebrated the Forth by a trip along the entire length of the battlefield. It had rained during the night previous, the dead were swollen and

black and the sight and smell to one not hardened as a soldier was simply intolerable. Detachments were busy burying the dead of both armies as Lee had retreated, leaving his dead on the field."[29]

Just as its major battle had ended, Cornelia Hancock's encounter with the Civil War began. On July 4, a boat carrying a horse and carriage belonging to Dr. Henry T. Child was making its way up the Delaware River. The boat arrived in Hancock's Bridge early the next day, and the horse and carriage were driven to the Hancock house. The young woman was still in bed, but she heard a commotion. It was her mother, fretful and worried, telling her not to leave for Gettysburg. Her mother had enough to worry about; her son, Cornelia's only brother, was already gone. Her mother begged her not to go. But Cornelia was determined to go to war. "So it proved," she recalled, "and in an hour's time I was off to Philadelphia."

She and Dr. Child passed through Salem, Cornelia hiding lest she be spotted by friends who would, she feared, parrot her mother. By late afternoon, she'd reached Philadelphia. The city was abuzz with news and rumor. There had been a massive battle somewhere in Pennsylvania—"no one knew exactly where." Further inquiries revealed the exact place: "a little town called Gettysburg." There was a false rumor that the rebel army was making its way to Philadelphia. Everyone was skittish. What was certain, though, was "the awful loss of life on both sides." Dr. Child and several other physicians were determined to leave for Gettysburg that night, on the eleven o'clock train, and Cornelia was to go with them. She would not be the only young lady, for Dr. Child and others had secured passes for several volunteer nurses, all older than Cornelia, and they were all headed to Gettysburg to tend to the wounded.

As Cornelia set off that night of July 5, her senses were on high alert. Philadelphia's darkness seemed heavy to her; at Havre de Grace, Maryland, she "heard the cars creaking weirdly on the pontoon bridges over the Susquehanna River." New and foreboding sounds and sights seemed to jump at her. However, neither Philadelphia nor Baltimore, where the train stopped briefly, he

anything special in terms of smell. For years, American cities had been making progress in containing odors. Throughout the antebellum period, various city and municipal authorities had started projects dedicated to efficient disposal of human and animal waste. Fearing that disease was spread through miasmatic stench, authorities started to mandate cleaner streets and suppress the reek of waste by shuttling at least some of it underground into rudimentary sewage systems. Although most of the nation's sewer systems were yet to be built, many Americans by 1860 were beginning to embrace an idea popular by the mid-nineteenth century: public safety owed a great deal to efforts at environmental deodorization and the control of smells.[30]

Personal hygiene also gained importance. People in the antebellum period had started to wash more, and use of soap and scents was increasingly common. Women were advised in a slew of books on the desirability of washing, subduing bodily odors, and the use of soap. Men, too—of all classes, from elites to servants—were instructed not to mask body odor with superficial scents. Entire bodies should be scrubbed. For forward-thinking Americans and nineteenth-century moderns everywhere, odor meant filth, suggesting lack of character and refinement; clean smells denoted not just cleanliness but also decency, a smell commensurate with civilization and godliness.[31]

And then there was the demonic smell of chaos. Cornelia and her party arrived in Gettysburg on the evening of July 6 and immediately went to one of the local churches "where I saw for the first time what war meant": hundreds of wounded soldiers "stretched out on boards laid across the high-backed pews as closely as they could be packed together," their bodies elevated high enough to be almost on a level with hers. There she stood, "breast-high in a sea of anguish." She tried to help them as best she could that night, writing letters home to their loved ones before they died.

The next morning, Cornelia ventured out to the fields around Gettysburg. She went to see a New Jersey regiment, the Twelfth,

a few miles outside the town. She saw the sort of sights that were being captured so powerfully in photographs: the wounded and contorted bodies, limbs spastic; frozen faces, the moment of death etched in their grimaces. But photography couldn't capture the sounds, the groans, or the rustle of twitching bodies that gave depth to what the camera couldn't.[32]

Above all, it was the sense of smell that engulfed Cornelia Hancock in Gettysburg, freighting it with a meaning that a photograph alone could never capture. She had no choice but to confront it, and she chose her words with care:

> Not the presence of the dead bodies themselves, swollen and disfigured as they were and lying in heaps on every side was as awful to the spectator as that deadly, nauseating atmosphere which robbed the battlefield of its glory the survivors of their victory and the wounded of what little chance of life was left to them.

Note her belief that smell—more than smell but "atmosphere"— would kill off the wounded. Smell was more than dangerous and oppressive to the living; it would rob the dead, repulsing glory. The smell had a physical presence:

> A sickening, overpowering, awful stench announced the presence of the unburied dead upon which the July sun was mercilessly shining and at every step the air grew heavier and fouler until it seemed to possess a palpable horrible density that could be seen and felt and cut with a knife.

Gettysburg's odors were as violent as the action that had caused them, and they had to be fought against.[33]

Cornelia Hancock's nose was far from alone. A dispatch from "Mr. N. Davidson," published in the *New York Herald*, described the conditions of various Confederate and Union hospitals in and around Gettysburg on July 17. The account offers an olfactory map of the aftermath of battle and in the process makes claims about the superior medical expertise and cleanliness of Union hospitals and physicians and the utter barbarity of Confederates. To support the claims, to harden the distinction between Confederate and Union, Davidson uses smells, depicting Union hospitals as far superior to Confederate hospitals. Union field "hospitals are sweet, and the air pure." "If the rebels excel us in the discipline in their army," mused Davidson, "it certainly does not extend to the Medical Department." Neither was it for want of facilities. "Pennsylvania College Hospital," home to hundreds of injured Confederate soldiers, was "beautiful," "a large structure, very well adapted for hospital purposes . . . with unobstructed circulation of air." A shortage of nurses and pure and simple laziness, thought Davidson, was the chief cause of the appalling conditions, conditions best measured by "the atmosphere within," which was "close and fetid."[34]

Others attempted to escape the insistent smell, which, once again, had risen to the density of "atmosphere." "We saw the rifle-pits, the dead horses, the shattered windows and the stone walls, all scattered and many soldiers' graves. But who shall describe the horrible atmosphere which meets us continually?" Closing eyes offered temporary relief from the appalling sights, but escaping the stench was harder: "Chloride of lime has been freely used in the broad streets of the town and to-day the hospital was much improved by the same means; but it is needful to close the eyes on sights of horror and to shut the ears against sounds of anguish and to extinguish, as far as possible, the sense of smelling."[35]

Important lessons for future battles were learned, and, later in the war, some soldiers took scents with them to fight. "Thanks to a previous and somewhat similar experience at Gettysburg, when the streaming ground and murky atmosphere was surcharged with the stench of the unburied horses and half buried men, I had something with me more agreeable than the sanitary smudge," wrote one soldier a year after Gettysburg. He took along with him a "precious *vinaigrette* to stay the ceaseless nausea," a sort of "French aromatic vinegar."[36]

We can perhaps only see Gettysburg through smell, and we should look again at Gardner's pictures with Cornelia's words in mind. That he and his colleagues were not above staging their photographs, arranging bodies for artistic effect, matters little for our purposes. What is important is the suggestive power of the photograph, the way the image captures the grim sight of war but withholds sensory potential; it can only be animated by Cornelia Hancock's nose, by which this image becomes one of profound depth.[37]

Cornelia Hancock was not alone. Gettysburg resident Susan Broadhead's diary entry for Saturday, July 11, 1863, a week after battle's end, reads: "The atmosphere is loaded with the horrid smell of decaying horses and the remains of slaughtered animals, and, it is said, from the bodies of men imperfectly buried. I fear we shall be visited with pestilence, for every breath we draw is made ugly by the stench."[38] Burning the horses en masse seemed only to exacerbate the problem, the stench, "like a hateful charnel house," being carried for miles and miles.[39]

In purely visual terms, this photograph, by Timothy H. O'Sullivan, is powerful (figure 3.3), leaving us in no doubt about the scale of the event. But Broadhead's description gives the scene "atmosphere." O'Sullivan's photograph keeps us in a place, a visual frame; Broadhead's diary entry allows us to venture into it. Smell lends atmosphere to the photograph, animating death.

The olfactory experience of Gettysburg lingered long after among men who had fought on those hot fields in early July. Like all soldiers, they remembered—sometimes relived—war by smell. A year after the battle, at a July Fourth celebration in Philadelphia, youths were seen setting off fireworks. Not "until the 'weesma hours's' of the 5th will the atmosphere cease to be ladened with the fumes of villainous saltpetre!" wrote a reporter. But the smell triggered recollections: "Those returned veteran regiments now in our midst will again, in imagination, revisit the bloody field of Gettysburg, and

FIGURE 3.3. *Dead Horses of Bigelow's (Ninth Massachusetts) Battery, 1863.*

Timothy H. O'Sullivan. Reproduction Number: LC-USZC4-1831 (color film copy transparency), Library of Congress Prints and Photographs Division, Washington, D.C.

tell to their wives and little ones how, on a certain Fourth of July, brave Pennsylvania troops drove the Rebel invader from the soil of our noble State, and insured to her citizens that peace and security which, for so many years past, they had enjoyed."[40]

Gettysburg was not the only battle of the Civil War notable for its stench. The technology for killing en masse was so effective, so massively efficient at generating dead bodies, that it outpaced the technology for recovery and burial of those same bodies.[41] Other battles were thus similarly noted for their rancid odor. The Battle of Iuka in 1862 occurred in hot conditions, and in less than twenty-four hours, bodies were beginning to decompose "and the stench arising was horrible"; failed Union attacks at Vicksburg left many dead on the field "and the stench is awful"; after Petersburg "it required a good nose and a better stomach to carry one through the ordeal"—to name just a few.[42]

Sometimes, the technology of war itself was explicitly and deliberately olfactory. Both sides experimented with "stink balls." Union artillery men developed a shell containing ether and guano, which they happily lobbed into Charleston while besieging the city in 1863. The idea seems to have been to force surrender by smell. Certainly, the stink bombs were highly unpleasant: their stench was, according to one account, "suffocating and insufferable, besides being inextinguishable." For its part, the Confederacy considered the use of "a stink-shell" to create a "suffocating effect" in enemy trenches.[43]

Gettysburg, however, was exceptional. The scale of the battle, the roughly 6 million pounds of human and horse flesh, bone, and offal coating the hot fields and soaking into Pennsylvania soil, the numbing smell of 22,000 wounded people—all this made it olfactorily unprecedented. According to accounts, the reek lasted until October, nearing the time of the first frost.[44]

For many people, the stench constituted a very powerful form of meaning. Union and Confederate alike found it profoundly disconcerting. It brought in, against their will, death. The nation itself seemed to be decomposing. Gettysburg was the stench of war certainly, but it was also the living stench of the Union literally coming apart. This was a degenerative moment, one that had to be rescued later by powerful speeches, endless visits, and solemn, postwar reconciliatory commemorations.[45]

Years after the battle, when veterans met again on those same fields, they found something missing. When 50,000 veterans converged on Gettysburg in 1912, the atmosphere was clean. "The sanitary arrangements are perfect, no foul smells, no flies," wrote one, admiringly. Almost fifty years later, Gettysburg had become civilized.[46]

Chapter Four

The Hollowing of Vicksburg

Imagine a giant finger, as might belong to "the Lord of Creation," carving out the Mississippi River. For much of the immense river's length, the finger moves lazily, gouging inlets here and there, meandering occasionally, like a child drawing in sand. Always, the finger heads insistently south. At the beginning—at the most northern point of the river—the tip of the nail does the work, tracing little veins in the soil; by river's end in the Gulf of Mexico, the finger has dug deep and wide. At some point, something made the giant finger jerk violently, causing the river to almost double back on itself and creating a little pocket of land, the De Soto Peninsula. Here, the finger dug deep, pushing loamy soil high, creating steep slopes of loess, accumulating until it soared 140 feet high above the river. The loess had the consistency of icing on a cake, providing a stable foundation to what was built atop it but also permitting digging into its sides. The giant finger paused to tap the top of what it had created, flattening it and forming an earthen platform, a giant's table offering splendid views to anyone who would live on it (map 4.1).[1]

By the start of the Civil War, some 4,500 people had gathered atop the bluffs, making their home on this high bulge of land lodged in the river's throat and building the city of Vicksburg, Mississippi—the terraced City of the Hills, as a later statesman would call it, a pinnacle of civilization. In 1860, about sixty percent of the city's residents were white, the rest mostly slaves and free blacks.[2] For more than a decade, Vicksburg had been beginning

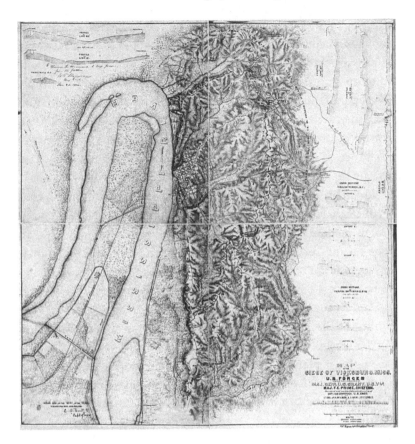

MAP 4.1. *Vicksburg.*

"Map of the siege of Vicksburg, Miss.," Aug. 20th, 1863 (Vicksburg, Miss., Head Qrs. of the Dept. of the Tenn., 1863), Call Number G3984.V8S5 1864. S59, Library of Congress Geography and Map Division, Washington, D.C.

to live up to its elevation over the Mississippi, due to the growing number of merchants, its railroad connections to the east, and the highly productive soil around the city. And with that influx of cash, the town became home to some of Mississippi's most refined citizens, presenting in 1862 "a fine appearance when viewed from below" and equally impressive from within, dotted with "elegant private residences" and a large, imposing courthouse that was considered the finest in the entire state. It was a bustling, business-oriented place, boasting tanneries, sawmills, wholesale and retail stores, schools, churches in abundance, and three daily newspapers. This was a city at once cultured and, by antebellum standards, varied. In fact, because of its geographic placement, Vicksburg attracted a greater variety and perhaps even greater abundance of goods, goods that it both consumed and sold, than most antebellum southern cities of similar size.[3]

Not all was airy and light, of course. From its official incorporation in 1825 right through the 1850s, the city assumed an industrial and commercial feel, due to the railroad shops, cotton gins, and all of the businesses necessary for servicing the surrounding plantations (grand but not quite as grand as those of nearby Natchez) and their large cotton crops. Vicksburg had slave pens, and those enslaved in the city and its environs certainly didn't share in the delights of the planter class. Like other urban areas in the Old South, Vicksburg was a city whose social hierarchy was rigid: slaves at the bottom, planters and slaveholders at the top, poor whites and an emerging white middle class wedged in between. Order mattered here because it had to. Everything—jobs, functions, public and private spaces—were arranged according to the protocols of a Southern slaveholding society. In this regard, Vicksburg was like any other Southern city.[4]

The essential character of this slaveholding city can be gauged by what it ate. By the 1850s, Vicksburg residents were used to food that was wholesome, plentiful, and fresh. The burgeoning market revolution—and Vicksburg, courtesy of river and rail, was very much a part of that development—allowed foodstuffs to be transported interregionally and aided in creating an ever richer and more varied diet. Vicksburg had its signature dishes. Native American, African American, and Euro-American traditions braided to create a range of distinctive Southern cuisines, heavily inflected with pork, rice, and cornbread. Southerners ate less beef and lamb than their Northern counterparts, preferred whiskey over ale, and consumed fewer fresh vegetables. Although buffeted by the vagaries of nature and periodic scarcity, Southerners, white ones of all classes, generally ate well and often, though what they ate was closely indexed to their place in the social hierarchy.[5]

Elite palates had access to tasty meats especially. Hotels in Southern cities offered legs of mutton swimming in caper sauce, veal loins, chicken (fried, of course), trout, and corned beef and cabbage. Vegetables were plentiful. At the American Hotel in Richmond in the early 1850s, patrons consumed boiled potatoes, onions, beets, cucumbers, turnips, tomatoes (stewed and raw), black-eyed peas, and rice, washed down with wine: port, champagne, claret, or sherry. If they had room for dessert, they could tuck in to puddings, a variety of pies (apple, peach, cherry), or dried fruit for dessert. The tastes of the world—wines imported from Europe—and the tastes of the South were on offer.[6]

By virtue of Vicksburg's location and its importance as a railroad hub, residents were fed especially well, having access to western corn, a food that was not that common elsewhere in the South.[7] Indeed, fresh food, tasty food seemed abundant and affordable. Although elites such as Vicksburg's Emma Balfour almost certainly exaggerated when she opined that "the poorest person can afford to spend 50cts for a [peach] tree & in two years they make enough to live on some time by selling the fruit," the city was a conduit for a wide variety of fresh foods, shuttled up from New Orleans, down from the Mississippi's upper reaches, and from the west. The sheer range of fresh food grown in and around the city was impressive. Fruit—grapes, cherries, guava trees, raspberries—abounded on plantations and in gardens; vegetables—corn, tomatoes, green peas, asparagus, artichokes—were consumed fresh or canned for winter consumption. White palates enjoyed variety, experiencing not just peas but "Red onion pease" and "Blue Prussian pease."[8]

The affluent—especially the planter class—feasted uproariously, especially on holidays. Eggnog greeted early risers even before breakfast on Miriam Brannin Hilliard's plantation on New Year's Day in 1840; later that month, "jelly, macaroons & plum pudding" were the order of the day.[9] Parties and social affairs brought out truly delicious offerings that could include large juicy hams, fried chicken, sponge cakes, tarts, biscuits, cake with whipped cream, all washed down with lemonade, coffee, and tea.[10]

Venues of taste were nestled within the city. Scattered among iron and brass foundries, tailors, dentists, law offices, cooking stove suppliers, and general merchants was Quigg's Bakery—on China Street, near the steamboat landing—which touted its "fresh" articles, including varieties of bread, crackers, sugar cakes, and gingerbread. Brown & Kuhn, on Washington Street, boasted "fine groceries" and "all kinds of Western produce." Wines, liquors, fruit, nuts, confectioneries, cigars, and tobacco were on offer: "All the above articles we have just received, and are fresh and new, and we are daily receiving fresh supplies of the best articles." No spoiled or stale food for Vicksburg tongues. The city also boasted several coffeehouses, hotels, and other bakeries, confectioners, and grocers. The availability and—above all—freshness of food was not an issue for most residents in this Southern city.[11]

Travelers got a taste of the city at the hotels. Eating at the Washington Hotel was an experience, both of sound and taste. "Gen. McMakin," the owner, offered a *"viva voce 'bill of fare,'"* whereby he "takes his position at the *head* of the *Side* table Surrounded by the Waiters and in a voice audible throughout the entire dining room names over the dishes."[12] Even if travelers never made it into the city proper, they could taste the flavor of the region from the steamboats that plied the Mississippi, feasting on board. Chicken, fried or broiled, was popular, but mackerel, lamb chops, beefsteak—plain, with mushrooms, onions, tomatoes, and fried potatoes—and any number of delectable goodies could be had on the riverboats by 1860.[13]

Food choices in the antebellum South were not simply about nutrition. In fact, the choice of what to consume reflected refinement and civilization, the two touchstones of the South's social order. In this sense, "taste" bestowed status, interlacing consumption with aesthetic worth.[14]

The meanings of taste were intertwined. Antebellum Americans placed a great deal of significance on the mouth, lips, tongue, and throat. The mouth, argued one writer on the subject in 1855, was far more than a mere delivery system for food. No, he argued in the widely read pages of *Harper's*, animals eat, too, and man, of course, was no mere animal. It was his ability to discriminate between food good and bad, high and low, that marked man as human. Indeed, the importance of tongue, lips, and mouth was best understood through explicit comparisons to those of animals. Man's mouth "is not like the mouth of animals, intended for grazing on herbs, or seizing or tearing bloody prey. It has no menial, degrading labor to perform; it but receives the food handed up by its obedient servants, the hands . . . ." More than this, man's mouth was elevated by "the higher power and . . . the loftier duty of uttering speech." Indeed, the power of the mouth was its ability to marry cerebral with sensual functions and, in the process, adjudicate on matters of gustatory and social taste. The "simple touch of lip" was at once sensual but courted the intellect to judge the quality of the touch, anticipating taste. Not all lips were created equal, of course. Animal lips were coarse and rough, and those of the "Negro . . . are thick, fleshy, and protruding," suggesting "a much duller, more material nature of mind and of senses." The idea that the lips and tongues of slaves were physically unrefined and, by extension, aesthetically immature was, of course, a deeply cherished stereotype maintained by the master class, justifying the allocation of plain, functional, and flavorless food to slaves on plantations.[15]

Within the mouth existed a powerful arbiter: "that wondrous 'little member that no man can tame,' and in whose 'power are death and life'—the Tongue." The tongue is at once private (concealed visually from others; "to show it without necessity is a vulgarity") and highly public: the source of discourse. Such a "delicate," "perfectly developed" part of the body stood in marked contrast to the rough, clumsy, indiscriminate tongues of animals—or those of slaves, whose diets, by contrast, were terrible and, apart from illicit ventures into the woods and creeks at night when slaves managed to supplement their diets through hunting and fishing, largely beyond their control. The bulk of their diet, courtesy of the slaveholders, was distinctly impoverished. The fare was numbingly bland, geared to giving them energy for work. It was nutritionally feeble, frequently monotonous, and, in the estimation of white Southerners, wholly in keeping with the unrefined black palate. Why waste good food on unappreciative tongues?[16]

No, the white man's tongue was at once "faithful watchman," tasting and testing what entered the body and, in the process, arbiter of the "inequalities" and qualities of food: what was worthy and what was not. "For taste was evidently given to man in proportion to the higher development and the greater refinement of his physical structure." Taste was at once innate and yet could be refined: tastes "may be trained" to distinguish good food from a truly "exquisite delicacy." Regardless, man's tongue was not suited to base foods, especially when those tongues occupied elite positions; eating base foods might well count as an act of decivilization.[17]

It was this understanding of taste that made hunger so deeply terrorizing to antebellum Americans generally. Most Americans, regardless of their class and wealth, had not experienced famine, at least in the years before the Civil War; it was something this "people of plenty" tended to associate with the stagnation and darkness of the Old World and a much earlier age. Hunger threatened to catapult man back in space and time, rendering him more animal than human. European famines in the thirteenth and fourteenth centuries "turned everything into food and compelled human teeth to chew things that were not even customarily eaten by animals," as one thirteenth-century writer put it. During the fourteenth century's Great Famine, starving people "gnawed, just like dogs, the raw dead bodies of cattle" and, in the darkest moments, "grazed like cows" on grass. Scarcity of food peeled back civilized man's exterior and revealed an animal that would eat anything to survive.[18]

Americans—antebellum Southerners included—were far removed from this past by 1860, increasingly beneficiaries of their resource-abundant land, and sufficiently able to extract and transport a variety of food at a low cost to not fear slipping into the dark famines of the past. Although the age of true exceptional abundance would have to wait until the twentieth century, resource-rich America, even in the antebellum period, meant people on the whole ate well and often, at least compared with their European counterparts. To be deprived of food when there was so much was unnatural. Nothing less than "humanity" dictated "that in a land of plenty no one should suffer the pangs of hunger." So wrote Ulysses S. Grant.[19]

Vicksburg's success and its importance as an economic center—its railroads—were the very things that drew the attention of Union forces to the city during the war. After Fort Sumter fell, Secretary of the Navy Gideon Welles, at Abraham Lincoln's behest, moved to close off the Mississippi River, in effect starting a policy of slow strangulation of the Southern ports scattered up and down that river, Vicksburg included. By November, Lincoln had apparently become convinced of Vicksburg's worth, calling it "the key" to future Union success. But such strangulation would take time, and Vicksburg would not feel the fuller effects for quite a while. For now, the summer of 1861, Vicksburg residents—at least those who had not enlisted to fight for the Confederacy—scurried around the city, fretting over whether spies and Union supporters were hiding in their midst, even contemplating forcing citizens to wear identification badges so that authorities could tell friend from foe. A thousand miles to the east, at a place some called Manassas, some wished that they had had similar foresight.[20]

General Ulysses S. Grant—tobacco-stained, rugged, determined, and quite ruthless, his five-foot-eight, 135-pound frame giving him a bearish, burrowing air—had not expected a prolonged

siege of Vicksburg. Indeed, neither he nor, for that matter, anyone else had thought much about sieges generally. They were Old
World battle tactics, common in medieval Europe, rare in this New
World. Though Grant was a quick study, besieging Vicksburg was
not going to be easy. Vicksburg's setting made scaling to or even
firing on the city a challenge; moreover, the city residents seemed
determined not to surrender. Grant, with his dislike of the sight of
blood (odd for someone who spilled so much of it), came to appreciate just how difficult taking the city would be.[21] Gifted and certainly relentless tactician though he was, he failed multiple times
and faced miserable losses throughout 1862 in attempting to claim
it, attacking it both by water and on land. Finally, he was convinced
to, as he put it, "outcamp the enemy." This he did sans siege train
and with relatively modest materiel. But once Grant had decided
on this course of action, he was characteristically relentless,
always pushing, "investment by inches," creeping up and nearer
the Confederate defensive works, digging down and pushing up.
Every day, he got nearer the Confederate lines, so that by late June
his soldiers were within 120 yards of the enemy lines at ten different points. Grant squeezed the base of the city, constricting and
pressing, keeping everything out and forcing everything within to
remain in.[22] He began the slow process of strangulation on May 25,
1863 (figure 4.1).

Grant, more than any other general, Union or Confederate,
understood what a siege was. The term, which originated in refer-
ence to the only vacant seat at King Arthur's table, meant sitting
down at a table—a fortress, a city—and, quite literally, denying
civilians and soldiers alike in the city access to anything, especially food. Grant knew that creating an artificial famine, while
possibly a lengthy process, would eventually wear down resistance. It could end only in abject, humiliating, gut-gnawing surrender and was designed to achieve that very particular end. He
made no apology. He was a merchant of war. His only remit was
to win. And so in May, following two major failed assaults on May

FIGURE 4.1. *The Siege of Vicksburg.*

Lithograph by Kurz and Allison, 1888. Reproduction Number: LC-USZC4-1754, Library of Congress Prints and Photographs Division, Washington, D.C.

19 and 22 to take the city that left hundreds of Union troops dead, bodies littering the city's slopes, General Grant started to carve out a seat at the foot of the city-fortress and proceeded to dig in. To buoy his troops' morale, Grant did his best to fill their bellies, knowing full well that filling food meant a lot when it came to keeping spirits high. His men fed on what arrived on boats and barges "laden" with grain.[23]

Humiliation of the enemy was part and parcel of this process. One Indiana soldier scoffed: "We live principally on the produce of the planter—I think excellent 'war policy' to quarter a hungry army on the produce of the enemy and on his own land." Grant

fully appreciated the strategic advantage of allowing his troops
to feed off Southern land: their voracious gobbling left less food
for Confederate troops.[24] The word *stripped* was commonplace;
tongues of those who had endured siege spat the word often.
Warfare, wrote a young Mississippi woman, Ida Barlow Trotter,
"had well-nigh stripped our Southland of its supply of feed stuff."
Gardens, orchards, all were stripped, and then turned into pas-
tures for Union horses.[25] The surrounding plantations were raided
for supplies. "They stripped our smokehouse and storeroom of all
provisions," recalled city resident Eliza Ann Lanier years after the
siege. Grant's troops were like locusts, ingesting food at an incredible rate: lard, bacon, flour—anything and everything was consumed. "They left a little sugar," moaned Eliza Ann. "That is all my
children had to eat for three days until one of our neighbors baked
a pan of cornbread and sent it to us." Grant's troops had done their
job, and "in ten days or less time there was not a hoof of anything
left."[26] Food was so scarce in and around the city that it took on
the quality of precious metal, something to be hoarded, hidden,
and protected. Families' jewels and silver were buried, "and to
keep some meat where we could get to it," one woman "put two
mattresses on a bed and placed a layer of bacon, hams between
them." A woman then got on the bed and feigned illness, hoping to
fool prying Yankee eyes.[27] As Vicksburg residents slowly starved,
Union troops enjoyed "pure air and shade," springs of "excellent
water," and "buckets full of mulberries, blackberries and red and
yellow wild plums."[28]

Grant had lost men in his two assaults, lots of them, and laying
siege to the daunting city was at once an admission of failure and
a statement of determination. He would tolerate no more Union
losses, certainly not on the scale he'd just witnessed. He wanted
to win and punish at the same time. Now he had the men to bring
that punishment to bear: about 35,000 of them, with more to follow. And so they began to dig, in earnest, tunneling, excavating a
twelve-mile series of binding trenches.[29]

The hapless Confederate General John C. Pemberton, who was in charge of the forces within Vicksburg, found himself increasingly surrounded. Although he'd been born in Philadelphia, he'd married a Virginian woman and opted to fight for the Confederacy, even while his two brothers donned Union blue. This bushy-bearded, recently promoted lieutenant general was now in the position of resisting the efforts of Grant, whom he knew from his days fighting for the US Army during the Mexican War. He was determined not to surrender the city, but the odds were against him from the start. Union forces were multiplying, squeezing, cutting off the remaining routes from the city to the countryside. With mounting casualties and his troops plagued by sickness and hunger, Pemberton could only wait for help that would never arrive. He tried stratagems to ease his predicament, but Grant refused to bite; rather, he had others do the biting. Because food was so scarce in the city by June 22, Pemberton released five hundred slaves to seek food and shelter with the besieging army. Grant apparently accepted the men, kept the strongest to assist federal labor, "and promptly returned the remainder" to Pemberton. "Grant knew what he was about," wrote a New York reporter. "He needed men to eat up the bread and bacon of the rebels even more than he wanted soldiers to use spades and firearms in repelling Joe Johnston from the rear."[30] So day after day, Pemberton's troops dug, fired back, and attempted to keep at bay the massing Union forces and the 22,000 shells, some of them as big as hogs, Grant lobbed into the city. It was, in hindsight, a pathetically futile attempt to halt the inevitable. The note of surrender Pemberton sent to Grant on July 3 should have been written two months earlier.[31]

If Confederates thought the siege was only about starvation, they were wrong. Grant knew the art of war and understood that closing off this city, while aimed at the gut, would affect every aspect of life—every sense—for those men, women, and children trapped inside. "The Federals fought the garrison in part, but the city mainly," as the Confederates began to understand. "The city was a target in itself, and was hit every time"; the shells—parrots, preachers, mortars of many sorts, all with their distinctive audible signature—dropped their "deadly hail of iron," alternating between different parts of the city throughout the forty nights, denying the trapped men, women, and children sleep, gradually demoralizing them by reducing their ability to think, and draining them of memories of what it was like to lead a normal life.[32]

The sounds of siege were, like Grant, relentless: "day after day the flare and boom of cannon and the whizzing balls were our constant companion."[33] So constant was the noise that residents became deafened to the awful rhythm of flying death, the sky-borne funeral dirge. "The slow shelling of Vicksburg goes on all the time," wrote one woman in March, "and we have grown indifferent." Daily labors—mending clothes, locating food, the signatures of daily life in the besieged city—"are performed while the shells are leisurely screaming through the air." The shrill nightly shellings—"phenomenal" in their loudness, "thundering," in fact, their loudness magnified by the darkness, and the seemingly constant "dragging about of cannon" in the "echoing gullies" of Vicksburg's nighttime streets—interrupted sleep.[34] As mortars and shells neared, lobbed with terrific force from the guns below the city, the "noise became more deafening," depriving civilians of "mental rest."[35]

"Added to all this is the indescribable Confederate yell, which is a soul-harrowing sound to hear," wrote Dora Richards Miller in her diary. "I have gained respect for the mechanism of the human ear, which stands it all without injury."[36] The federal fire was now "constant" and increasingly accurate. Beneath ground, sounds were more muffled but similarly ubiquitous. The pick, pick of miners was loud enough underground for Confederate and federal sappers to hear one another's mining.[37] The siege rearranged cues and coordinates. It broke "down of the ordinary partition between the days of the week, as well as the walls which make safe and sound domestic life." Church bells were increasingly muted, as were songs of praise, replaced by the screams of the mortars, missiles of destruction without almanac.[38] Mechanical sounds took on the quality of animal and human voices, throaty and visceral: "We heard the bellowing of the great guns, and heard the screams of the frantic and wounded men." Even the big guns "sound like a tortured thing."[39]

The unceasing sounds, the perpetual "shistling" of bullets around heads, also contorted bodies. Walking upright during the hottest exchanges was no easy matter—something Grant intended—and the men and women trapped in the city moved around, crouching, scuttling animal-like, learning the different sounds the shells made as they headed toward the city, echoing among the hills.[40] Increasingly, civilians became like soldiers who felt like animals, "cramped all day in the pits" and hardly "daring to change their positions and stand erect" for fear of federal sharpshooters.[41]

This "city full of stirs," this once "joyous city," now began to assume "the aspect of a camp or a trench, devoid of the attendants of home and pleasure."[42] Everything was getting smaller, leaner, and stingier. Even the *Vicksburg Daily Citizen* newspaper was reduced to a "tiny sheet" by the end of May; by June 18, it was being printed on wallpaper.[43] Amid this gnawing carnage of noise, residents could find sensory delights. Birds sung merrily, and in late May the air was "heavy with the perfume of jasmine and honeysuckle."[44] But ever diminishing comfort and increasing sensory assault were the rule, not the exception. Skin used to fine clothes was now rubbed by fabric coarse and old. "Nothing is thrown away now," and even rags were reconstituted to adorn increasingly thin bodies.[45] Sight was diminished as well. Even during daylight hours, the clouds of dust generated by the fighting armies in the dry heat gave the air—and vision—a hazy quality.[46]

Grant's assault on the senses was felt keenly by civilians, especially those forced to dig in during the siege. Noncombatants were, in late March of 1863, "order[ed] to leave or prepare accordingly." Those opting for the latter turned to the geography of Vicksburg, taking advantage of the high slopes and penetrable but dependable earth. Digging seemed ubiquitous during the siege. But instead of the Mississippi Creator's giant finger, thousands of smaller human digits dug the excavation. The soil, "light and friable" but "sufficiently stiff to answer the purposes of excavation," invited the besieged to construct caves.[47]

Cave diggers, many of them "Negroes," could be employed— and were paid up to fifty dollars, depending on the size of the cave. But what price for relative safety? Dora Richards Miller couldn't stand her cave, bigger than average and well braced though it was; it even featured a shelf carved into the earth. For her, having to enter felt like premature death. "We went in this evening and sat down," she wrote on March 20, "the earthy, suffocating feeling, as of a living tomb, was dreadful to me. I fear I shall risk death outside rather than melt in that dark furnace."[48]

Her instincts were right. Heavy shelling caused caves to collapse, burying people inside and necessitating rescue digs to save them.[49] Reports of people being buried alive in the caves that honeycombed everywhere only frayed already stretched nerves. Fear of being buried alive was real for the cave dwellers, with constant trembling of the earth and jolting of the soil, the cracks appearing in ceilings, courtesy of shells, the perpetual, haunting reminders of their precarious, fragile situation.[50]

When it came to digging, civilian and soldier endured similar experiences. For Confederate and Union forces around the city, digging became something of a way of life. Capturing Vicksburg meant mining through the soft, workable loess, using the labor power of federal soldiers, some experienced coal and lead miners, and freed slaves. Grant instructed these sappers to work their way toward Confederate trenches on May 25; Confederates, meanwhile, were also hard at work, mining and countermining, increasingly relying on slave labor to do so. By the time the siege ended, the foundation of Vicksburg was riddled with excavations, tunnels, and warrens, as well as thousands of bullet marks pitting the land "like a man with smallpox." A good deal of this work occurred under a cloak of invisibility. Sappers dug air holes while they worked, hidden under the soil. Sound mattered, too, with federal troops using tools that would not alert Confederates, often just a few feet away under the soil, to their presence[51] (figure 4.2).

The caves challenged sensibilities. The refined were now animal-like, people who "burrowed," tribal cave dwellers. Some protocols of the old existence were preserved in the caves: out of a sense of honor, men supposedly rarely used them, reserving them for women and children. But the caves were cramped, crowded places, with dozens in them at times, the pillars and joists occupying a good deal of the available room. Possessions were limited.[52] The caves literally swallowed those who sought shelter in them; entry beyond the cave mouth was an act of seeking "refuge under

FIGURE 4.2. *Vicksburg Riddled.*

"Quarters of Logan's Division in the trenches in front of Vicksburg" 1863, LOT 4203, no. 9 [P&P], Library of Congress Prints and Photographs Division, Washington, D.C.

the earth." Here, bodies again contorted to a new environment. Even the most spacious caves, replete with mirrors, furniture from the houses, and rugs on the dirt floors, demanded "constant contact with the soft earthy walls," the inhalation and feel of perpetual dampness. The caves, now "a necessity," rendered the upright lowly. Formerly proud society matrons now "crouched" and cowered in caves, literally bowing down to enter their hovels, skittish as mortars landed at the mouths of caves, threatening to bounce down the cavernous throats into the chambers.[53]

Civilians experienced what it was like to step back in time and, by association, down in class. Here they were—men and women of high social standing—digging or paying to dig, living underground, scurrying in a sedimentary past. Time began to surround them, layered time, ancient time. Huddled, they sat in the dark, millions of years of geologic history surrounding them, time embedded in the thick, heavy loam gouged by the giant finger.

Squirreled away in caves and cellars for much of the day, darkness became the norm for these poor souls, the few available candles too puny and too corrupted—"dirty brown," often, that "spluttered and wasted like any vulgar tallow thing"—to illuminate the spaces. These were the dark ages.[54] Determination sounded pitifully defensive and hollow. "We'll just burrow into these hills and let them batter away as hard as they please," boasted one cave-dwelling woman.[55]

Release from the caves felt just like temporary freedom. Lulls in the shelling allowed these prisoners of the loess, who "had been confined for so long a time in a narrow space of earth," the joy of seeing and feeling "daylight, green trees, and ample room."[56] But release was also bittersweet; they knew that when shelling resumed, they would return once again to the dark and dank.

The federal siege of Vicksburg was not only a major military turning point of the Civil War, granting Union access to the interior of the Confederacy; it also represented a profound shift in taste, at least for the Confederate soldiers and civilians trapped in the city. Barely a dozen Southern civilians died during the siege, but the cost of Vicksburg isn't best measured in lives. Vicksburg revealed what those on the home front would have to do to survive. It involved the abandonment of former tastes and the concomitant leveling of palates. The color of the skin, by siege's end, held little sway over what went into mouths. Eventually even Union soldiers besieging the city were forced to eat mediocre food—one Illinois soldier hankered after the food his sister fed her dogs, so tired was he of sowbelly, tainted food, and appalling water—but on the whole they ate better fare than either Confederate soldiers or civilians trapped in Vicksburg.

At the beginning of the siege, the gustatory hierarchy of antebellum days—elite whites ate better than poor whites, who, in turn, ate better than black slaves—held fast. But siege brought a radical transformation in what people of all races and classes could and would eat. Everyone was starving. There was nothing palatable left to eat. But eat they nonetheless did.[57]

By 1863, war often centered around food: its quality, quantity, and rationing; these matters were, in turn, indicative of military strength, weakness, and even national character. By the spring, Northern newspapers were triumphantly reporting that the cotton states were "very near a general famine," one that the fall of Vicksburg—the only conduit left to shuttle the "surplus crops of Western Louisiana and Texas" to the Deep South—would exacerbate. The poor in Richmond were already hungry—cases of "actual starvation" not unknown, said the papers. Lose Vicksburg and the Confederacy "must be starved into submission." But first, Vicksburg had to undergo that punishment.[58]

Although Grant began the siege of the city on May 25, Union efforts to control the city and surrounding area during the preceding months meant that residents' stomachs were already being hollowed out long before the general began the siege of the city. As early as the autumn of 1861, Vicksburg residents got a taste of things to come. Courtesy of Union blockading, imperfect though it was, river traffic from New Orleans and from upriver had come to a standstill. Food shortages were beginning to dig in.[59] They did what they could to prepare. The buildup to the siege and the repeated efforts by Grant and Union forces to take the city helped citizens brace for a siege by cultivating more food—especially fruits and vegetables—and less cotton.[60]

The start of the new year in 1862 was marked by want. Supplies of certain items, courtesy of federal activity up and down the Mississippi River north and south of Vicksburg, were already short. In January, for example, paper was "a serious want," as were books. Sustenance for the mind was an early casualty—as was sustenance for the body. Soon, certainly by the end of February, food, good food, the sort of food necessary for returning the sick to health, was hard to get. Dora Richards Miller found it hard to secure food to help her ill husband recover. "I got with great difficulty two chickens. The doctor made the drug-store sell two of their six bottles of port; he said his patient's life depended on it. An egg is a rare and precious thing."[61]

By March, tastes of things to come were being felt along the Confederate Mississippi, partly due to federal forces in New Orleans but also due to initiatives by Pemberton—Vicksburg's supposed custodian, who was out in the field at this point—and, ironically enough, Jefferson Davis. Southern papers bemoaned that Pemberton's prohibition of "the shipment of flour and meal southwards" was starving Mobile—"famine appears to be imminent"—and chastised him for having "brought starvation upon the people." For his part, Davis, without a hint of irony, was busily calling for a day of fasting to be held on March 27, presumably to get God on his side.[62]

As hunger hit, "the ordinary rules of good breeding" went out of fashion. Confederate soldiers stole increasingly precious food, raiding civilian gardens especially. The siege was taking its toll by the spring of 1863, tormenting palates used to eating certain kinds of fruits and vegetables at certain times of the year. "As the spring comes," moaned one woman in late March, "one has the craving for fresh, green food." The palate's clock, an anchor of civility, was being altered by this siege.[63] By late April, the reality of the situation was hitting hard. "I never understood before the full force of those questions—what shall we eat? What shall we drink?" wrote Dora Richards Miller in her diary.[64]

When Grant decided to besiege the city, Confederates initially fought back with defiance. "Vicksburg has five months supplies of every kind, and can be taken only by hunger," intoned the *Charleston Mercury* on May 25.[65] Southern newspapers reprinted Pemberton's bold claim, made in response to withering criticism that he had fully intended to abandon the bluff city: "When the last pound of beef, bacon and flour; the last grain of corn, the last cow, and hog, and horse, and dog shall have been consumed, and the last man shall have perished in the trenches, then, and only then, will I sell Vicksburg."[66]

For all the bravado, however, the newly crowded city—a "trap," Emma Balfour called it, without "ingress or egress"—seemed crushing, close, suffocating. Filled with the "thousands of women and children who have fled here for safety," the number of newly arrived soldiers, and the "mules and horses," susceptible to stampede, the city seemed to be choking. Thank God for the mules, wrote Balfour, for "we can live on them" if necessary.[67] But even that sad hope went unrealized: a week later, she saw almost two thousand mules "driven beyond our lines given to the Yankees or to starvation—because we have not the food to feed them." The only corn issued to horses was for those being used by officers in the field.[68]

Things got worse, beginning on May 17, when Pemberton's defeated armies scurried back to Vicksburg, putting immense pressure on the already shaky infrastructure and straining scarce resources to their limits. Thirty thousand troops descended on a place that customarily was home to about 4,500 people. Emma Balfour captured the chaotic retreat of the "routed army": "I hope never to witness again such a scene . . . . From twelve o'clock until late in the night the streets and roads were *jammed* with wagons, cannons, horses, men, mules . . . ." Already, the soldiers' basic needs were obvious: they were parched and starving. Residents who could afford to help did. Emma Balfour arranged buckets of water to quench dust-stung lips; she then "had everything that was eatable put out—and fed as many as I could." The sight was pitiful: "it made my heart ache to see them."[69]

The question of what to eat and how to eat it was constant. Civilians who found cave dwelling simply too coarse—and who could afford alternatives—retreated to cellars, seeking to protect themselves alongside bottles of wine, but life in these dark, dank subterranean squares was little better than being holed up in ancient soil, and the issue of scarcity remained. Published recipes "for making delicious preparations" out of rice flour proved disappointing: "no manner of cooking I had heard or invented contrived to make it edible." Money mattered, though, and those with it, at least in early May, could get food—albeit at extortionate prices. Some foodstuffs, such as meal, though, were beyond dollars: "there is no more for sale at any price." What was left was directed to the hospital and to soldiers.[70] Eventually, neither love nor money could secure even the most repulsive meals: "I think all the dogs and cats must be killed or starved, we don't see any more pitiful animals prowling around," wrote one woman on May 28.[71]

The city's rulers now had to make hard choices, choices that they had never really entertained making. Dora Richards Miller put it this way at the end of May: "We are lucky to get a quart of milk daily from a family near who have a cow they hourly expect to be killed. I send five dollars to market each morning, and it buys a small piece of mule meat. Rice and milk is my main food; I can't eat the mule-meat. We boil the rice and eat it cold with milk for supper. Martha runs the gauntlet to buy the meat and milk once a day in a perfect terror."[72] Upper-class women, slaveholding women, now subsisted on cornbread and bacon, "the only luxury of the meal consisting in its warmth"; lips used to prepared food now had to contend with "tough biscuit," "there being no soda or yeast to be procured." Eating was joyless, something done merely "to sustain life, without the slightest relish for the food I was compelled to masticate and swallow." Little separated these people from cud-chewing bovines.[73]

By mid-June, Grant's grip around the city had tightened. As Union trenches penetrated the base of Vicksburg, digging away its foundation, the city began to take on a new appearance. "Vicksburg was in a deplorable condition." The city was being hollowed out, literally, taking on the "appearance of a half ruined pile of buildings." Starvation had begun to level class distinctions. Even "families of wealth had eaten the last mouthful of food in their possession, and the poor of non-combatants were on the verge of starvation." The affluent were still able to buy what morsels were left for sale, but the astronomic prices being charged meant starvation for the poorest residents. Basic foodstuffs were appallingly expensive: flour was selling at five dollars a pound (almost a thousand dollars a barrel); meal was fetching 140 dollars a bushel.[74] Rats eventually reached a dollar apiece; demand for them, though, apparently outpaced supply.[75] Even children were affected: one was so hungry she ate her pet bird.[76] And it wasn't only lack of food but also lack of water that hurt. Good, potable water was increasingly scarce, its absence visible on horribly "parched lips" during that hot, miserable summer. The first rains since the start of the siege did not come until June 23.[77]

If there had been any salt left, Grant would have rubbed it in Confederate wounds. Outside Vicksburg, he started feeding hungry rebels. Peace for food was a potent temptation, serving to undermine support for the Confederacy. In late June, Grant sent four or five wagons of food a couple of miles from the city. Three hundred Southern families—rich, poor, old and young—descended on a grove where each family "was supplied pro rata to the number of individuals comprising it." In all, ten days' rations were distributed, with each adult receiving a soldier ration, each child under twelve a half ration. The federal soldiers distributing the food expected gratitude; they were disappointed. Instead, they encountered hostility and humiliation in the faces of those they fed, particularly those of women. Grant likely expected that reaction—it was an appropriate response to the profound sense of dependency and weakness he hoped to inculcate.[78]

By July, the hunger was relentless, grinding. Brief respites—a bit of food scavenged here and there—seemed only to taunt the gut. There was almost nothing left. "Hunger and starvation was the inevitable, as everything had been eaten that would sustain life," lamented Ida Barlow. Anything living—"Fowls, cattle, horses, mules, dogs, cats, frogs," pretty much "any living thing in reach, except the gaunt human creatures who stared at one another with blood shot eyes"—had been consumed.[79] Citizens were said to be "Living on Air."[80]

The siege, as one contemporary put it, "abolished the unwritten law of caste." Now, all tongues tasted equally awful fare, and the simple mechanism of hunger drove those with taste to suspend it, so desperate were they to get something inside them. Hunger reduced planter to slave and human to animal. Just beneath the veneer of a carefully cultivated civility, poise, and demeanor, centuries in the making, stood a visceral human-animal, motivated by base instincts.[81] Even when elites managed to acquire beef—sometimes stray cows were killed by shell—the mode of preparing and consuming the meat, which was smoking it and hanging it around the caves, made them feel "quite like an Indian," reluctant members of a putatively inferior, savage civilization.[82] And therein was the agony for the Vicksburg elite: whatever food was on offer was food they had rarely consumed prior to the war. It was coarse food, food for the unrefined tongue. Now it was all that was left, and it was what they had to eat to simply survive. In this devolution of taste rested a revolution in the tongue, a revolution for those wholly unaccustomed to eating filth.[83]

Gnawing hunger, and all the class implications embedded in that need, was accentuated by another quality of gustation endured by the residents: monotony. The astonishing variety of food before the siege was replaced with crushing gustatory tedium. Some tried to vary diets, and luck very occasionally intervened: Precious gifts of June apples—"large, yellow, ripe"—recalled variety of old: "they were as much variety to me as pineapples would have been."[84] But on the whole, luck was a stranger to residents, and the limited range of food available meant that variety was now understood in terms of how many ways one could cook cornmeal.[85] The monotony of the diet was beginning to take its toll psychologically by the end of May. Dora Richards Miller confessed to her diary: "I am so tired of corn-bread, which I never liked, that I eat it with tears in my eyes."[86]

Most insufferably, most insultingly, eating even this monotonous, subpar food was often rushed and hurried, people forced to scoff slop. Wretched food crammed down throats in the brief intervals while Union guns cooled and the gunners themselves ate realigned mealtimes and forced Vicksburg residents to stuff their mouths regardless of how awful the food was. But perhaps there was a perverse relief in that. Perhaps "people . . . eating their poor suppers at the cave doors, ready to plunge in again" spared them. Scoffing awful fare might well have been preferable to the slow forcing of the inedible down tired throats.[87]

Civilians seemed to suffer more than soldiers. After Day Ten of the siege, soldiers were on half rations—a quarter pound of bacon, a half pound of beef, five-eighths of a quart of meal, some rice, peas, sugar, and molasses a day; "the citizens must have had less." By June 10, Confederate soldiers at Vicksburg described rations as "short" but "still enough."[88]

Soldiers still had better access to hunger-stifling foods. Tobacco—widely chewed among all classes of men at the time—was issued to Confederate troops and might have helped with the hunger. Suppressing the senses of smell and taste,

tobacco—chewed, snuffed, smoked—could alleviate the gnawing. The sense of taste was, argued physician Joel Shew in 1860,
especially dulled by tobacco chewing, making "plain and wholesome food" insipid. Social strictures had prevented women
from using tobacco, and so they were denied its numbing and
hunger-stifling effects.[89]

As the siege went on, the worlds of civilian and soldier began
to overlap, and increasingly, they were all forced to eat from the
same table. Confederate soldiers who had managed to make it
back to Vicksburg after Pemberton's loss at Baker's Creek and
Big Black were already starving, the city having little to offer men
visibly "wan, hollow-eyed, ragged, footsore, bloody."[90] This siege
was wretched for everyone, regardless of rank or caste. "I have
read of besieged cities and the suffering of the inhabitants," wrote
one Confederate soldier from Vicksburg on June 10, musing, "but
always thought the picture too highly painted. But now I have witnessed one and can believe all that is written about the subject."[91]

Civilian women of high social standing now "drew our rations
just like the soldiers did ("and awful living it was to[o] fat pickled
pork, so old it had bugs in it, a little flour and coffee.") Not much
could be done to flavor this fare, a nasty mush of pea bread, the
effects of which "on the human system . . . may be probably imagined without any inquiry of the doctors." "My grandmother soaked
her hard tack in water over night to soften it, then fried it in the
grease that came out of the meat."[92]

Civilians, as we've seen, ate mule flesh in an effort to add variety
to a mind-warpingly monotonous diet; soldiers did, too, but also
ate it in the hope that it would ward off scurvy, which was beginning to make its presence felt in the ranks.[93] By late June, wrote one
soldier, there was "talk of our being compelled to eat mule beef if
not relieved very soon." Talk turned into reality a week later. "We
have been eating mule 'beef,'" wrote Joseph Dill Alison on July 4,
"but it has not been issued to the whole army as rations yet." "I have
not tasted it yet but hear it very good." Men in the trenches would

likely have agreed if they could have gotten their hands on it. "Many of them die for the want of proper food to support their strength."[94] Sometimes even starving soldiers couldn't stomach the stuff. "The stench from dead mules and horses (killed by shell) is intolerable," noted one Confederate soldier. The smell helped dampen hunger pangs and also protected people from consuming dangerous food.[95] Yet food preoccupied Confederate soldiers so much that even that sentinel faltered at times. One Mississippian talked in the same breath about his main source of abundant food—mule meat, courtesy of federal shells—and the "intolerable" stench of those same creatures when rotting.[96]

While all Confederate tongues suffered, some suffered in particular ways. Confederate soldiers holed up in Vicksburg seemed to have had access to water. Joseph Dill Alison, for example, noted that the soldiers "have good water most of the time, so do not yet suffer on that source." Dora Richards Miller knew she was lucky. The house in which she stayed had underground cisterns of "good cool water," one of which she "had to give up to the soldiers"; the other, though, was all hers. Most were not as fortunate: "the weather has been dry a long time, and we hear of others dipping up the water from ditches and mud-holes."[97] For men in the trenches, the scarcity and quality of water was a real problem. "Muddy and warm," it "caused many of the disorders which prevailed with effects so fatal." While some civilians like Dora Richards Miller had access to cisterns, the best the soldiers in the trenches could hope for was water hauled from the river.[98]

While the majority of soldiers seem to have been better off than civilians, some suffered so badly that civilians felt sorry for them. Brave men had been reduced to animals through hunger. Dora Richards Miller felt this way: the war-worn soldiers "swarm about like hungry animals seeking something to devour. Poor fellows! My heart bleeds for them." There was something deeply humbling and humiliating seeing soldiers—hard, toughened defenders—reduced to begging black slaves for food, scoffing "spoiled, greasy bacon, and bread made of musty pea-flour." Miller could see these men, some of whom "crawled" to her kitchen, were "ashamed," gratefully eating even "corn-meal gruel" while "tears ran from his eyes."[99]

Many on both sides availed themselves of blackberries ripening around the city, which could produce diarrhea; the rancid, brackish, downright dangerous water, polluted with the flesh of dead mules and horses, caused similar maladies.[100] Starving soldiers became food themselves, their bodies host to a variety of parasites, ticks, ants, and beetles.[101]

It was all over on Independence Day. Pemberton surrendered Vicksburg and the twelve thousand fighting men (excluding the wounded) under his command to Grant.

Pemberton bore the brunt of soldiers' anger after the surrender, his hand in starving his own troops coming in for greatest condemnation. Precisely because the residents and soldiers offered, as the *Charleston Mercury* put it, "a most heroic defense," defeated only by "hunger and fatigue," Pemberton's actions seemed shameful.[102] The men in Vicksburg "will never forgive Pemberton," said one soldier. He "shut men up in this cursed trap to starve like vermin . . . . Starve to death because we had a fool for a general." Pemberton had not only denied his men glory in life but also consigned them to humiliation in survival and shame in death.[103]

The Northern press was quick to pile on. "The immediate cause of surrender," crowed the *New York Herald*, was General Joseph E. Johnston's failure to relieve the city and, simply, "exhaustion," humiliating, gut-gnawing exhaustion. "Crippled," "exhausted," starved, dispirited, and prostrated were increasingly the words used to describe the Confederacy.[104] Within days of Vicksburg's fall, news of what the besieged had been eating trickled into national papers. Provisions were "almost exhausted," announced the *New York Herald* in an article, ending with "for days numbers had been eating mule flesh." Thus had the plume- and feather-wearing ladies, subscribers to "the latest fashion," and eager importers of English clothes "at fabulous prices" been reduced.[105] The *Chicago*

Tribune ran a piece listing meals available at "Hôtel de Vicksburg," with mule meat offered for every course. The bill of fare concluded: "Gentlemen to wait on themselves." Tasteless journalism it may have been, but the *Tribune* writer hit upon the essential truth: the reduction in diet was closely related to the humiliation of a social class.[106]

The surrender was a study in contrasts: decay and degeneration in the city, verdant freshness outside; the bitter taste of defeat, the sweetness of victory. For the victors, the day of surrender was infused with "balmy sunlit air," "cheer after cheer" wafting, the whole place having a "fresh" feel, a "luxuriant verdure," an atmosphere of "quietude" hovering over the place, troops now relaxed, even "listless." "Everywhere," wrote a correspondent for the *Herald*, "silence and relaxation reigned," peppered only by human voices, excitable and relieved that the siege was done and heard clearly against the backdrop of "a cloudless sky." Such were the sensations among the victorious.[107]

And for the vanquished? Briefly, very briefly, the end of the siege brought a return to normalcy. It was the quiet that many residents noticed first—or, rather, the absence of noise and shelling. "All is still. Silence and night are once again united." Then it was the light: candles were lighted. And then some decent food: "We have had wheat supper and wheat bread once more."[108] The surrender had something of a surreal quality, the "quietness" lending it an air of "volition, and not of compulsion." But within four hours of the surrender, the city seemed to reanimate, becoming "once more a living city," wrote Dora Richards Miller. Steamers now lined the levees "as far as the eye could reach," crowded, bustling, underwritten with a sense of relief and the need to leave. Vicksburg "had not experienced the interregnum of intercourse with the outer world" for nearly two years, and people wanted out. And in truth, there was not much reason to stay, at least for now. People wanted to eat, and Vicksburg's tables were empty. Only "mule meat of an inferior quality, old rice, a small quantity of corn meal, and a scant supply of vegetables" remained in the commissariat.[109]

Despite the reanimation of the city, the principal signatures of postsiege Vicksburg nonetheless remained humiliation and anger. Consumption of mule meat by soldiers had, as it turns out, been unnecessary. It had been served as army rations only on the last day of the surrender, and by that time Grant had "issued abundant supplies of the best that his army had" to Confederate soldiers and civilians. Bitter though that food must have been to swallow, swallowed it nonetheless was.[110] As Grant wrote to his father on July 6 from Vicksburg, "The enemy still had about four days' rations of flour and meat and a large quantity of sugar."[111]

Months after the end of the siege, came news bad enough to make everyone gag: "it now appears, officially, that PEMBERTON had, at the time of the surrender, about 40,000 pounds of pork and bacon, which had been reserved for the subsistence of his troops in the event of attempting to cut his way out of the city." The report— General Johnston's "official report"—went on: Pemberton also had stashed more than 50,000 pounds of rice, 5,000 bushels of peas, 112,234 pounds of sugar. Soap? There was plenty left: 3,240 pounds. And certainly more than enough salt—428,000 pounds— to rub into the collective wounds of every Vicksburg soldier and civilian who had experienced rat meat. Pemberton's defense was that he had stashed the food in the belief that help would come. When it didn't, he elected to surrender sooner rather than later. The papers were scathing: "So there appears to have been nothing but a general occasion for the surrender of Vicksburg." And that he selected July 4 as the day of surrender—believing "that, upon that day, I should obtain better terms"—was a further source of utter "humiliation on the part of the Confederacy."[112]

That bitter pill swallowed, by August 18, reports about the "Trans-Mississippi West" were making their way into Southern newspapers. "Never," wrote one, "did Providence bless any land with such treasures from the soil." "The cornucopia of plenty has been so prodigally emptied in the laps of our people that it is believed the present crop would supply all the wants of this department for three years to come, even if we should, in the future, be denied the ordinary harvest."[113]

There was no gainsaying the most fundamental effect of the siege on the city of Vicksburg. Underwriting the profound sense of shame was a feeling even more disturbing. The scale of the siege, the way it served to rearrange behavior and bend instincts, generated a sense of hollowness, a feeling that those who had endured the siege had lost their decency. "A state of siege fulfills, in more ways than would be imagined by the uninitiated, all that is involved in the suspension of civilization," recalled one soldier. Civilization was eroded by the constant fear, the constant hunger, and "the troglodyte existence." More than that, it was the act of becoming "easily habituated" to the deprivations that had emptied out the last vestiges of civilization. Everything had changed during the siege—all the habits of taste and decorum. But it was the act of "becoming accustomed" to it all that stuck most in their craw.[114]

Federal troops were not exempt from experiencing the feeling that the veneer of civilization had been stripped away. Those on burial duty at the foot of the city following Grant's early failures to take the city were aghast. Hundreds of corpses, blackened by the sun, gnawed on by countless maggots, produced a "stifling" stench, an "effluvia" unendurable. "I saw sights that I pray God I may never see again," gulped one burial-duty soldier. "Awful! Awful! Not civilized warfare," lamented another federal soldier.[115]

But it was the white Southern elite who felt this degradation most keenly. The siege and time in the caves led Mary Ann Webster Loughborough to lament: "I vegetate, like other unfortunate plants—grow wan, spindling, and white!"[116]

Vicksburg was but a shell of its former self: "the gardens, with gates half open, the cattle standing amid the loveliest flowers and verdure," the whole place marked by "carelessness of appearance."[117] Federal troops saw it, too. Once inside the city, they witnessed in ways powerful and disturbing just what the siege had done: "When we beheld the emaciated condition of the women and children at the entrance of their cave dwellings, along the roadside, on our way in, we didn't feel a bit like cheering. The boys emptied their haversacks for the little ones, and watched them devour the rations like starved animals."[118]

As residents left the beleaguered city, they glanced back and saw the ground plowed violently by the hundreds of shells and shrapnel, "scattered over . . . like giants' pepper, in numberless quantity." Gone was the sculpted table courtesy of the giant finger. The "savage horde"—as the Confederates called the federals—would capitalize on their victory and proceed to work their way into the entrails of the Confederacy. If there was one meal left to eat, federals would soon enough be spooning it down the South's throat. Humble pie would be plentiful.[119]

Chapter Five

The *Hunley*'s Impact

Eyes strained hard, the chilly winter air and cold Atlantic breeze inducing a watery squint. These eyes were accustomed to looking out. A sailor on a cathead was staring at the water, and so was Acting Master J. K. Crosby. Both were on the deck of the USS *Housatonic*—a state-of-the-art steam-powered sloop boasting twelve guns and three hundred crewmen, the pride of the US Navy. The ship was part of a fleet whose purpose was to blockade Charleston Harbor, to keep Confederates from leaving and help from arriving. This nautical siege—part of Anaconda—was far from perfect, but it had done its main job: to constrict the Confederacy. Any effort to break the blockade had to be thwarted, and for that reason, Crosby's and the sailor's eyes scanned the water that cold night of February 17, 1864, with focused determination.

8:45 P.M. Something odd appeared in the dark, glassy waters. It wasn't a wave—the water was too smooth. Nor was it a ripple, though those were there, lapping the ship. A plank? A log? Neither. It was moving too quickly and was far too straight and linear for an aquatic animal. There was, unmistakably, "something in the water."[1]

For both Crosby and the sailor, that "something" was nerve-wracking. Rumors abounded about a Confederate submarine, an underwater machine, hard to see or detect, but neither man could be sure that that was what they were seeing.[2] Crosby was an experienced naval man whose eyes were trained to scan vast horizons and search the skies. But he couldn't make sense of it.

And yet the weather was clear, "the night bright," moonlight generous, revealing any movement in the water. That water was calm. The moderate wind and the half-ebbed tide did little to excite the waters, leaving them "smooth." Moreover, the *Housatonic*, anchored about five and a half miles from Fort Sumter, had been afloat on the margins of Charleston's harbor for some time, blockading the city, and its crew knew how to survey the often choppy Atlantic waters for Confederate privateers and blockade runners. The object had the benefit of being cloaked by both the darkness and twenty-seven feet of murky ocean. Only a bit of the object pierced the surface; the rest of it—whatever it was—remained submerged. Crosby was certain of one thing, however: this "something" was headed directly toward his ship. He judged it to be 100 yards out and heading not just for the ship but for its most exposed and dangerous part: "forward of the mizzenmast, on the starboard side, in a line with the magazine." And whatever it was, it was coming straight and, from Crosby's eye-straining perspective, fast.[3]

What Crosby was struggling to identify was a piece of Confederate technology that was about to make history: the *H. L. Hunley* submarine. Eight men were crammed into what amounted to a repurposed boiler (strengthened with a skeletal frame) made of iron three-eighths of an inch thick, in a space forty-eight inches high, forty-two inches wide, and forty feet long.[4]

What Crosby couldn't hear was the furious labor, the urgent grunting, the creaking and groaning of iron, muscle, bone, and sinew, several feet beneath Charleston Harbor's heavy waters. What he couldn't know was that the men below could see almost as little as he, despite remnants of white paint intended to reflect weak candlelight and milky moonlight let in by eighteen glass ports. The crew lived in a dim, shadowy world.[5] What Crosby couldn't imagine was the stench of sweat produced by the men inside the iron husk and a lingering, distant, but still pungent smell of the men who had died in the submarine during doomed trials.

Or the air saturated with body odor and sea salt. As rank as it undoubtedly was, the men, their muscles and lungs straining, sucked down the life-sustaining oxygen. The *Hunley's* snorkel and air-pump system fed the men a stingy diet of it.

And what Crosby couldn't fully appreciate, standing as he was under the expansive night sky filled with distant horizons marking space, was the size of the world inside that contraption. For these eight men, the horizons were not the Atlantic or Charleston or the yawning star-speckled sky but, rather, the rough, industrial iron skin of the sub's interior, just inches from their feverishly rotating hands, spinning arms, heaving shoulders, stooped necks, and straining knuckles. Such labor was a product of incredible focus and ferocious drive. These were not pampered men—their captain had complained loudly earlier that year that his submariners were given mere soldiers' rations (cornmeal and rice, cornbread, no meat). It was remarkable that through sheer muscle power they could achieve a top speed of about three, maybe four knots.[6]

Such extreme confinement would have been alien even to a sailor like Crosby, who was more accustomed to close quarters than were many soldiers on land. Being inside the *Hunley* was an experience quite unlike anything else endured by other combatants before or during the Civil War. It was born of necessity and creativity. Breaking Anaconda meant pushing men to the limits of endurance.

This submarine had been conceived and built expressly to challenge the blockade. Building on knowledge of previous iterations and prototypes (most notably the *Pioneer*), the *Hunley* was assembled in Mobile, Alabama, and, after trials, taken by train to Charleston, arriving in the city on August 12, 1863, and it was later handed over to the Confederate Navy.

Death haunted the submarine. Twice, once in August 1863 and again in October that same year, the vessel sank during trials in Charleston Harbor. The first time, five of the eight crewmen drowned. The *Hunley* was then retrieved and, with its benefactor,

Horace Hunley, inside, sank again in October on a training mission, lodged in silt and sand at a thirty-degree angle. Everyone inside was dragged to a choking, smothering death.

But the Confederacy had faith in the machine and again excavated the submarine, bodies and all. Now under the command of Lieutenant George Dixon, who had urged a now-ambivalent General Beauregard to give the submarine a third chance, the *Hunley* was repaired, modified, and readied (figure 5.1). And so, for the third time, men, knowing full well the tragic history of the iron coffin—as everyone conceived it—squeezed in and prepared themselves for grueling labor.[7]

In precise order they sat, on a bench about a foot wide. Before them, not quite down the center of the vessel (to allow for the bench), was a long iron bar, a crankshaft, indented at the position for each seated crewmember. Each of the seven indents was possibly wrapped with a wooden sheath, enabling the men to rotate the entire crankshaft in sync. The crankshaft, in turn, was connected to a differential gearbox, which converted human energy

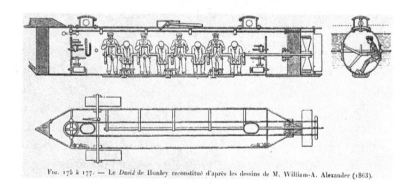

Fig. 175 à 177. — Le *David* de Hunley reconstitué d'après les dessins de M. William-A. Alexander (1863).

FIGURE 5.1. *Schematic of the* **H. L. Hunley** *submarine.*

Confederate submarine *H. L. Hunley* (1863–1864). Cutaway drawings published in France, based on sketches by William A. Alexander, who directed its construction. Photograph #: NH 58769 U.S. Naval Historical Center Photograph.

power into propeller power, giving the submarine locomotion under the water.[8]

At the helm was George Dixon. Dixon was likely from the Midwest, though he enlisted in Company E of the Alabama Twenty-First Infantry in October 1861. Injured at the Battle of Shiloh, Dixon became intimately familiar with the submarine, working first at the Park and Lyons machine shop in Mobile during the *Hunley*'s construction and then accompanying the vessel to Charleston. Dixon "requested Commodore Tucker to furnish him some "men," which he did."[9] Seated directly behind Dixon was the youngest and shortest of the crew members, Arnold Becker, a recent arrival from Europe (where is not known). For reasons unclear, he had joined the Confederate States Navy in October 1861. Serving on the *General Polk* and then on the CSS *Chicora*, Becker was later assigned to the CSS *Indian Chief*, and from that vessel, he was recruited for the *Hunley*. Age twenty and five feet, five inches, Becker was at the first crank position, muscling the propeller in circles, but he was also responsible for the air-circulation system, managing the forward pump and, critically, checking the position of the valves when the sub needed positive buoyancy.

As for the second cranker, there was surely more to his name, but we know him, simply, as "Lumpkin," likely his last name. From his remains, forensic science has determined that his was a life of physical exertion—and physical abuse: he was a heavy pipe smoker with the grooves worn into his teeth to prove it. He'd probably served, like Becker, on the *Indian Chief* before joining the *Hunley*.

Two men down from the diminutive Becker—next to Lumpkin—sat a large man, well over six feet. This was Frank Collins. A Virginian, Collins signed up with the Confederate Navy in 1861. Like the others, he'd served on the *Indian Chief*. His position at third crank situated him mid-vessel. In the event of a sinking, escape through either of the boat's two conning towers, situated forward and aft, would be unlikely.

In the equally sticky fourth crank was Corporal C. F. Carlsen, in his early twenties, whom Dixon recruited from the German Artillery. Carlsen, like the others, had naval experience, having served on the *Jefferson Davis*. He also saw battle at Fort Walker on Hilton Head, South Carolina, in November 1861. It is likely that nothing had truly prepared him for the position he found himself in on that cold February night in 1864.

Like Lumpkin, we know the man at fifth position only by his last name, Miller (his first name might have been Augustus). And we don't know much more than that. He might have served with Carlsen on the *Jefferson Davis*, and he might have been a recent immigrant from Europe. Either way, he volunteered to serve on the *Hunley*.

About the man in the sixth crank position, James A. Wicks, we know a bit more. Wicks had served the US Navy early in the war, aboard the USS *Congress*. When the *Congress* was destroyed at the Battle of Hampton Roads in 1862 by the CSS *Virginia*, Wicks swam ashore and enlisted in the Confederacy. He, like other crew members, ended up on the *Indian Chief* and from there volunteered for *Hunley* duty. He returned from a mission in New Bern, North Carolina, just days before the *Hunley* was launched to attack the *Housatonic*.

Another former sailor on the *Indian Chief* secured the last crank position, a Marylander named Joseph Ridgaway. The son of a sea captain, Ridgaway was well versed in nautical matters, so much so that Dixon recruited him directly for the *Hunley*, not only having him man the seventh crank position but also making him responsible for securing the hatch and operating the flywheel and the pump.[10]

Two of the eight men, Dixon and Ridgaway, used more than muscle. Dixon used his eyes and ears to navigate, and Ridgaway employed his eyes and fingers for stabilizing the sub by tweaking and feathering the levers controlling the ballast tanks at the vessel's fore.[11] And yet, like the other crewmen, they had to contort their bodies into position.

As advanced as the *Hunley* was, it relied on the oldest form of power—not horsepower, not steam power, both increasingly driving

Southern trains and cotton gins, but, rather, the same power that was used to pick cotton, tend rice, and run plantations: human strength, usually effected through the hands. Despite the wooden sheaths and leather protection, blisters likely erupted. Ridgaway found his knuckles so bruised, rasped, and mangled by banging into the bench positioned close to the lever system that he carved out the shape of his knuckles from the wood, hoping to spare his skin and bone.[12]

Seven or eight men "turning cranks attached to the propeller shaft" could move the boat, "when working at their best," those three to four knots per hour (figure 5.2). Maneuvering was very hard, and no amount of manhandling could make turning a speedy affair. That the boat could "sink at a moment's notice and at times

FIGURE 5.2. *Interior view of the* **H. L. Hunley** *showing crankshaft and bench.*

Courtesy of Friends of the Hunley.

without it" and had, as one Confederate engineer claimed, been coffin to thirty-three men between its completion and the sinking of the *Housatonic*, meant that only the very brave crewed it.[13] The push for Confederate victory at sea demanded a great deal, but these men were willing to pay the price.

Ever more anxious, Crosby continued to squint into the water. A minute, perhaps a minute and a half, passed. The object was now only fifty yards away, trajectory the same. It was coming closer. In desperation, the *Housatonic* put its engine into reverse, trying to back away. All hands were called to quarters. Two officers started firing at the object with their small arms, to no avail. Rapid musket fire followed, "without effect." This was turning out to be a deadly game of tag. Onward came this "suspicious" object, "exhibiting two protuberances" and rippling through the water. Would the object ram the hull? If so, what would happen? That it was lasering in on the ship's magazine did not bode well at all.[14]

By this point, the existence of these vessels was known, and the technology it employed was considered mischievous and sneaky by Union commanders.[15] Rear Admiral John A. Dahlgren, commander of the Union's South Atlantic Blockading Squadron, complained that "the whole line of blockade will be infested with these cheap, convenient, and formidable" vessels. It was a fear he had harbored for a while, and now the threat of these invisible or only partly visible weapons had been realized. The only solution was for the Union to develop and deploy "similar contrivances." And if that meant cramming men into spaces, so be it. Without these machines, even the "utmost vigilance" was futile.[16]

There was an irony to the fact that, while advanced for its time, the *Hunley*'s technology was still powered by hand. Eight white men in incredibly close contact for prolonged periods suggested the world of the classical triremes rather than anything modern. That a highly civilized, impressively modern ship of the US Navy could be threatened, and possibly destroyed, by such a machine stretched the definitions of strength and superiority as understood by men of the day.

In many ways, the *Hunley* was the most intensely intimate sensory environment experienced by soldiers or sailors during the Civil War. The men aboard it understood that it meant almost certain suicide. War generally places people at risk, forcing them to expose their bodies to violence and great pain, to become intimate with death.

The violence of the Civil War on human flesh was novel in its variety and scale. Weapons used against soldiers lacerated, shot, punctured, bayoneted, mashed, pulverized, extracted, amputated, and burned. Flesh was torn asunder; the sight of brain and bone became commonplace. Intimacy with death meant intimacy with its causes—massive, traumatic destruction of the flesh. Shot and shell did most of the damage. At the bloody mess called Antietam— or Sharpsburg—on September 17, 1862, shells acted like scythes, and men were found wandering the fields clutching a severed arm.[17]

Most fighting was done outside, in open areas. But some engagements demanded more intimate quarters. Confederate soldiers manning the Stevens or Iron Battery on Cummings Point, Morris Island, described the small, sandbagged caves around the guns as "rat-holes," low-ceiling affairs designed to offer protection against bombardment.[18] Civilians during the Vicksburg siege, as we have seen, understood this feeling only too well. High society was forced to crouch like animals in caves, rustle around in dirt, scraping against tree roots. Trenches provided their own body-crushing experience, as did transportation to them. Union soldiers loaded onto troop transport ships during the siege of Vicksburg, for example, were "huddled together like hogs in a pen—jostled and jammed from side to side—compelled to eat and sleep on the filthy decks—without exercise during the day, and trampled upon at night while endeavoring to sleep—with rations of half cooked meat and tasteless pilot bread, and constantly inhaling the impure atmosphere engendered by the dense crowd on board, and arising from mules and horses on the lower deck."[19]

The *Hunley*'s submariners experienced this on an unprecedented scale. A common—and wholly understandable—gripe among

Civil War soldiers on land concerned rain and the bone-aching, skin-numbing effects of watery environments. Soldiers on land hated "drenched skin," loathed the "drip, drip, from the tents." The *Hunley's* crew knew these conditions only too well, and while they didn't have to put up with the mud that clung to soldiers on land, forming second skins, they were continuously drenched.[20]

The crew of the Union ironclads would have understood something of the *Hunley's* conditions. We know most about the experience aboard the USS *Monitor*, which famously battled the CSS ironclad *Virginia* at Hampton Roads in March 1862. Like the *Hunley*, the *Monitor* offered its crew a claustrophobic space. The *Monitor* even sounded closed. "The dash of the waves as they roll over our heads is the only audible sound that reaches us from the outer world. One would hardly suppose from the quiet stillness that pervades our submarine abode that a gale was raging around us." Those were the words of a *Monitor* man; they could just as easily have been written by a *Hunley* crew member.[21]

The interior worlds of the *Hunley* and *Monitor* were, however, very different. In terms of scale, the *Monitor* was much larger: 179 feet long overall and a beam of 41 feet, 6 inches, enough for a crew of forty-nine officers and enlisted men. Unlike the Confederate submarine, the *Monitor* did not go below the waves. When it was covered by water on four sides, the water above wasn't thick, heavy, or constant. Rather, waves rolled over the vessel, smothering it but only temporarily. Not that this couldn't be a frightening experience. The "accumulative weight" seemed to one *Monitor* man "sufficient to bury us forever."[22]

The *Monitor* was a haven of comfort compared with the inside of the *Hunley*. Moreover, the *Monitor* did not tax the muscle power of its crew in the same way or to the same extent; the *Monitor* was powered by steam. There were residual benefits to that as well. Steam operated two large blowers, giving the crewmen generous ventilation, indeed almost inundating the crew with "fresh air." Light, too, was plentiful. There was some grumbling—inevitably, given the function of the boat—about it being too hard to write without the use of candlelight. But "lamps are always burning" in some rooms, and, during the day, sunlight soaked through six-inch-diameter skylights, allowing, on bright days, the crew to read and write. The inside of the *Monitor* was, generally, comfortable. Rooms were "bright cheerful well-lighted" and "cozy"; men even delighted in their "little snuggery." Nathaniel Hawthorne, who had occasion to visit the boat, found it "a palace, with all its conveniences, under the sea," reminiscent of a luxury yacht. The presence of fine soups, champagne glasses, and brandy made this a world wholly apart from the dingy deathtrap interior of the *Hunley*.[23]

The men ensconced in the *Hunley* experienced something unique, something that wouldn't be matched for another half-century and the development of submarines and U-boats during the First World War and, of course, tank warfare. Intimacy meant contact with others.[24] The men in the *Hunley* experienced a world more familiar to fighting in earlier ages. There were the triremes, of course, but the siege machines of both the ancient and medieval worlds offer comparisons.

By contrast, most antebellum Americans embraced an arm-stretching culture of open space. Partly, this was a product of the country's size. News didn't always come by word of mouth and human contact. Print and growing literacy and the intellectual forces underwriting the Enlightenment conspired to promote a more distanced, noncontact form of social interaction. Bathing, like bodily excretions, was now a private affair, and dining was now individuated at the table. While servants in medieval Europe had often slept in the same bedroom as the master, servants in the nineteenth century had been relegated to a separate space, to quarters near enough for them to be summoned but removed. Touching was less necessary.[25]

Human contact had changed, and beginning in the eighteenth century, the idea of private, individuated comfort began to spread from the elite downward to the middle class. By the early nineteenth century, ideas about comfort were understood in terms of room temperature, not body heat.[26]

Clothing took on especial meaning, since what you put in contact with your skin was a matter of individual choice, not a group function. It formed an outer shell against contact with the environment and with others. What people wore against their skin, in other words, said much about their station in life and their inner worth and beliefs. It also diminished the need for constant intimacy. We could be self-sustaining.[27]

The men aboard the *Hunley* were practically working as a single body; their parts intertwined with the others'. In antebellum America generally, touching, particularly between men, was subject to protocol and especially evident in handshaking. Handshaking was the sine qua non of social contact. Seventeenth-century Quakers, for example, preferred the handshake as an egalitarian form of gesture to doffing hats, bowing, and similar "dirty customs" that communicated a social relationship they regarded as inauthentic.[28] Moreover, handshaking seems to have been increasingly understood as American and masculine in the antebellum period. Unlike French and British elite men, who prided themselves on "the degree of delicacy of the hand" and who considered the American habit of handshaking slightly disgusting, Americans generally cast their touch in more democratic terms.[29]

Even in war, touching between men was prescribed and regimented. And certainly in peacetime, free white men were not really accustomed to either this intimacy or the contortions that it provided. Few, very few occupations even began to approach the world of the submariners, and those that did were held in contempt. American observers of nineteenth-century English coal mines were aghast at how the mineshafts made men crawl over each other, animal-like, "with back and legs at an angle quite as acute as the pain thereby caused through underground passages that were apparently constructed for some Lilliputian race yet to be discovered." Theirs was an unnatural world. The lack of air, the smell, the closeness of it all were a throwback to an uncivilized age, when men "naked from head to waist are at work all the time, in narrow out-of-the-way passages, where without a lamp one might consider himself as completely lost to the world in general as if imbedded in the heart of a Brazilian forest."[30]

With this in mind, we return to the men in the *Hunley*. Their bodies were "stowed so close" in quarters so low that they were not permitted "the indulgence of an erect posture." The close, cramped quarters meant the "exclusion of the fresh air." Even in cold water, the physical exertion of the crankers likely meant that inside the "climate was too warm to admit the wearing of anything but a shirt," which so that the "skin," especially on "the prominent parts of the shoulders, elbows, and hips," was "rubbed" aggressively by the "friction of the ship." Dank, cramped, and forcing skin-rubbing closeness: this was the *Hunley*.[31]

But this description is not, in fact, of the *Hunley*. It is a description of a ship of enslaved black men, women, and children.

The *Hunley*'s men were where they were by choice. Their skin was never lacerated by a whip held by another. But in a world where white men resisted mightily any comparison to slaves, where race meant everything, where white Southern men fought duels and civil wars to prove they were free and not slave, the similarity between the world of the *Hunley* and a slave ship seems uncanny. The way the skins of slaves were treated meant something that didn't bear uttering at the time. It was this willing proximity to the experience of slavery that reveals the depth of sacrifice these men were willing to make to pursue the Confederate cause.

The crewmen wore clothes suited to their particular environment and their class, clothes consistent with their laboring bodies. Dixon donned the most refined, comfortable clothing. His boots were made of supple leather; his vest and coat were cashmere; he wore suspenders with silver buckles; he had a brass buckle from Paris. He was the only crewman not to remove his coat while in the submarine. Unlike the rest, Dixon didn't have to crank the shaft.

The others were dressed differently. The roughness of the vessel's interior meant that everyone wore boots, but those of the cranking crew were crafted of hard, stiff leather—workingmen's brogans—made marginally softer only by woolen socks, which likely rubbed skin raw when wet. Crew members took off their woolen coats, tucked them under the bench, and cranked in cotton shirts simply because their exertions—the ferocious rowing motions—were so great they generated significant body heat. Even Dixon's garb, given the environment, did little to cater to his sense of physical, bodily ease. It was, rather, a way to retain his status, his being primus inter pares, not to afford him warmth or the state of ease or bodily freedom associated with comfortable clothes and white liberty.[32]

Volunteers or not, not only were these white men stooped in quarters similar to those of the Middle Passage but also the constant turning of the cranks was reminiscent of slaves ginning cotton (figure 5.3). The mechanism in the *Hunley* was roughly equivalent to the gin to shuttle cotton and seed through cylinders, separating them, also in forward motion. Actually, though, the gin was more efficient, particularly after it had ceased to be powered by hand and used steam locomotion. By the 1860s, the hand-powered gin was considered backward, superior to the earlier foot-powered gin but now retrograde in the face of the saw gin and mechanically powered devices. The locomotive power of the *Hunley*, then, was behind even the technology used on slave plantations.[33]

The *Hunley* volunteers weren't slaves, but they had willingly placed themselves in the condition of slaves—in the fight to preserve slavery. Indeed, it was a wonder that Beauregard didn't crew the *Hunley* with at least some slaves. Why not have Dixon guide and direct the boat while slaves provided the manpower to propel it through the water? We can't say with certainty why slave labor was not used to power the *Hunley*, but the answer probably has something to do with the fact that slaves were expensive (their death and loss was, after all, quite likely) and also with the same logic that kept the South from using armed blacks in combat. Manning the

THE FIRST COTTON-GIN.—Drawn by William L. Sheppard.—(See Page 811.)

FIGURE 5.3. *The First Cotton Gin.*

William L. Sheppard, "The first Cotton-Gin," *Harper's Weekly*, 13 (December 1869), p. 813. Reproduction Number: LC-USZ62-103801 (b&w film copy neg.), Library of Congress Prints and Photographs Division, Washington, D.C.

boat, this piece of proud Confederate technology that might break the blockade, was understood as an honor befitting only white men.

And so the Confederate crankers turned and rotated the shaft as fast as their muscles would allow, in reeking quarters so cramped their skins rubbed and chafed, in light so dim they knew each other's presence by contact and smell rather than by sight. But such was the importance of their suicidal mission that these men were willing to endure them all. For now, they had but one object in mind: to deliver, by hand, a torpedo.

The *Housatonic* was far too large a vessel to be redirected easily and quickly. Crosby had spotted the "something," but it was too late: a minute after, the object beneath the ocean was alongside his ship. Hurriedly, Union sailors tried to pivot their aft guns but "were unable to bring a gun to bear upon" the object, the angle too downwardly steep, presumably. And then something hit.[34]

The extent of the explosion revealed the object below the waves: it was a torpedo boat, a submarine, armed with an explosive device attached to a long, projecting arm—a torpedo on a spear, if you will. Mounted to the boat's bottom—which made it very difficult, if not impossible, to see from the surface—the hollow iron spar jutted out seventeen feet. It looked now for all the world like a gaping fish, replete with sheeny scales. But this was the Singer torpedo after it exploded, courtesy of its 135 pounds of black powder. Bolted to the spar, the copper-clad torpedo was, through the sheer momentum of the *Hunley*, plunged into the guts of the warship and activated by a trigger fingered by Dixon.[35]

In some ways, the torpedo had a medieval quality to it, looking not unlike a knight's lance used in jousting. But this spar was a powerful piece of nineteenth-century stealth technology. Its invisibility was by choice. The alternative—a torpedo dragged behind the sub and designed to hit an object when the sub dove—was far more obvious to lookouts and vigilant eyes. And it was a target easily shot at. Dixon, following trials of both torpedo designs, elected for the spar because it had the redoubtable virtue of being below the waterline and very hard to see.[36]

Like a clenched fist at the end of a stiff arm, the torpedo was also a technology of touch. It had to be. Unlike warfare above the sea and on land, where shells could be lobbed greater distances anonymously, this underwater technology was less distanced. It required men to plant it, even in this prosthetic manner. This was maritime hand-to-hand combat, and deadly. The torpedo rammed hard into the ship's magazine, just as Crosby feared. Then came a painful delay. The device seems to have pierced the hull, but there was, perhaps for a minute, no immediate explosion, and then a veritable eruption. The *Housatonic* plunged, sinking stern first. Some sailors were stunned by the concussion; others flung themselves on the rigging, clinging for dear life. It had been all of three minutes from the sighting of "the something" to detonation.[37]

The *Hunley* sank the *Housatonic* between 8.45 and 9.00 P.M.[38] Within the hour, the Union ship was swallowed by the cold waters of the bay, five of its crew missing, presumed drowned; the rest, twenty-one officers and 129 men, some injured by the explosion, were rescued by the USS *Canandaigua*.[39] The effect was profound, the loss of the ship causing "great consternation in the fleet." All wooden vessels were "ordered to keep up steam and go out to sea every night, not being allowed to anchor inside" the harbor. For the Confederacy, this was "the glorious success of our little torpedo boat," which "raised the hopes of our people."[40]

One source at the US Navy thought "undoubtedly" that the *Hunley* "sank at the time of the concussion, with all hands."[41] Right or wrong, we do know that no one on the sub survived.

Ironies haunted the crew of the *Hunley*, even in death. It was, after all, a man by the name of Tomb, J. H. Tomb, an engineer with the Confederate Navy, who believed the vessel "a veritable coffin." Tomb believed there was only one relatively safe way for the *Hunley* to sink a ship, and that was to forgo invisibility. A spar torpedo was an effective weapon only when the boat was at the surface. "Should she attempt to use a torpedo as Lieutenant Dixon intended, by submerging the boat and striking from below, the level of the torpedo would be above his own boat, and as she had little buoyancy and no power, the chances were the suction caused by the water passing into the sinking ship would prevent her rising to the surface, besides the possibility of his own boat being disabled." Tomb had told Dixon this before Dixon had launched his daring raid on the *Housatonic*; he'd insisted that it was dangerous. None of this was news to Dixon. He and Tomb had even witnessed the *Hunley* sink on a previous dive, killing its entire crew. It was a ruthless boat.[42]

That warning was too late now. As the submarine sank, the men—assuming they were still conscious and not knocked out by the explosion—must have known they were doomed. The only question was how long it would take for them to die. Agonizingly, they might well have known even as the sub sank. In January, before the *Hunley* went on its nocturnal mission, the men had deliberately let the sub sink to the ocean floor to see how long they could go without fresh infusions of air. Dixon had estimated the crew could last half an hour. It turned out they got stuck and barely escaped with their lives—two and a half hours later.[43]

Now, time was not on their side, and the sub sank ever deeper. There was something both serene and cruel in the way the men of the *Hunley* faced their final moments. Decades later, their bodies were not found clumped together; each man was at his station. There had been no apparent efforts to hold hands or cling to one another. Perhaps the concussion from the explosion had knocked them out. We simply don't know. There seems to have been no scrambling, no desperate lurch for escape, no clambering over one another, no bruising, no ripping. We know that the seven men on the *Hunley* who died earlier were "found in a bunch near the manhole" when the boat was brought to the surface following a failed trial run. But not the crew of the *Hunley* on that fateful night.[44] Even though they were in excruciating proximity, each man died alone at his station.

Had the men survived their successful destruction of the *Housatonic*, they might well have forgotten all the aching, stooping, and skin-rubbing and told tales of victory in the comfort of warm homes. Instead, the sub sank, dragging its already entombed crewmen to a sarcophageal grave. There they sat, at station: the dandy captain, Mr. Dixon; the anonymous Mr. Lumpkin, pipe smoker; the diminutive twenty-year-old immigrant, Mr. Becker, dwarfed by the man from Virginia next to him, Mr. Collins; Mr. Carlsen, whom Dixon had recruited from the German artillery; the man known only as Mr. Miller; the erstwhile Union sailor, Mr. Wicks; and the sailor responsible for securing the hatch, the Marylander,

Mr. Ridgaway. They died together in the closest of worlds, but rarely have eight men been so solitary, so alone.

They remained at the bottom of the ocean until their remains, and the *Hunley*, were raised and brought to Charleston's shore in 2000. Then, for the first time in 136 years, these men—water-logged skeletons—were touched by other human hands.

Epilogue

Experiencing Total War

And so Vicksburg fell, and the Union cautiously rejoiced—anything more seemed fate tempting, even unseemly. Still, federal commanders were now more secure in their knowledge that, at long last, they had gained the advantage of interior lines, so that a column of soldiers could march through the Confederacy's soft belly. They turned to a man who knew how to do the work: Major General William Tecumseh Sherman.[1] His commanding officer, Ulysses S. Grant, insisted in April 1864 that he slice through the interior of the South—"break it up," he said, "inflicting all the damage you can."[2]

Sherman was expected to battle, parry, and bully his way to Atlanta and take that city. This he did. With his army of 60,000 men, he started, on November 12, 1864, to destroy railroad tracks, shops, mills, and homes from the city center to sixty miles north of Atlanta. Four days later, the city gently smoldered, wisps of smoke testimony to its capture.[3]

From there, Sherman's giant raiding party split into two phalanxes, machinelike columns designed to destroy Palladian ones. One massive column, more of a huge, ragged arc, became the Left Wing, made up of the Fourteenth and Twentieth Corps (the Army of Georgia). It left Atlanta, went to the capital, Milledgeville, and then rolled through small towns toward Savannah. The Right Wing (the Fifteenth and Seventeenth Corps) muscled farther south, toward Macon, and then, too, on to Savannah. The port city was captured on December 21.[4]

Without missing a beat, Sherman initiated his campaign to eviscerate the Carolinas. Chunks of the Fifteenth Corps and all of the Seventeenth headed to Beaufort; everyone else powered north, through Lexington, Winnsboro, and Columbia and then into North Carolina. On April 12, 1865, Grant would alert Sherman that, at long last, Lee had surrendered.[5]

In 1864, the war in the eastern theater had been a nasty, gummy business, with Grant and Lee buried in trench warfare at Petersburg, which lasted from June 1864 to March 1865. This slow-motion fighting stood in marked contrast to what was expected of Sherman and his men. They were mobile, encountering, thrusting, and, as such, thoroughly sensory. Sherman understood that to destroy the Southern will to fight meant depriving civilians of their customary experience of the world. Intuitively, he knew this meant doing things in such a way as to stun their senses, throwing them back into the howling-wilderness past that white Southerners fancied they had long left behind. Making Southerners "feel that war," making them equate "war and individual ruin," and impressing "upon the minds of sensible men" the cost of continuing the fight inevitably entailed retailing in the unpleasant economy of pain, taste, touch, smell, sight, and sound.[6] Sherman's march was a thoroughgoing sensory revolution, and to effect it, he had to have men who could remain numb to its effects.

The soldiers executing Sherman's march were hard men whose time in war had inured them. Senses dulled by war, they were inclined to exact very hard revenge on the people they blamed for starting this bloody nastiness. Their origins, a modernizing Northern society, seemed like a distant place now. They had become like soldiers from an earlier age.

Of the four corps in Sherman's army, three came from the western theater, where long, hard marching had been the norm.[7] This toughened army of self-reliant veterans, who had fought so much in so many places, swaggered their way through the Deep South. Leathered, wizened bodies enacted the iron hand of war. They marched, with skin as tough as *Hunley* men, as loud as the secession screamers, eating food as vile as that digested at Vicksburg, smelling as expansively as Gettysburg, and leaving sights as visually disorienting as those at First Bull Run. As Sherman's men marched through Georgia and South Carolina, their encounters with slavery increased, and so, too, did their revulsion at it. Despite their own roughness, they saw slavery as uncivilized, an institution incompatible with their country, and something to be rooted out.[8] These living atavists brought about something noble and civilized: freedom. Liberty, Sherman's men knew, depended on their savagery.

The men looked different from others in the Union Army, the more conventional, spit-and-polish eastern types. Sherman's men looked the part. Their clothes were loose, often dirty, and worn. They had to be, for these men lived largely off the land.

These were raucous men, men used to noise. Some of them had become addicted to the gritty sounds of battle and destruction and were unable to sleep in quiet camps at night. They needed the sound of strife, of war, of bullets and shells, simply to feel comfortable. "I feel the most at home, where there is the most noise, about me," wrote one.[9] They were not immune to attack, of course, and they, too, could sometimes be heard "groaning, begging for assistance and gasping in death" when Confederates managed a direct hit.[10] They were not immune to the sounds of white Southern women, whose virulent and "obscene words" were abhorrent to the ear of even the "roughest and most brutal soldier."[11] Still, many found other aspects of the Southern soundscape, notably the singing of slaves, incredibly moving and "melodious."[12]

Sight became necessary to survival on the march. Confederates buried mines—"torpedoes," the federals called them. Sherman considered them, like submarines, dishonest, even uncivilized warfare, which was saying something, given his own ruthlessness. Blowing up men with hidden, invisible bombs was treacherous, he thought, which is one reason he had Confederate prisoners of war remove them.[13]

Marching through the South, they felt exposed to a different world. Slavery was a revelation to them. Their skins were tanned and leathery. They looked, said one slave, "about as black as we alls." To a Northern man in South Carolina, the soldiers "seem like a gang of coal-heavers."[14]

It had been so from the beginning of the march. One federal wrote: "reached Memphis at 9 A.M.—Marched down Poplar to Main . . . . Our boys made a sorry appearance into the city—No music our tired band having walked through the fields barefooted . . . . About one third of our men were barefooted, one third without breeches, plenty without shirts & hardly a man with a full suit."[15] The new recruits on the march learned quickly, and within a few weeks of accompanying the veterans, they became accustomed to drenched skin and erupting blisters. By the time the army reached North Carolina's towns, they looked "very hard," as one soldier noted, faces blackened by smoke, feet often without shoes, bodies and hands dirty and ragged.[16]

Awful cold combined with equally awful shoes rendered Sherman's men "so numb I could hardly step," legs and feet moving on pure instinct, skin mere prosthetic. They were the lucky ones: "My right foot is worn through on the bottom, and my toes are wet with blood every day," wrote one soldier.[17]

The men frequently treated one another with contempt. Soldiers beat and choked each other for minor offenses; officers punished infractions by hanging men up by their thumbs or trussing their bodies to artillery wheels. Still, a rough sort of tactile egalitarianism seemed to prevail, with officers and men performing similar manual labor, carrying knapsacks for one another.[18]

Their skins roughened by weather, rain, sun, dust, bone-chilling dampness, cloying mud that caked moisture to skin, and ever-present lice, these hardened men were emotionally numbed when they encountered Southerners, treating them as roughly as they did themselves.[19] This is how Sherman wanted it. He had tried to select men as tough as possible. He wanted "men whose bodies were so inured to hardship that disease could make no impression upon them."[20] And hard skin meant hardened emotions, perfect for the sort of manhandling needed to crush Southern civilians.

Thick skins were matched by tough constitutions. Although food was sometimes plentiful and flavorful enough to make the men "fat and saucy," and despite some delicious encounters in Savannah where the men had access to spices and tasty potables, average soldiers, especially when they hit the Carolinas, where foraging was hard and morsels few and far between, moaned about the "dry rations" that were their lot. And yet, for the most part, they complained little. Sherman's men "were jolly on parched corn, cow beans, or whatever they could find." The revolution in taste resulting from the war was nothing to their palates; their heavy reliance on what they could carry in their haversacks—mainly coffee, hardtack, sugar, and salt—was enough to help power them through the wet, muddy, and difficult South Carolina terrain.[21] And it wasn't just food; fresh water was at a premium. The soldiers shared precious water from canteens, but their tongues were often dry. White Southern women sometimes refused to give them water, at least in potable form. The most some would offer was their spit.[22]

With only 1.2 million rations to begin with and relying on stingy land, Sherman's men, also charged with destruction of Southern war resources, including food, were locustlike, devouring whatever fare they encountered.[23] Ephraim Cutler Dawes, an officer in the Fifty-Third Ohio Volunteer Infantry, captured this quality. In late July 1864, as Sherman marched toward Atlanta, his company "halted at noon at Germantown eat [sic] one onion for dinner— During the halt the 8th Mo cleaned Germantown completely."[24]

For the most part, they harbored no pity for white Southerners. The rebels deserved starvation in their view, and so they took food from Southern women with glee and happily, even eagerly, destroyed cotton crops. They blamed the women for firing up their men, supporting the war with their "wild enthusiasms," and happily paid them back, destroying "Anything and Everything." They wanted them on "Bended Knees," pathetic and supine, and the soldiers fully understood how deprivation might achieve that.[25]

When food was very scarce, the men hacked flesh off dead animals they encountered along the way, raw hunger trumping taste. They devoured food whenever they could, wolfing down precious supplies hoarded by Southern civilizations. These men were "hungry wolves," without civility. This tension between the need to survive and the impulse to preserve a sense of decency was common during the march and amounted to what one soldier called "a conflict between appetite and noble sensibilities." Victors had to play the savage if they were to win this fight.[26]

Sherman's 60,000 or so troops, cutting a swath up to sixty miles wide through the Confederate heartland, were a sensory assault on the South—heard, seen, smelled, tasted, and felt.[27]

Typically, Sherman's imminent arrival in Southern towns and cities was heard before it was seen. Rumors of their arrival, their viciousness, and their contempt for Southern whites circulated long before the soldiers arrived. In Savannah, word had it that Yankees cut off fingers to get rings, that burning homes was perfectly standard. Many Southerners tried to avoid the encounters.[28] Union soldiers fanned the flames of rumor and spread word of what Sherman's men might or might not do. In Columbia, South Carolina, a Union guard mentioned that the city would likely be burned, the troops allowed to run riot, and all food and possessions taken.[29]

Many white Southern women were indeed "frightened . . . out of their senses" by rumors about what the troops might do to them.[30] Even rumor of the arrival of the scythelike phalanx changed the soundscape of Southern towns. At Milledgeville, "the excitement increased," men and women ran around madly, "dogs howled and yelped, mules brayed, Negro drivers swore, while Negro girls giggled."[31]

Rumor was followed by the awesome sound of a massive army moving ever closer, the ground between them and the civilians being eaten up at an impressive and relentless pace.

Sherman's army could be heard, through martial song and sheer vibration, miles before they came into view, the sound of feet and voice an aural vanguard sending shivers through white Southerners. The sound of musket fire sometimes announced the approach of the men. At other times, as during their approach to Winnsboro, South Carolina, it was the "lowing of driven cattle, the squawking of poultry, and the squealing of pigs" that signaled the coming of the army.[32] Often, it was the sound of axes chopping— the customary sound of civilization, ironically enough—that announced the coming. Retreating Confederates hacked down southern pines and left them strewn on roads, a pathetic attempt to slow the inevitable.[33]

And then they were there in force, full throated in Southern ears. To white Southerners, they sounded like the noise of the mob that slaveholders had fought so long to contain. In Beaufort, South Carolina, the "marauders" came "trooping" through the streets, audible everywhere, "roaring out songs and jokes."[34] Yankee voices, "cussing and swearing," filled the dark swamps of Georgia. Columbia's women bemoaned "the coarse language of this mass of ruffians sounding in our ears."[35] Everywhere Sherman's war machine moved, in every town it laid waste, Southerners heard, for the first time in four years, a sound they had come to loathe: the "reveling," "roaring," riling notes of "Yankee Doodle."[36]

With perverse harmony, sights matched sounds. Seeing such vast numbers of Union men wading through the Confederate heartland was wholly new to most civilians; hitherto, they had only read about and imagined what war on this scale might look like.

Carefully cultivated Southern civilization could be seen—and heard—crumbling. At Hardeeville, South Carolina, Yankee hands systematically destroyed a church. Axes vibrated as they chewed up pulpit and pew; in Archimedean fashion, long poles, fashioned from trees, leveraged the church spire, which sank down "with a screeching groan." And then, for twenty, even thirty miles around, the "black columns of smoke" could be seen, as the men burned the church to the ground.[37]

One sight in particular stayed with white Southerners: the sight of the Union flag. Union soldiers ran it up on the state capitols in Georgia and South Carolina, marking their turf, cowing Confederates: "Our degradation was bitter" was the Southern refrain.[38] Emma LeConte saw her beloved Columbia humiliated, degraded by the "horrid sight" of the American flag flown atop the statehouse during Sherman's occupation of the city. The sights of destruction were so mortifying that LeConte looked away, believing it was "a contamination even to look at these devils." New sights announced the death of an old way of life, at least for the time being.[39]

And then, eventually, the men would leave. In their wake, the countryside and towns were unrecognizable. Grain fields once proud and tall were now flat, trampled by thousands of feet; animals—hogs, horses, cattle—once carefully penned and contained were now roaming, and those that weren't lay strewn, carcasses lining the roads. Orderliness had vanished. City buildings, once proudly straight and vertical, were now obscenely jagged, "shattered brick walls" the signature of defeat. Windowpanes, once beautifully demarcating in from out and soundproofing homes, were now sharp, broken, and oddly audible, with winds and gusts whistling grotesque music.[40] Books and papers from ransacked libraries covered streets, the litter in turn blanketed by "a stillness almost Sabbath."[41]

Confederate noses could smell Sherman's army miles before it arrived and for days after it left. Houses, whole cities, were cindered; decades of settlement, of carefully cultivated society, were left drifting on the air, the impressive physicality of a civilization reduced to an evaporating smell. Total war meant total destruction of anything that might be of use to the Confederacy—houses, barns, railways, mills, anything, everything. As such, total war also entailed overwhelming the senses. Sherman's march, directed at civilian and soldier, had the effect of not only crushing the Southern heartland physically but, in the process, also generating overwhelming sights, smells, sounds, tastes, and touches. This march was, in short, a sensory event of unprecedented scale, intensity, and scope, for Southern civilians especially.[42]

Deliberate torching was deemed the most efficient means of achieving destruction. "Old Sherman's Smokehouse Rangers" had one mantra: Burn. Nights in Atlanta were made so bright some soldiers could read their newspapers from the fuel of Southern civilization.[43] South Carolina generally, the capital of Columbia in particular, was left so charred, the scale of the burning so great, that even federal soldiers were choked, almost suffocated by the consuming blazes (figure 6.1). And in the wake was left behind "a howling wilderness," not unlike the one the first settlers had encountered hundreds of years before.[44]

This was the stench of the uncivilized. An Ohio sergeant said as much from South Carolina: "Every house, barn, fence and cotton gin gets an application of the torch. That prospect is revolting, but war is an uncivil game and can't be civilized."[45] "Never in *modern* times," wrote a Wisconsin man about Columbia, "did soldiers have such fun . . . fire and soldiery had full swing."[46]

Destruction achieved, the army left behind not just burned buildings but the carcasses of the animals they had killed and a memory of their consumption, the fetid smell of their garbage circulating wildly in Southern air. This was the stench of degenerating matter—vegetable, animal, fecal—left behind by a massive army on the move. Women sniffed cologne to mask the odor of the Yankee invasion, but to little avail.[47]

FIGURE 6.1. *Columbia, South Carolina, after Sherman.*

George N. Barnard, *Barnard's Photographic Views of the Sherman Campaign,* *ca. 1866* (New York: Press of Wynkoop & Hallenbeck, 1866).

The effect was like a moving Vicksburg. A Wisconsin private wrote to his wife that the army devoured whatever food it encountered, leaving "not enough in the country to support the women and children," who were left "crying and begging" to be left "a little meal or something to eat; yet the last morsel would be taken and they left to suffer." Starving women and children was an effective way to break the Southern will.[48]

It was not the only way. When Sherman's bummers—men operating relatively independently of his command—swooped on plantations and city houses, they handled whites in ways new and alien. Southern white women, especially plantation mistresses, used to the delicate touch, found themselves having to do the dirty work of digging holes to hide family jewels in anticipation of the federal arrival. The unlucky ones were manhandled, prodded, choked, sometimes raped.[49]

Often, the men were as hard on slaves. Certainly, the slaves who ran to Sherman's line impressed them, with "men, women, and children . . . willing to endure the hardships of a long march," just like the soldiers.[50] But the men in blue were impatient with the slaves; the sheer numbers who ran to the lines (around 10,000 followed the army to Savannah; about 7,000 tailed them in the Carolinas) caused problems, testing not only supplies but the patience of tired men. It was not unknown for soldiers to beat, rape, and abuse slaves, treating them not unlike slaveholders did. Slaves who either watched the soldiers march or who joined the lines were sometimes stabbed, hit, even shot.[51] Despite the noble cause they championed, Sherman's men, in an effort to break Southern will and enact total defeat, stooped to a kind of primitive savagery, perpetrating acts of violence and dehumanization intended to humiliate and terrorize.

For all that violence, poignant scenes could touch the troops emotionally. When soldiers saw a slave mother reunited with her daughter (who had been sold a decade earlier), many wept openly. So, too, with gestures of kindness. Seeing a barefoot soldier, one slave offered him his shoes, so that his feet might be spared. Soldier and slave knew what the abuse felt like, and the slave certainly shared empathy with the soldier.[52]

For African American slaves, Sherman's march brought the sensory signatures of freedom, no matter how poorly they were treated by some Union men. When, like Southern whites, they heard, saw, and smelled Sherman coming, slaves fled to his lines, happy to trade slavery for the taste of Union rations.[53]

The Civil War began with a bang. And at least for the Confederacy, it ended with deafening silence. By 1865, its bells had been melted for cannon, and erstwhile voices clamoring for war had been muted. Familiar soundscapes in Charleston, the sound of markets, the din of commerce, the songs of celebration, were now gone (figure 6.2).

"Did you think of this when you hurrahed for Secession?" one Union soldier asked a white man in Columbia as he gestured to

FIGURE 6.2. *Charleston, South Carolina, at War's End.*

George N. Barnard, stereo card, "Circular Ch., St Philip's Ch., Secession Hall, Charleston, S.C.," LOT 13461, no. 20 [P&P], Library of Congress Prints and Photographs Division, Washington, D.C.

the flames engulfing the city. "Your mouth is silenced now and it is worth every damn year of this bloody war." "How do you like it, hey?" His answer, if there was one, would have been drowned by the incredible noise of consuming fire, the "palpitating blaze" creating a "terrible roar."[54]

Other sounds, equally humbling to white Southern ears, lasted long after the men in blue left. They denoted the deafening crash of their world order. Black voices were no longer constrained (figure 6.3). "God bless you, Yanks! Come at last! God knows how long I been waitin'," shouted one Georgia slave after Sherman's men had captured Milledgeville. In Columbia, they ran to touch Sherman's hand. For these men and women, that hard hand of war was the hand of freedom. They celebrated against the keynotes of "Yankee Doodle" and, ironically, "Hail, Columbia," courtesy of the Union army band. "I think the day of Jubilo has come," cheered one slave. The words punctured the Southern air as surely as the

FIGURE 6.3. *The Sounds of Freedom.*

Wood engraving, "Emancipation Day in South Carolina," January 1, 1863.
Reproduction Number: LC-USZ62-88808 (b&w film copy neg.), Library of
Congress Prints and Photographs Division, Washington, D.C.

first shells launched at Fort Sumter those long four years before.[55]
This was all to the good and wholly necessary, for from the degradation came national dignity—the new birth of freedom. Yet
to realize it, to claim their place in modernity, Americans had to
endure a wrenching war, one that reminded them of the past that
they had believed they had escaped but that, when it arrived, overwhelmed them.

ACKNOWLEDGMENTS

A book many years in the making incurs many debts. Important aspects of it were shaped by conversations, some of them formal, many of them not, all of them invaluable. One of the first was with Geraldine Brooks in 2006, when we had the opportunity to discuss the sensory language of her Pulitzer Prize-winning treatment of the Civil War, *March*. Over the years, I benefited from similar conversations with, and support from, Daniel Bender, Vernon Burton, Walter Edgar, Eric Foner, William Freehling, Eugene Genovese, Paul MacKenzie, David Moltke-Hansen, and Johanna Rivera.

Lisa Brady, John Mayfield, Cary Mock, Megan Kate Nelson, and Sam Thomas kindly shared evidence they thought helpful to my project; Peter Carmichael's generosity in this regard was simply astonishing. For granting me access to the nation's largest private collection of Civil War artifacts and for educating me on their meaning, I remain most grateful to Beverly M. DuBose III and Bronson Smith. My thanks also go to Sheffield Hale and Gordon L. Jones of the Atlanta History Center for sharing with me their knowledge of the DuBose collection.

As chairs of the history department at the University of South Carolina during the research and writing of this book, Lacy Ford and Larry Glickman were steadfast in their support, as was the dean of the College of Arts and Sciences at Carolina, Mary Anne

Fitzpatrick. A good deal of this book was written while I was a fellow at the University of South Carolina's Institute of African American Research. I remain most grateful to Daniel C. Littlefield, the Institute's Director, for his kind hospitality and support.

I have been honored to be able to test many of the ideas offered in this book at a variety of conferences around the world. On each of those occasions, my hosts were gracious, and the book has benefited from the hard questions offered by commentators and audiences alike. Doug Kahn offered invaluable insights on my initial effort to chart the acoustemology of the Civil War at a conference on "Listening to Archives" at the University of Technology, Sydney, Australia, in 2001. Constructive and helpful comments were offered, too, when I spoke on the sensory history of the Civil War at the Department of History, University of Illinois, Urbana-Champaign (2005); the Department of History, University of Northern Colorado (2008); the Department of African American Studies, Yale University (2008); the Chicago History Museum (2011); the University of Georgia (2011; thanks to Vince and Barbara Dooley for hosting my presentation in their home); at a conference arranged by Raviv Ganchrow on sound in Tallinn, Estonia (2011); Carleton University, Ottawa, Canada (2012); the Imperial War Museum, London (2013); Griffith University, Brisbane, Australia (2013); the Hagley Museum and Library, Wilmington, Delaware (2013); Gettysburg College, Pennsylvania (2013); the University of Toronto, Canada (2013); and at Rice University, Houston, Texas (2014), where I was honored to deliver the David Potter Lecture, courtesy of John Boles and Randal Hall. I am also grateful to James McHugh, Alex Rehding, and Alison Simmons for inviting me to participate in a colloquium on the limits of sensory perception in 2011 at the Radcliffe Institute for Advanced Study at Harvard University.

Thanks go to Joan Cashin for urging me to offer my early ideas about the sounds of the war in the form of an essay in her edited book, *The War Was You and Me: Civilians and the American Civil*

War (2002), and to Leo G. Mazow for inviting me to test my ideas about battle smells and photography in the journal *American Art* in 2010.

Students and former students have generously shared tidbits from their own research over the years, and I would like to thank especially Parker Ainsworth, Ehren Foley, Ali Nabours, Dave Prior, Jay Richardson, Cheryl Wells, and Michael Woods in this regard. My sincere thanks go to Angela Riotto for invaluable research assistance on the Vicksburg siege, Francesca Fair for her considerable help with Gettysburg, and, especially, to Evan Kutzler, whose assistance has been nothing short of remarkable.

For reading earlier iterations of the manuscript, my sincere thanks go to Steve Berry, Tracey Green, and Sarah Gardner, all of whom helped improve the book. Jackie Jones also read a later version and, as always, did her best to keep me on track with extensive, gracious, and insistently insightful comments. Any failure to make the most of their suggestions and recommendations is, of course, mine alone.

My agent, Geri Thoma, displayed great patience and forbearance and offered sage advice when it was most needed. At Oxford University Press, Keely Latcham took care of any number of matters with great efficiency and aplomb. There is no adequately thanking Tim Bent, my redoubtable editor. Tim did wonders with the manuscript I gave him, and I remain deeply impressed by his exemplary editing. I am very grateful, indeed, for the incredible care he took with my work.

My family has lived with this book for quite a while. For allowing me to research, write, and think about war and for making my world the sensory delight that it is, one full of laughter, happiness, and smiles, Sophie, Bennett, Connor, and Raegan have my enduring thanks and deepest love.

NOTE ON SOURCES

This book represents a marriage between a relatively new way of doing history and an established historical subject. The Civil War ranks among the most examined, interpreted, and written-about subjects in history. "Sensory history," by contrast, is an approach, perhaps best understood as a habit of thinking historically rather than as a delineated field of inquiry. Regardless of the place and time—from ancient Rome to modern America—it endeavors to apply the senses to our understanding of the past. Certainly, it attends to the primary way people view events: sight. This visual or ocular way of understanding historical evidence is extremely common in all fields of historical inquiry, and some theorists have argued that our inclination to understand the past through the eyes of historical actors is indebted to any number of "modern" technologies and ways of thinking, including the visual bias of the Enlightenment, the invention of print, and eye-empowering tech-nologies, such as telescopes and photography (see, for example, Jonathan Crary, *Techniques of the Observer: On Vision and Modernity in the Nineteenth Century* [Cambridge, Mass.: MIT Press, 1992]; David Michael Levin, ed., *Modernity and the Hegemony of Vision* [Berkeley: University of California Press, 1993]). Yet sensory his-tory moves beyond purely visually mediated evidence and tries to understand the ways in which hearing, olfaction, taste, and tactility also shaped the way people experienced and remembered certain events. Although the writing of sensory history is older than is sometimes assumed (examples of historians and other scholars writing about the senses can be found in the mid-twentieth century), this way of writing about the past has blossomed in the last thirty years, especially in the last decade. I offer what I hope is a helpful summary and interpretation of a great deal of this work, as well as an indication of just how wide-ranging the historical study of the senses has become (historians of all periods and many places have made the sensory turn), in my book *Sensing the Past: Seeing, Hearing, Smelling, Tasting, and Touching in History* (Berkeley: University of California Press, 2008). Readers interested in a more recent overview would be well advised to consult David Howes and Constance Classen, *Ways of Seeing: Understanding the Senses in Society* (New York: Routledge, 2014).

Some of the nonvisual senses have received more attention than others. A great deal has been written on the history of sound especially, and *The Oxford Handbook of Sound Studies*, edited by Trevor Punch and Karin Bijsterveld (New York: Oxford University Press, 2012), is a good point of access to some of this work. Work on the other senses, meanwhile, is beginning to catch up in terms of both quantity and quality. On touch, see the detailed treatment offered by Constance Classen in *The Deepest Sense: A Cultural History of Touch* (Urbana: University of Illinois Press, 2012). Carolyn Korsmeyer has helpfully collected some key essays on taste (*The Taste Culture Reader: Experiencing Food and Drink* [Oxford: Berg, 2005]), and the historiography of smell is well served by Jonathan Reinarz's *Past Scents: Historical Perspectives on Smell* (Urbana: University of Illinois Press, 2014).

A word on method seems in order. In this book, I've aspired to move beyond the mere cataloguing of sounds, smells, tastes, and the like, which was a hallmark of the very earliest historical treatments of the senses. Instead, I follow Alain Corbin's insistence that, above all, sensory history must try to tease meaning from the evidence and go beyond simple listing. See his seminal *Time, Desire, and Horror: Towards a History of the Senses*, trans. Jean Birrell (Cambridge: Polity Press, 1995). I outline some of the methodological challenges facing sensory historians as they continue to excavate the sensate past in my essay "Producing Sense, Consuming Sense, Making Sense: Perils and Prospects for Sensory History," *Journal of Social History* 40 (June 2007), pp. 841–858.

As I note in the introduction to this book, relatively few historians of the Civil War have attended to the sensory experience of its participants, at least in an explicitly historicized fashion. I have noted the exceptions throughout the study, but it is worth highlighting here a few who have begun to document, historicize, and refer to the senses and sensory experience in their work. Earl J. Hess's *The Union Soldier in Battle: Enduring the Ordeal of Combat* (Lawrence: University Press of Kansas, 1997), pp. 15–29, 140–160, is among the most sensory treatments we have of battle and soldiering. The sense of smell appropriately informs some of Drew Gilpin Faust's brilliant examination of death during the war in her book, *This Republic of Suffering: Death and the American Civil War* (New York: Vintage, 2008). Allen C. Guelzo's award-winning *Gettysburg: The Last Invasion* (New York: Knopf, 2013) speaks perceptively if briefly about sound and touch. Jacqueline Jones's absorbing study, *Saving Savannah: The City and the Civil War* (New York: Alfred A. Knopf, 2008), is highly attentive to sound. The gold standard for placing the Civil War in its full context, and one that is also sensitive to the sounds and noises of battle, remains James M. McPherson's *Battle Cry of Freedom: The Civil War Era* (New York: Oxford University Press, 1988).

These examples notwithstanding, there are surprisingly few books about the sensory history of any war. An exception is the pioneering work by Santanu Das, *Touch and Intimacy in First World War Literature* (New York: Cambridge University Press, 2005). Much more could be written on the topic, and using this approach, I offer this book in the hope that it is the first of many.

NOTES

Introduction

1. "The Cultivation of the Senses," *Harper's New Monthly Magazine*, 6, no. 31 (December 1852), p. 81.

2. Recent, exceptional treatments of the war, regardless of whether it was fought over slavery or preservation of Union, as well as superb attention to all of the knotty struggles that underwrote the conflict, are Eric Foner, *The Fiery Trial: Abraham Lincoln and American Slavery* (New York: Norton, 2010); James Oakes, *Freedom National: The Destruction of Slavery in the United States, 1861–1865* (New York: Norton, 2013); and Gary Gallagher, *The Union War* (Cambridge, Mass.: Harvard University Press, 2011).

3. See Tony Horwitz, *Confederates in the Attic: Dispatches from the Unfinished Civil War* (New York: Vintage, 1999). For a balanced, thoughtful, and engaging assessment of the nature and meaning of Civil War re-enactment that is also useful for highlighting key scholarly works on the topic, see Paul Mullins, "Imagining War: The Material Experience of Civil War Reenactment," available at: http://paulmullins.wordpress.com/2013/06/23/imagining-war-the-material-experience-of-civil-war-reenactment/.

4. On these matters, see my commentary in "Producing Sense, Consuming Sense, Making Sense: Perils and Prospects for Sensory History," *Journal of Social History* 40 (summer 2007), pp. 841–858.

5. Charles D. Ross, *Civil War Acoustic Shadows* (Shippensburg, Pa.: White Mane Press, 2001).

6. These authors were prolific. But see, for example, the descriptions offered in Shelby Foote, *The Civil War, a Narrative* (New York: Random House,

1958), pp. 4–6, 76, 81; Bruce Catton, *A Stillness at Appomattox* (1952; repr., New York: Anchor, 1990), pp. 67–68, 74, 88, 98; and Bell Irvin Wiley, *The Life of Johnny Reb: The Common Soldier of the Confederacy* (1943; repr., Baton Rouge: Louisiana State University Press, 2008), pp. 71–73, 150–159, and *The Life of Billy Yank: The Common Soldier of the Union* (1952; repr., Baton Rouge: Louisiana State University Press, 2008).

7. I survey the emergence of sensory history in my *Sensing the Past: Seeing, Hearing, Smelling, Tasting, and Touching in History* (Berkeley: University of California Press, 2008).

8. On this unpleasant intimacy with the war, see the exceptional essays in Stephen Berry, ed., *Weirding the War: Stories from the Civil War's Ragged Edges* (Athens: University of Georgia Press, 2011).

9. The list of possible topics is almost endless and could include, among many others, sensory treatments of other key battles and sieges, the Northern home front, and the war at sea. Important work on the sensory experiences of Civil War prisoners is already underway. See Evan Kutzler, "Captive Audiences: Sound, Silence, and Listening in Civil War Prisons," *Journal of Social History* (forthcoming, December 2014), as well as his forthcoming PhD dissertation being written at the University of South Carolina.

10. Relevant literature on this topic is surveyed in Smith, *Sensing the Past*, pp. 1–40 especially.

Chapter One

1. Although rudimentary streetlighting in the city had existed since the 1760s, Charleston did not acquire reliable gaslights until the 1840s. See Peter A. Coclanis, *The Shadow of a Dream: Economic Life and Death in the South Carolina Lowcountry, 1670–1920* (New York: Oxford University Press, 1989), p. 7; Phillip C. Richardson Jr., "Gaslight, Progress, and the Old South, 1801–1865" (PhD dissertation, University of South Carolina, 2012), ch. 1 esp.; N. H. Campbell, Apr. 3, 1848, Charleston, [SC], to Dr. J. H. Dean, Greenville, S.C., South Caroliniana Library, University of South Carolina [hereafter SCL].

2. For the meteorological conditions that night, I am indebted to the generosity of Professor Cary Mock of the University of South Carolina's Geography Department, who kindly shared George Plezer's weather records he kept for the Charleston Board of Health in December 1860.

3. "Who Major Anderson Is—His Career," in *The Battle of Fort Sumter and First Victory of Southern Troops, April 13, 1861* ... (Charleston, S.C.: Evans & Cogswell, 1861), pp. 29–30.

4. Quotation from the Charleston *Courier* in Walter Edgar, *South Carolina: A History* (Columbia: University of South Carolina Press, 1998), p. 356.

5. Edgar, *South Carolina*, pp. 291–292, 321; Raimondo Luraghi, *The Rise and Fall of the Plantation South* (New York: Franklin Watts, 1978), pp. 164–166; Coclanis, *Shadow of a Dream*, p. 7; John Radford, "The Charleston Planters in 1860," *South Carolina Historical Magazine* 77 (October 1976), pp. 227–235; George C. Rogers Jr., *Charleston in the Age of the Pinckneys* (Columbia: University of South Carolina Press, 1980), pp. 161–164. Quotations, in order: William E. Surtees, *Recollections of North America, in 1849–50–51* (London: Chapman and Hall, 1852), p. 30; Jane M. Turnbull and Marion T. Turnbull, *American Photographs* (London: T. C. Newby, 1860), vol. 1, p. 92. See also Ivan D. Steen, "Charleston in the 1850's: As Described by British Travelers," *South Carolina Historical Magazine* 71 (January 1970), pp. 36–38, quotations on 38, 41. Census data from the immensely useful Historical Census Browser, University of Virginia, http://mapserver.lib.virginia.edu/php/county.php.

6. A clearly composite argument summarizing an impossibly complex development. But see James Henley Thornwell, *National Sins: A Fast-Day Sermon: Preached in the Presbyterian Church, Columbia, S.C, Wednesday, November 21, 1860* (Columbia, S.C.: Southern Guardian Steam-Power Press, 1860), pp. 33–37 esp.; Elizabeth Fox-Genovese and Eugene D. Genovese, *The Mind of the Master Class: History and Faith in the Southern Slaveholders' Worldview* (New York: Cambridge University Press, 2005).

7. Quotation in Edgar, *South Carolina*, p. 295.

8. Quotation in Edgar, *South Carolina*, p. 295; J. Benwell, *An Englishman's Travels in America: His Observations of Life and Manners in the Free and Slave States* (London: Binns and Goodwin, 1853), p. 187.

9. Mark M. Smith, *Listening to Nineteenth-Century America* (Chapel Hill: University of North Carolina Press, 2001). Quotations in "The Senses. IV. Hearing," *Harper's New Monthly Magazine*, 12, no. 71 (April 1856), pp. 635, 639.

10. Quotations: William Gilmore Simms, "Walterboro," *Southern Literary Gazette*, October 15, 1829, p. 257; Henry A. Murray, *Lands of the Slave and*

the Free: or, Cuba, the United States, and Canada (London: John W. Parker and Son, 1855), vol. 1, p. 380.

11. A., "Idle Hours—No.1. Twilight," *Southern Rose*, 7 (December 22, 1838), p. 135.

12. See, for example, John Edwards, "An Ordinance for Establishing a Guard and Watch in the City of Charleston . . .," February 20, 1796, in Edwards, *Ordinances of the City Council of Charleston . . . (1804–1807)* (Charleston, S.C.: W. P. Young, 1802 [*sic*]), p. 144; Mark M. Smith, *Listening to Nineteenth-Century America*, p. 57; Mark M. Smith, *Mastered by the Clock: Time, Slavery, and Freedom in the American South* (Chapel Hill: University of North Carolina Press, 2001), pp. 19, 46–48.

13. Smith, *Listening to Nineteenth-Century America*; Smith, *Mastered by the Clock*; Steen, "Charleston in the 1850's," pp. 44–45.

14. Quotation in Karl Bernhard, Duke of Saxe-Weimar Eisenach, *Travels through North America during the Years 1825 and 1826. In Two Volumes. Volume 2* (Philadelphia: Carey, Lea & Carey, 1828), p. 7. Gina Haney, "In Complete Order: Social Control and Architectural Organization in the Charleston Back Lot" (MA thesis, University of Virginia, 1996), p. 46; Rogers, *Charleston in the Age of the Pinckneys*, pp. 147–148; Steen, "Charleston in the 1850's," pp. 43–44.

15. Margaret Izard Manigault to Gabriel Manigault, November 23, 1792, Manigault Family Papers, SCL; Frances Ann Kemble, *Records of Later Life* (New York: Henry Holt, 1882), pp. 123–124. On the few lamps and their inability to pierce the dark streets at night in the city, see William E. Baxter, *America and the Americans* (London: J. Routledge, 1855), p. 175.

16. Quotations from Mary Boykin Chesnut, *A Diary from Dixie*, ed. Ben Ames Williams (Boston, Mass.: Houghton Mifflin, 1949), p. 147; John George Clinckscales, *On the Old Plantation: Reminiscences of His Childhood* (Spartanburg, S.C.: Band and White, 1916), p. 104. The broader discussion is based on my *Listening to Nineteenth-Century America*, pp. 80–89. But see also Haney, "In Complete Order"; Rebecca Ginsburg, "Freedom and the Slave Landscape," *Landscape Journal*, 26 (January 2007), pp. 36–44.

17. Abner Doubleday, *Reminiscences of Forts Sumter and Moultrie in 1860–'61* (1876; repr., Charleston, S.C., Nautical and Aviation Publishing Company, 1998), pp. 32–33; "Diary of John Berkley Grimball," *South Carolina Historical Magazine*, 56 (April 1955), p. 101.

18. Sophia Rosenfeld, "*AHR FORUM*: On Being Heard: A Case for Paying Attention to the Historical Ear," *American Historical Review*, 116 (April 2011), pp. 326–328 esp.

19. Charles Edward Cauthen, *South Carolina Goes to War, 1860–1865* (1950; repr., Columbia: University of South Carolina Press, 2005), pp. 45, 47.

20. Samuel Wylie Crawford, *The Genesis of the Civil War: The Story of Sumter, 1860–1861* (New York: Charles L. Webster, 1887), pp. 10–12, 13.

21. Doubleday, *Reminiscences*, pp. 14, 16, 19.

22. Crawford, *Genesis of the Civil War*, p. 50.

23. Doubleday, *Reminiscences*, pp. 31–32.

24. Crawford, *Genesis of the Civil War*, p. 7; James Chester, "Inside Sumter in '61," in *Battles and Leaders of the Civil War* (Secausus, N.J.: Castle, n.d), p. 50.

25. Crawford, *Genesis of the Civil War*, p. 13.

26. Crawford, *Genesis of the Civil War*, pp. 13, 16.

27. Crawford, *Genesis of the Civil War*, pp. 52–53. Traveler James Stirling observed in the 1850s that Charleston's streets were the first paved ones he had encountered outside of New Orleans. See Steen, "Charleston in the 1850's," p. 41.

28. Crawford, *Genesis of the Civil War*, p. 53.

29. Crawford, *Genesis of the Civil War*, pp. 52–54.

30. Crawford, *Genesis of the Civil War*, pp. 54–55.

31. Crawford, *Genesis of the Civil War*, p. 55; "Diary of John Berkley Grimball," p. 102; Cauthen, *South Carolina Goes to War*, p. 30; Richardson, "Gaslight, Progress, and the Old South, 1801–1865," p. 208.

32. Charleston *Mercury*, December 21, 1860; Crawford, *Genesis of the Civil War*, pp. 54–55. For Union evaluations, see Doubleday, *Reminiscences*, p. 55.

33. Doubleday, *Reminiscences*, p. 26. "There is a great deal of dissatisfaction of the silence of yr self and Chesnut already and it will increase," I. W. Hayne told James Henry Hammond in September 1860. Hayne to J. H. Hammond, September 15, 1860, Hammond Papers, Library of Congress [hereafter LOC]. See, too, Cauthen, *South Carolina Goes to War*, p. 50.

34. Doubleday, *Reminiscences*, p. 26.

35. Crawford, *The Genesis of the Civil War,* p. 2; Doubleday, *Reminiscences,* p. 100. Note, too, "Description of Fort Sumter," in *The Battle of Fort Sumter,* p. 28.

36. Doubleday, *Reminiscences,* pp. 35–36.

37. Crawford, *Genesis of the Civil War,* pp. 60–61.

38. Crawford, *Genesis of the Civil War,* pp. 62–63, 64. See also Doubleday, *Reminiscences,* pp. 49–51.

39. Crawford, *Genesis of the Civil War,* pp. 63, 64–65, quotation on p. 68.

40. Quoted in Crawford, *Genesis of the Civil War,* p. 73.

41. Crawford, *Genesis of the Civil War,* pp. 71, 74; Doubleday, *Reminiscences,* p. 57.

42. Doubleday, *Reminiscences,* pp. 58–61, quotation on p. 58; David Detzer, *Allegiance: Fort Sumter, Charleston, and the Beginning of the Civil War* (New York: Harcourt, 2001), p. 111. See also [Jefferson C. Davis], "Charleston Harbor, 1860–1861: A Memoir from the Union Garrison," ed. James P. Jones, *South Carolina Historical Magazine,* 61 (July 1961), p. 149.

43. Doubleday, *Reminiscences,* pp. 61–63.

44. Quotations: John Thompson to "My Dear Father," Fort Sumter, South Carolina, February 14, 1861, in John Thompson, "A Union Soldier at Fort Sumter, 1860–1861," *South Carolina Historical Magazine,* 67 (April 1966), pp. 99–100; Doubleday, *Reminiscences,* p. 64.

45. Doubleday, *Reminiscences,* pp. 64–66; Thompson, "Union Soldier at Fort Sumter," pp. 99–100; Detzer, *Allegiance,* pp. 117–118; Maury Klein, *Days of Defiance: Sumter, Secession, and the Coming of the Civil War* (New York: Vintage, 1997), pp. 155–156. See also, [Davis], "Charleston Harbor," p. 149; Chester, "Inside Sumter," p. 51.

46. Doubleday, *Reminiscences,* pp. 66–67; James Chester, "Inside Sumter," p. 51.

47. Doubleday, *Reminiscences,* pp. 68–69, 71, 73. Soldier observations in Thompson, "Union Soldier at Fort Sumter," pp. 100–101.

48. Doubleday, *Reminiscences,* pp. 83, 84, 103, 177; "Under the Union Guns," *New York Times,* May 10, 1891.

49. On rations, see Thompson, "Union Soldier at Fort Sumter," p. 102.

50. Doubleday, *Reminiscences,* pp. 86, 88, 89, 100, 102, 112, 113, 115, 116; Chester, "Inside Sumter," p. 56. Detzer, *Allegiance,* pp. 233–234. But see, too, A. R. Chisolm, "Notes on the Surrender of Fort Sumter," Alexander R. Chisolm Papers (New York: New York Historical Society), pp. 82–83.

51. "The Battle of Fort Sumter. First Day's Bombardment," Friday, April 12, 1861, in *The Battle of Fort Sumter*, p. 3.

52. "Battle of Fort Sumter," in *Battle of Fort Sumter*, p. 3.

53. "Battle of Fort Sumter," in *Battle of Fort Sumter*, p. 4.

54. "Battle of Fort Sumter," in *Battle of Fort Sumter*, p. 4; Robert Lebby, "The First Shot on Fort Sumter," *South Carolina Historical and Genealogical Magazine*, 12 (July 1911), pp. 143–144; Chester, "Inside Sumter," p. 66. For an observation that shells were seen before they were heard, see John W. Urban, *My Experiences Mid Shot and Shell and in Rebel Den* (Lancaster, Pa.: privately printed, 1882), pp. 607–608.

55. "Battle of Fort Sumter," *Battle of Fort Sumter*, p. 4.

56. "Battle of Fort Sumter," *Battle of Fort Sumter*, p. 4; Stephen D. Lee, "The First Step in the War," in *Battles and Leaders*, vol. 1, pp. 76–77.

57. "The Fight as Seen from Cummings' Point (from a special correspondent on Morris Island)," in *Battle of Fort Sumter*, p. 12. For the distance, see Chester, "Inside Sumter," p. 55. For a helpful map, see T. Seymour, "Morris Island and Cumming's Point as seen from Fort Sumter," http://digitalcollections.baylor.edu/cdm/singleitem/collection/tx-wotr/id/1495/rec/15.

58. "Cummings' Point," in *Battle of Fort Sumter*, pp. 12–13.

59. Johnson Hagood, *Memoirs of the War of Secession* . . . (Germantown, Tenn.: Guild Bindery Press, 1994), p. 32.

60. "Cummings' Point," in *Battle of Fort Sumter*, pp. 15, 16.

61. Thompson, "Union Solider at Fort Sumter," pp. 102–103.

62. "Cummings' Point," in *Battle of Fort Sumter*, pp. 16–17.

63. "Battle of Fort Sumter," in *Battle of Fort Sumter*, p. 5.

64. "Battle of Fort Sumter," in *Battle of Fort Sumter*, p. 5; "A Night in the Harbor—A Cruise after the Enemy," in *Battle of Fort Sumter*, p. 20.

65. "Close of the Bombardment," April 13, 1861, in *Battle of Fort Sumter*, pp. 7–8. On wind direction and the sound of guns from Sumter, see *New York Times*, April 14, 1861.

66. "Close of the Bombardment," in *Battle of Fort Sumter*, pp. 8–9; "Cummings' Point," in *Battle of Fort Sumter*, pp. 12; *New York Times*, April 16, 1861.

67. "The Surrender of Fort Sumter," April 14, 1861, in *Battle of Fort Sumter*, pp. 10–11. At the announcement of the major's surrender, voices on the point

joined those in Charleston and those on water, knitting sounds over varied geographies, blanketing the bay. They "cheered and cheered again ... and the whole shore rang with the glad shouts of thousands." "Cummings' Point," in *Battle of Fort Sumter*, p. 18. See, too, "Night in the Harbor," in *Battle of Fort Sumter*, pp. 20, 21. See also Klein, *Days of Defiance*, pp. 418–419.

68. "Scenes and Incidents of the Bombardment," in *Battle of Fort Sumter*, pp. 21, 22.

69. Doubleday, *Reminiscences*, pp. 157, 158.

70. "Scenes and Incidents," in *Battle of Fort Sumter*, pp. 22, 23.

Chapter Two

1. William C. Davis, *Battle at Bull Run: A History of the First Major Campaign of the Civil War* (Baton Rouge: Louisiana State University, 1982), pp. 49, 51, 64, 67; T. Harry Williams, *P. G. T. Beauregard: Napoleon in Gray* (Baton Rouge: Louisiana State University Press, 1954), pp. 8–12, 72–73; Alfred Roman, *The Military Operations of General Beauregard in the War between the States 1861 to 1865* (New York: Harper & Brothers, 1884), vol. 1, pp. 77–78. Quotation from Jubal A. Early, *War Memoirs: Autobiographical Sketch and Narrative of the War between the States* (Bloomington: Indiana University Press, 1960), p. 5. On maps and their visual qualities, see Martin Bruckner, *The Geographic Revolution in Early America: Maps, Literacy, and National Identity* (Chapel Hill: University of North Carolina Press, 2006).

2. Details and quotation from Davis, *Battle at Bull Run*, pp. 51–52.

3. "The Battle of Bull Run, Fought July 18, 1861. Official report of Gen'l Beauregard," *Charleston Mercury*, September 5, 1861.

4. Davis, *Battle at Bull Run*, p. 10; Warren W. Hassler Jr., *Commanders of the Army of the Potomac* (Baton Rouge: Louisiana State University Press, 1962), p. 4; James B. Fry, *McDowell and Tyler in the Campaign of Bull Run, 1861* (New York: D. Van Nostrand, 1884), p. 7.

5. Davis, *Battle at Bull Run*, pp. 74, 78; Samuel P. Heintzelman Diary, July 11, 1861, Samuel P. Heintzelman Papers, LOC.

6. Baron [Antoine] Henri Jomini, *The Art of War. A New Edition, with Appendices and Maps. Translated from the French* (Philadelphia: J. B. Lippincott, 1862), pp. 166, 186, 342, quotations on 343–344. Jomini's famous text was translated and published in the United States in 1854 and widely used at West Point. John Keegan, *The American Civil War*

(New York: Knopf, 2009), pp. 96–97. On sound and sight for reconnoitering, see "The Advance into Virginia—the News from the Advanced Arm," *Christian Recorder* (Philadelphia), July 27, 1861.

7. D. B. Conrad, "History of the First Battle of Manassas and the Organization of the Stonewall Brigade," *Southern Historical Society Papers*, 19 (1891), p. 83.

8. Davis, *Battle at Bull Run*, p. 67.

9. "The Great Battle of Manassas," *Charleston Mercury*, July 27, 1861. See also the appropriately entitled chapter, "A Bird's Eye View of Wartime Journalism," in J. Cutler Andrews, *The South Reports the Civil War* (Princeton, N.J.: Princeton University Press, 1970), ch. 1, and pp. 79–87. See also Andrews, *The North Reports the Civil War* (Pittsburgh, Pa.: University of Pittsburgh Press, 1955), p. 89 esp.

10. "Great Battle of Manassas," July 27, 1861; last quotation from "Great Battle of Manassas," *Charleston Mercury*, July 25, 1861.

11. "Battle of Manassas," *Charleston Mercury*, July 27, 1861.

12. "Battle of Manassas," July 27, 1861. The newspaper men were not alone. This battle had to be seen. "A great many citizens of Washington and representatives from Northern cities came out in carriages to witness and take part in the triumphal entry into Richmond," wrote a member of the Palmetto Guard, elaborating: "The officers of the army and the civilian spectators brought with them every conceivable comfort and delicacy, and confidently expected to pass Manassas without even a fight." "Extracts of a Letter," *Charleston Mercury*, August 5, 1861. [James Butler Suddath], "From Sumter to the Wilderness: Letters of Sergeant James Butler Suddath, Co. E, 7th Regiment, S.C.V." *South Carolina Historical Magazine*, 62 (January 1962), p. 5.

13. On Oken, see Brenda Farnell, "Kinesthetic Sense and Dynamic Embodied Action," *Journal for the Anthropological Study of Human Movement*, 12 (2003), p. 133; Constance Classen, "Foundations for an Anthropology of the Senses," *International Social Science Journal*, 153 (September 1997), pp. 401–412; David Howes, *Sensual Relations: Engaging the Senses in Culture and Social Theory* (Ann Arbor: University of Michigan Press, 2003), p. 5.

14. "The Senses. V.—Sight," *Harper's New Monthly Magazine*, 12, no. 72 (May 1856), pp. 801–802.

15. "Senses," pp. 801–802.

16. Thomas Pitts to "Lizzie," May 28, 1861, Thomas Henry Pitts Papers, Emory University Library, Atlanta, Ga.

17. Donald Grant Mitchell, *Daniel Tyler: A Memorial Volume Containing His Autobiography and War Record* . . . (New Haven, Conn.: privately printed), p. 56. See, too, Daniel G. Crotty, *Four Years Campaigning in the Army of the Potomac* (Grand Rapids, Mich.: Dygert Bros., 1874), p. 24.

18. Davis, *Battle at Bull Run*, pp. 92–94; Thomas S. Allen, "The Second Wisconsin at the First Battle of Bull Run," in *War Papers Read before the Commandery of the State of Wisconsin, Military Order of the Loyal Legion of the United States* (Milwaukee, Wis.: The Commandery, 1896), vol. 1, p. 380; William Todd, *The Seventy-Ninth Highlanders* (Albany, N.Y.: Brandow, Barton, 1886), p. 20. Men from Massachusetts accustomed to eating with knife and fork now found themselves eating meat with fingers, a habit more medieval than modern. But at least they had fresh meat. A soldier from the New York Seventeenth found his meat "a little too fresh and lively" for his taste. Grinding heat and only stagnant water to combat it were common complaints, and the constant drilling made camp life "the daily round of the galley slave." Modern habits were being tested even before the first shot of the battle was fired. Quotations in Davis, *Battle at Bull Run*, pp. 37, 58.

19. Alexander Hunter, *Johnny Reb and Billy Yank* (New York: Neal, 1905), p. 54.

20. Davis, *Battle at Bull Run*, pp. 220, 225; Warren H. Cudworth, *History of the First Regiment Massachusetts Infantry* (Boston: Walker, Fuller, 1866), p. 41.

21. Davis, *Battle at Bull Run*, p. 223; "The Battle of Manassas. Official Report of Col. Kershaw," *Charleston Mercury*, August 8, 1861.

22. Davis, *Battle at Bull Run*, pp. 92–97, 230; Charles C. Perkins Diary, July 21, 1861, Civil War Times Illustrated Collection, US Army Heritage Education Center, Carlisle, Pa. [hereafter AHEC].

23. John C. Gregg to "Friend Heber," Arlington Heights, July 25, 1861, p. 1, Dr. Peter Schmitt Collection, Western Michigan University Archives and Regional History Collections [hereafter WMU].

24. John N. Opie, *A Rebel Cavalryman with Lee, Stuart, and Jackson* (Chicago: W. B. Conkey, 1899), pp. 25, 26. Last quotation in Conrad, "First Battle of Manassas," p. 84. See, too, p. 91. On the role of music in the war, see two exceptional, highly innovative, and penetrating studies: Christian McWhirter, *Battle Hymns: The Power and Popularity of Music in the Civil War* (Chapel Hill: University of North Carolina Press, 2012); James Davis, *Music along the Rapidan: Civil War Soldiers, Music,*

and Community during Winter Quarters, Virginia (Lincoln: University of Nebraska Press, 2014).

25. Gregg to "Friend Heber," Schmitt Collection, WMU; George Miller to "Dear Parents," Bull Run, July 20, 1861, p. 2, John F. Lane Collection, WMU. See also Charles B. Haydon Diary, July 18–19, 1861, p. 89, Michigan Historical Collection, University of Michigan, Ann Arbor [hereafter MHC]. On the feel of the bullets whistling past skin, see Davis, *Battle at Bull Run*, p. 109. Raw troops found their bodies jumping at certain sounds, particularly the eerie timbre of the long roll, the keynote of imminent engagement with the enemy. The effect could be powerful, emotionally and physiologically. For one Confederate soldier, it "quickened every nerve, and made all hearts bound with joy." "The fire-bell in the city is the alarm drum of the camp." Alexander Hunter, "Four Years in the Ranks," p. 30, Virginia Historical Society; second quotation, Hunter, *Johnny Reb and Billy Yank*, p. 4. Also on the long roll, see Opie, *A Rebel Cavalryman*, p. 26.

26. Hunter, "Four Years," pp. 34–35.

27. Quotation in Davis, *Battle at Bull Run*, p. 127.

28. Gregg to "Friend Heber," Schmitt Collection, WMU; [Suddath], "From Sumter to the Wilderness," p. 4. See also Haydon Diary, July 18–19, 1861, p. 93, MHC. "We are in plain sight of the rebel artillery, which opens on us with shot and shell." At that moment, they knew no better. "There are some nice blackberries nearby, and we cannot resist the temptation, and so fall too and eat as though nothing was happening." Crotty, *Four Years Campaigning*, p. 22.

29. Miller to "Dear Parents," Lane Collection, WMU; Davis, *Battle at Bull Run*, p. 123; Allen, "Second Wisconsin," p. 384.

30. Todd, *Seventy-Ninth Highlanders*, p. 25. See, too, Hunter, *Johnny Reb and Billy Yank*, p. 55; P. F. Ellis, "On That Hot Sunday Afternoon, July 21, 1861," *Confederate Veteran*, 5 (December 1897), p. 624.

31. Davis, *Battle at Bull Run*, p. 225, first quotation on p. 230; second quotation, Elnathan B. Tyler, *"Wooden Nutmegs" at Bull Run* (Hartford, Conn.: George L. Coburn, 1872), p. 66. Note, too, Allen, "Second Wisconsin," p. 377; Cudworth, *First Regiment Massachusetts Infantry*, p. 49.

32. Tyler, *"Wooden Nutmegs,"* p. 67.

33. Davis, *Battle at Bull Run*, p. 226; Conrad, "First Battle of Manassas," p. 88.

34. Tyler, *"Wooden Nutmegs,"* p. 66.

35. Quotation in Davis, *Battle at Bull Run*, p. 225.

36. Quotations from "Our Richmond Correspondence," *Charleston Mercury,* July 24, 1861. See, too, Todd, *Seventy-Ninth Highlanders,* p. 24; George Baylor, *Bull Run to Bull Run or Four Years in the Army of Northern Virginia* (Richmond, Va.: R. F. Johnson, 1900), p. 21.

37. Davis, *Battle at Bull Run,* p. 119.

38. Davis, *Battle at Bull Run,* p. 120. See, too, "The Battle Field," *Richmond Enquirer,* August 2, 1861.

39. James Chester, "Inside Sumter in '61," in *Battles and Leaders of the Civil War* (Secausus, N.J.: Castle, n.d.), p. 62. Note, too, Hunter, "Four Years in the Ranks," p. 30.

40. "Extract of a Private Letter, Camp Beauregard, Bull's Run," *Charleston Mercury,* June 15, 1861.

41. C. P. Fisher to his sister, July 17, 1861, Peter Hairston Papers, Southern Historical Collection, University of North Carolina, Chapel Hill [hereafter SHC].

42. Miller to "Dear Parents," Lane Collection, WMU.

43. Conrad, "First Battle of Manassas," p. 89.

44. "Official Report of Col. Kershaw," August 8, 1861.

45. " "Beauregard's Official Report," August, 1861, in Frank Moore, ed., *Rebellion Record: A Diary of American Events, with Documents, Narratives, Illustrative Incidents, Poetry Etc.* (New York: G. P. Putnam, 1862), vol. 2, p. 342.

46. "The Battle of Manassas. Official Report of Gen. Schenck," *Charleston Mercury,* August 7, 1861. Visual deception had, in fact, been important to First Bull Run long before battle. Female spies, for example, passed through enemy lines in disguise, offering information on federal troop movements to Confederate officers. Davis, *Battle at Bull Run,* pp. xi–xiii.

47. Quotations in "The Advance into Virginia—the News from the Advanced Arm," *Christian Recorder,* July 27, 1861; Todd, *Seventy-Ninth Highlanders,* p. 20; Perry Mayo to his parents, July 23, 1861, Mayo Family Papers, Michigan State University, East Lansing. On masked batteries, see also Allen, "Second Wisconsin," p. 379.

48. Miller to "Dear Parents," Lane Collection, WMU.

49. Gregg to "Friend Heber," Schmitt Collection, WMU.

50. Davis, *Battle at Bull Run,* p. 107.

51. John O. Casler, *Four Years in the Stonewall Brigade* (Guthrie, Okla.: State Capital, 1893), pp. 25, 27.

52. "Notes of the War," *Charleston Mercury*, August 27, 1861.

53. Casler, *Four Years in the Stonewall Brigade*, p. 26.

54. Davis, *Battle at Bull Run*, pp. 22, 24–25. See D. Augustus Dickert, *History of Kershaw's Brigade* (Newberry, S.C.: Elbert H. Aull, 1899), p. 34. General Orders No. 9 issued on June 6, 1861, stated that "All officers shall wear a tunic of gray cloth, known as cadet gray" and that "The uniform coat for all enlisted men shall be a double-breasted tunic of gray cloth, known as cadet gray"; see *War of the Rebellion: Official Records of the Union and Confederate Armies* (70 vols. in 128; Washington, D.C., 1880–1901) ser. IV, vol. I, 369 [hereafter *OR*].

55. Davis, *Battle at Bull Run*, p. 191.

56. Davis, *Battle at Bull Run*, p. 91. The requirement for these various blues depended on rank. As of August 1861, per the orders of Secretary of War Simon Cameron, commissioned officers were required to wear a " 'cloak coat' of dark blue cloth." Enlisted men were supposed to wear "sky blue." While these orders were not followed by everyone—there are instances of some Union troops electing to don their more comfortable, homemade gray uniforms and resisting the shoddy, uncomfortable blue ones dispensed by the quartermaster—the danger of being mistaken for the enemy, one supposes, eventually led most to wear the assigned blue. As Bell Irvin Wiley put it: "Not until the summer of 1862 could the term boys in blue be applied accurately to the Union forces, and deviations were to be found occasionally until the close of war." See his *The Life of Billy Yank: The Common Soldier of the Union* (1952; repr., Baton Rouge, Louisiana State University Press, 2008), p. 22. The 1861 dress requirements are in *Revised United States Army Regulations of 1861* . . . (Washington, D.C.: Government Printing Office, 1863), pp. 473–474.

57. Quotations in Davis, *Battle at Bull Run*, p. 159.

58. Davis, *Battle at Bull Run*, p. 166.

59. Davis, *Battle at Bull Run*, p. 168.

60. William Tecumseh Sherman, *Memoirs of General W. T. Sherman*, ed. Michael Fellman (New York: Penguin, 2000), p. 170; Report of Col. William T. Sherman, July 25, 1861, *OR*, ser. I, vol. II, pp. 369–370. Similarly, Captain Edward Hudson of the Fourteenth US Infantry saw a company of men ahead of him "whom I, from their gray uniform, at first took for Wisconsin troops." "Report of Captain Edward McK. Hudson," July 4, 1861, *OR*, ser. I, vol. II, p. 184.

61. "Official Report of Col. Kershaw," August 8, 1861.

62. Perkins Diary, July 21, 1861, AHEC.

63. Hunter, "Four Years in the Ranks," pp. 37–38.

64. William Smith, "Reminiscences of the First Battle of Manassas," *Southern Historical Society Papers*, 10 (1882), p. 439.

65. Allen, "Second Wisconsin," p. 382.

66. Cudworth, *First Regiment Massachusetts Infantry*, quotations on pp. 42–44; Davis, *Battle at Bull Run*, p. 116.

67. First quotation from Sherman, *Memoirs*, p. 170; details and other quotations from Davis, *Battle at Bull Run*, pp. 185–187.

68. Davis, *Battle at Bull Run*, pp. 188, 193–194.

69. Davis, *Battle at Bull Run*, pp. 194–195.

70. Quotations in Davis, *Battle at Bull Run*, pp. 194–195; penultimate quotation, Opie, *A Rebel Cavalryman*, p. 28. Note, too, p. 26.

71. Davis, *Battle at Bull Run*, pp. 195–199; Barton Rudolph, "Stonewall Brigade at Louisville," *Confederate Veteran*, 8 (November 1900), p. 482. Last quotation in Casler, *Four Years in the Stonewall Brigade*, p. 22.

72. Davis, *Battle at Bull Run*, pp. 201, 202, 205, quotation on p. 203. Last quotation in Opie, *A Rebel Cavalryman*, p. 31.

73. Details and quotations in Davis, *Battle at Bull Run*, pp. 205–206.

74. Quotations from Davis, *Battle at Bull Run*, pp. 206–207; quotation from soldier in Casler, *Four Years in the Stonewall Brigade*, p. 27.

75. Davis, *Battle at Bull Run*, pp. 207–208.

76. Davis, *Battle at Bull Run*, p. 211.

77. Davis, *Battle at Bull Run*, pp. 212–213.

78. Davis, *Battle at Bull Run*, pp. 237; Keyes's quotation, 239.

79. "The Advance into Virginia," July 27, 1861; "The Grand Battle at Bull Run," *Richmond Enquirer*, July 23, 1861; "The Field of the Second Battle," *Richmond Enquirer*, July 26, 1861.

80. Nathaniel H. R. Dawson to Elodie Dawson, July 24 and August 29, 1861, Nathaniel H. R. Dawson Papers, SHC.

81. Davis, *Battle at Bull Run*, p. 242. See also Alexander R. Chisolm, "Notes on Bull Run," p. 2, Alexander R. Chisolm Papers, New York Historical Society, New York.

82. "The Pursuit at Manassas," *Charleston Mercury*, July 31, 1861.

83. Quotations, in order: David E. Johnston, *Four Years a Soldier* (Princeton, W. Va.: n.p., 1887), p. 85; Early, *War Memoirs*, p. 14.

84. "Great Battle of Manassas," July 27, 1861.

85. Davis, *Battle at Bull Run*, pp. 218–219.

86. Samuel W. John, "The Importance of Accuracy," *Confederate Veteran*, 22 (August 1914), p. 343.

87. Davis, *Battle at Bull Run*, pp. 245, 251. Quotations in order: Davis, *Battle at Bull Run*, p. 251; Rudolph, "Stonewall Brigade at Louisville," p. 481; Benjamin White to J. J. Phillips, n.d. [August 1861], James J. Phillips Papers, North Carolina Office of Archives and History, Raleigh.

Chapter Three

1. John W. Kuhl, "Cornelia Hancock," in *New Jersey Goes to War: Biographies of 150 New Jerseyans Caught Up in the Struggle of the Civil War, including Soldiers, Civilians, Men, Women, Heroes, Scoundrels—and a Heroic Horse*, ed. Joseph G. Bilby (Wood-Ridge: New Jersey Civil War Heritage Association, 2010), p. 60.

2. Cornelia Hancock was born February 6, 1840, to an old Quaker family at Hancock's Bridge in Salem County, New Jersey. She became known as the "Florence Nightingale of America." After Gettysburg, she continued as an army nurse serving in the winter of 1863–1864 and on the Overland Campaign in the spring of 1864. She was one of the first Union women to enter Richmond after its capture. After the war, she moved to South Carolina and founded a school for ex-slaves. In 1875, she returned to Philadelphia, where she helped the poor in the neighborhood of Wrightsville. She died from nephritis on December 31, 1927, in Atlantic City. Kuhl, "Cornelia Hancock," p. 60.

3. "The Senses—Smell," *Harper's New Monthly Magazine*, 12, no. 70 (March 1856), pp. 495–496.

4. Quotations, in order, "The Senses—Smell," pp. 494, 495, 501, 497, 498, 499.

5. Numbers from Military History Online, "The Battle of Gettysburg: Casualties," www.militaryhistoryonline.com/gettysburg/getty4.aspx.

6. In some respects, Gettysburg and the war generally accelerated modernization, especially in efforts to deal with death, to contain and

preserve flesh, and, in the process, contain smell. See the masterful Drew Gilpin Faust, *This Republic of Suffering: Death and the American Civil War* (New York: Vintage, 2008).

7. Eileen F. Conklin, *Women at Gettysburg, 1863* (Gettysburg, Pa.: Thomas, 1993), p. 2. On the uniforms, see *Revised United States Army Regulations of 1861 . . .* (Washington, D.C.: Government Printing Office, 1863), pp. 473–474.

8. Conklin, *Women at Gettysburg*, pp. 2–3; quotations from Charlotte E. McKay, *Stories of Hospital and Camp* (Philadelphia: Claxton, Remsen, and Haffelfinger, 1876), pp. 86–88.

9. Henrietta Stratton Jaquette, ed., *South after Gettysburg: Letters of Cornelia Hancock from the Army of the Potomac 1863–1865* (Philadelphia: University of Pennsylvania Press, 1937), p. 2.

10. "Three Years with the Army of the Potomac," written by W. W. Potter, 1888, General Civil War Collection, Box 5, Folder 9, Buffalo and Erie County Historical Society, Buffalo, N.Y.

11. "Gettysburg by E. C. L." *The Old Guard*, 1, no. 1 (January 19, 1886).

12. Quotations in Conklin, *Women at Gettysburg*, p. 9.

13. Quotations in Conklin, *Women at Gettysburg*, p. 9.

14. Conklin, *Women at Gettysburg*, pp. 13, 15, 16, 18, 41, 42, 88. On the braiding of home and field, see *The War Was You and Me: Civilians and the American Civil War*, ed. Joan Cashin (Princeton, N.J.: Princeton University Press, 2002).

15. Conklin, *Women at Gettysburg*, p. 61.

16. Conklin, *Women at Gettysburg*, pp. 50, 66, 90–91.

17. Anne Kelly Knowles, "A Cutting-Edge Second Look at the Battle of Gettysburg," www.smithsonianmag.com/history-archaeology/A-Cutting-Edge-Second-Look-at-the-Battle-of-Gettysburg.html#ixzz2XXJ91OSW. This fascinating digital exercise reminds us how unreliable sight could be during battle, not unlike sound and the misleading effects of acoustic shadows. On this, see Charles D. Ross, *Civil War Acoustic Shadows* (Shippensburg, Pa.: White Mane Books, 2001). On the effect of not seeing on soldiers' other senses, see the brief but skilled and interesting treatment offered in Allen C. Guelzo, *Gettysburg: The Last Invasion* (New York: Alfred A. Knopf, 2013), pp.276–280.

18. "I have had a chance to *smell powder*," wrote a soldier from Maine after First Bull Run. That was proxy for fighting. Quoted in William C. Davis,

Battle at Bull Run: A History of the First Major Campaign of the Civil War (Baton Rouge: Louisiana State University, 1982), p. 254.

19. Asa W. Bartlett, *History of the Twelfth Regiment New Hampshire Volunteers in the War of the Rebellion* (Concord, N.H.: Ira C. Evans, 1897), p. 437.

20. John H. Rhodes, *The History of Battery B, First Regiment Rhode Island Light Artillery in the War to Preserve the Union, 1861–1865* (Providence, R.I.: Snow & Farnham, 1894), p. 226.

21. Conklin, *Women at Gettysburg*, p. 121; *Gettysburg Star and Sentinel*, July 2, 1913, p. 1; Harry W. Pfanz, *Gettysburg—Culp's Hill and Cemetery Hill* (Chapel Hill: University of North Carolina Press, 1993), pp. 354–364.

22. Conklin, *Women at Gettysburg*, p. 122.

23. Conklin, *Women at Gettysburg*, pp. 92, 128.

24. Conklin, *Women at Gettysburg*, p. 124. The line of dead bodies is based on a rough estimate. The average height of native-born American men and women in 1860 was 67.2 inches. See Richard H. Steckel, "A History of the Standard of Living in the United States," http://eh.net/encyclopedia/a-history-of-the-standard-of-living-in-the-united-states/.

25. C. E. Troutman, "The Second Corps. How Grandly It Met the Shock at Gettysburg. The Hurried March from the Rappahannock into Pennsylvania. The Giant Combat, as Seen and Graphically Told by a Jerseyman," *National Tribune* (Washington, D.C.) May 20, 1886.

26. Harold Adams Small, ed., *The Road to Richmond: The Civil War Memoirs of Maj. Abner R. Small of the 16th Maine Vols.; With His Diary as a Prisoner of War* (Berkeley: University of California Press, 1959), p. 105.

27. L. Leon Louis, *Diary of a Tar Heel Confederate Soldier* (Charlotte, N.C.: Stone, 1913), p. 37.

28. Quotations in Conklin, *Women at Gettysburg*, p. 145.

29. J. L. Porter, "After Forty Years: Experiences and Sensations Incident to a Visit to Washington and Gettysburg," *Akron Daily Democrat*, October 20, 1902, p. 5.

30. Although municipal efforts to sanitize American cities would increase markedly after the Civil War, by the standards of the time, many Americans in 1860 believed they were making some progress toward making their urban areas cleaner, a quality they tended to measure through smell. On the American situation, see Joel A. Tarr, *The Search for the Ultimate Sink: Urban*

Pollution in Historical Perspective (Akron, Ohio: University of Akron Press, 1996), pp. 111–158 esp.; Martin V. Melosi, *The Sanitary City: Environmental Services in Urban America from Colonial Times to the Present* (Pittsburgh, Pa.: University of Pittsburgh Press, 2008), pp. 1–70; Melanie Kiechle, "The Smell Detectives," *Chemical Heritage*, 29 (summer 2011), pp. 32–36. More generally, see Mark M. Smith, *Sensing the Past: Seeing, Hearing, Smelling, Tasting, and Touching in History* (Berkeley: University of California Press, 2008); David Inglis, "Sewers and Sensibilities: The Bourgeois Faecal Experience in the Nineteenth-Century City," in *The City and the Senses: Urban Culture since 1500s*, eds. Alexander Cowen and Jill Steward (Aldershot, England: Ashgate, 2007), pp. 105–130; Constance Classen, "The Deodorized City: Battling Urban Stench in the Nineteenth Century," in *Sense of the City: An Alternate Approach to Urbanism*, ed. Mirko Zardini (Baden, Switzerland: Lars Muller, 2005), pp. 292–321; David S. Barnes, *The Great Stink of Paris and the Nineteenth-Century Struggle against Filth and Germs* (Baltimore, Md.: Johns Hopkins University Press, 2006). In the mid-eighteenth century, Charlestonians used flowers and plants in an effort to improve "the odor of the town"; see Peter A. Coclanis, *The Shadow of a Dream: Economic Life and Death in the South Carolina Lowcountry, 1670–1920* (New York: Oxford University Press, 1989), p. 6.

31. See Kathleen M. Brown, *Foul Bodies: Cleanliness in Early America* (New Haven, Conn.: Yale University Press, 2009), pp. 244–247, 259, 327 esp.; Alain Corbin, *The Foul and the Fragrant: Odor and the French Social Imagination* (Cambridge, Mass.: Harvard University Press, 1986), pp. 70–90 esp.

32. Jaquette, ed., *South after Gettysburg*, pp. 2–4.

33. Jaquette, ed., *South after Gettysburg*, pp. 4–5.

34. "Our Wounded at Gettysburg. Arrangements for Their Comfort. Army Hospitals There," *New York Herald*, July 24, 1863. See also Carol Reardon, *Pickett's Charge in History and Memory* (Chapel Hill: University of North Carolina Press, 1997), p. 28 esp. There was some truth to Davidson's claim. As Drew Gilpin Faust has shown, federals were indeed buried better at Gettysburg than Confederates, the latter often bundled into shallow mass graves, the putrid stench far from contained. See Faust, *This Republic of Suffering*, pp. 72–82.

35. Field hospital of the Second Corps, July 15, 1863, in Mrs. Edmund A. Souder, *Leaves from the Battle-Field of Gettysburg. A Series of Letters from a Field Hospital. And National Poems* (Philadelphia: Caxton Press of C. Sherman, Son & Co., 1864), p. 17.

36. *Tenth Annual Report of the Secretary of the State Board of Health of the State of Michigan for the Fiscal Year Ending Sept. 30, 1882* (Lansing: W. S. George & Co., State Printers and Binders, 1883), p. 55. Even at First Bull Run, life's little comforts, such as "perfumed soap," were disbanded, packed into a box labeled the past, relegated to the soldier's salad days. Now, "Toilets" consisted of "a soldier's dry wash, which meant rubbing the face on a jacket sleeve." Alexander Hunter, *Johnny Reb and Billy Yank* (New York: Neal, 1905), pp. 4, 51–52.

37. See my *Sensing the Past: Seeing, Hearing, Smelling, Tasting, and Touching in History* (Berkeley: University of California Press, 2007).

38. http://voicesofgettysburg.com/.

39. Soldier's observation quoted in George Sheldon, *When the Smoke Cleared: The Tragic Aftermath of the Bloodiest Battle of the Civil War* (Nashville, Tenn.: Cumberland House, 2003), p. 171.

40. *Evening Telegraph* (Philadelphia), July 2, 1864, third edition, p. 2.

41. See Faust, *This Republic of Suffering*, pp. 66–68.

42. "Important News from the Southwest," *New York Herald*, October 2, 1862; "Telegraphic News," *Charleston Mercury*, May 30, 1863; "Scenes under a Flag of Truce," *Charleston Mercury*, August 12, 1864.

43. "Siege Matters," *Charleston Mercury*, October 13, 1863; order from W. N. Pendleton, Brigadier-General and Chief of Artillery at Headquarters Artillery Corps, June 10, 1864 to Lieutenant-Colonel Baldwin, Chief of Ordnance, Army of Northern Virginia, Confederate Correspondence, Orders, and Returns relating to Operations in Southeast Virginia and North Carolina, May 20, 1864–June 12, 1864, #4.

44. Faust, *This Republic of Suffering*, pp. 67–69.

45. On the evolving meanings of the battle and the turning of a bloody, chaotic mess into a sacred place, see Amy J. Kinsel, "From Turning Point to Peace Memorial: A Cultural Legacy," in *The Gettysburg Nobody Knows*, ed. Gabor S. Borrit (New York: Oxford University Press, 1997), pp. 203–222.

46. "The Re-Union at Gettysburg," *Laurens Advertiser* (Laurens, S.C.) August 6, 1912, p. 3. On the general fear of the process of decivilization in nineteenth-century American culture, see the suggestive book by Nick Yablon, *Untimely Ruins: An Archaeology of American Urban Modernity, 1819–1919* (Chicago: University of Chicago Press, 2009).

Chapter Four

1. First quotation from Michael B. Ballard, *Vicksburg: The Campaign That Opened the Mississippi* (Chapel Hill: University of North Carolina Press, 2004), p. 1. Warren E. Grabau, *Ninety-Eight Days: A Geographer's View of the Vicksburg Campaign* (Knoxville: University of Tennessee Press, 2000), p. 21; Preston E. James, "Vicksburg: A Study in Urban Geography," *Geographical Review*, 21 (April 1911), pp. 234–235. The arrangement and location of parts of Vicksburg shifted, sometimes considerably, following a flood in 1876. James, "Vicksburg," p. 235. Vicksburg's siege has attracted some talented writers. Of the more recent of them, Michael Ballard (noted above) and Winston Groom (*Vicksburg, 1863* [New York: Alfred Knopf, 2009]) rank among the most compelling and detailed. See also the important treatment of the siege from the perspective of an environmental historian: Lisa M. Brady, *War upon the Land: Military Strategy and the Transformation of Southern Landscapes during the American Civil War* (Athens: University of Georgia Press, 2012), pp. 49–71.

2. The phrase was used by Daniel Webster. See Edward S. Gregory, "Vicksburg during the Siege," *The Annals of the Army of Tennessee and Early Western History*, 1, no. 3 (June 1878), p. 97.

3. John Hebron Moore, *The Emergence of the Cotton Kingdom in the Old Southwest: Mississippi, 1770–1860* (Baton Rouge: Louisiana State University Press, 1988), pp. 196–197, contemporary description from *Harper's Weekly*, quoted on p. 196. See also A. A. Hoehling, *Vicksburg: 47 Days of Siege* (Mechanicsburg, Pa.: Stackpole Books, 1969), p. 1.

4. James, "Vicksburg", p. 238; Isaac Johnson, *Slavery Days in Old Kentucky. A True Story of a Father Who Sold His Wife and Four Children* (Electronic Edition: Documenting the American South, http://docsouth.unc.edu/neh/johnson/johnson.html), p. 21; Israel Campbell, *An Autobiography. Bond and Free: or, Yearnings for Freedom, from My Green Brier House. Being the Story of My Life in Bondage, and My Life in Freedom* (Philadelphia, Pa.: privately printed, 1861), pp. 40–47 esp.; Moore, *Emergence of the Cotton Kingdom*, p. 194.

5. On white food, see Sam Bowers Hilliard, *Hog Meat and Hoecake: Food Supply in the Old South, 1840–1860* (Carbondale: Southern Illinois Press, 1972), p. 61 esp.

6. *Richmond Whig*, March 1, 1853.

7. See Hilliard, *Hog Meat and Hoecake*, p. 227 esp.

8. Gordon A. Cotton, ed., *Dr. and Mrs. Balfour at Home: From the Letters of Emma Balfour, 1847–1857* (Vicksburg, Miss.: The Print Shop, 2006), pp. 94–97; Taylor Family Plantation Ledger, entry for 1845, Mississippi Department of Archives and History, Jackson, [hereafter MDAH].

9. Miriam Brannin Hilliard Diary, 1849–1850, entries for January 1 and 11, 1840, mfm., MDAH.

10. Cotton, *Dr. and Mrs. Balfour at Home*, pp. 138–139, 187.

11. H. C. Clarke, *General Directory for the City of Vicksburg: Containing the Name and Address of Every Professional and Business Man and Resident of the City* . . . (Vicksburg, Miss.: privately printed, 1860), quotations on pp. 18, 23.

12. Welles (Edward R.) Diary, Vicksburg, December 4, 1854, p. 14, MDAH; Ballard, *Vicksburg*, p. 22.

13. See Leonard V. Huber, *Advertisements of Lower Mississippi River Steamboats, 1812–1920* (West Barrington, R.I.: The Steamboat Historical Society of America, 1959).

14. Much has been written on the history of gustation, taste, and identity, national and otherwise. But for our purposes here, read James E. McWilliams, *A Revolution in Eating: How the Quest for Food Shaped America* (New York: Columbia University Press, 2005); Donna R. Gabbacia, "Colonial Creoles: The Formation of Tastes in Early America," in *The Taste Culture Reader: Experiencing Food and Drink*, ed. Carolyn Korsmeyer (Oxford, England: Berg, 2005), pp. 79–82 esp.; Stefan Halikoswski Smith, "Demystifying a Change in Taste: Spices, Space, and Social Hierarchy in Europe, 1380–1750," *International History Review*, 29 (June 2007), pp. 237–257; and, of course, Norbert Elias, *The Civilizing Process: The Development of Manners: Changes in the Code of Conduct and Feeling in Early Modern Times*, trans. E. Jephcott (New York: Urizen Books, 1978).

15. "The Senses. I—Taste," *Harper's New Monthly Magazine*, 12, no. 79 (December 1855), pp. 74–76; Mark M. Smith, *How Race Is Made: Slavery, Segregation, and the Senses* (Chapel Hill: University of North Carolina Press, 2006); pp. 21, 23.

16. "The Senses. I—Taste," pp. 74–76. On white perceptions of slave taste, see Smith, *How Race Is Made*. On slave diets in the Mississippi Valley, see Walter Johnson, *River of Dark Dreams: Slavery and Empire in the Cotton Kingdom* (Cambridge, Mass.: Harvard University Press, 2013), pp. 178–179, 185–188.

17. "The Senses. I—Taste," pp. 78–80. On cultivating taste and indexing to social class, see T. Sarah Peterson, *Acquired Taste: The French Origins*

of Modern Cooking (Ithaca, N.Y.: Cornell University Press, 1994); Sidney W. Mintz, *Tasting Food, Tasting Freedom: Excursions into Eating, Culture, and the Past* (Boston, Mass.: Beacon Press, 1996).

18. Quoted in Roger Daniel Sorrell, *St. Francis of Assisi and Nature* (Oxford: Oxford University Press, 1988), p. 53; William Chester Jordan, *The Great Famine: Northern Europe in the Early Fourteenth Century* (Princeton, N.J.: Princeton University Press, 1996), p. 115.

19. See David M. Potter, *People of Plenty: Economic Abundance and the American Character* (Chicago: University of Chicago Press, 1954). Grant quoted in Ballard, *Vicksburg*, p. 113. Throughout the war, the Confederacy generally suffered food shortages, although nothing came near to the starvation felt in Vicksburg. See Andrew F. Smith, *Starving the South: How the North Won the Civil War* (New York: St. Martin's Press, 2011).

20. Ballard, *Vicksburg*, pp. 8, 14–15, 21, 24, 25.

21. Ballard, *Vicksburg*, pp. 32–33; Groom, *Vicksburg*, pp. 355, 41; Hoehling, *Vicksburg*, p. 1.

22. F. Stansbury Haydon, "Grant's Wooden Mortars and Some Incidents of the Siege of Vicksburg," *Journal of the American Military Institute*, 4 (Spring 1940), pp. 30–38, quotations on pp. 30–32.

23. *New York Herald*, January 11, 1863; Ballard, *Vicksburg*, p. 333. For intelligent commentary on food scarcity and famine during and after the war generally in the South, see Joan E. Cashin, "Hungry People in the Wartime South: Civilians, Armies, and the Food Supply," in *Weirding the War: Stories from the Civil War's Ragged Edges*, ed. Stephen Berry (Athens: University of Georgia Press, 2011), pp. 160–175.

24. Quoted in Ballard, *Vicksburg*, pp. 248–249, 361.

25. Ida Barlow Trotter, "Story of the Siege of Vicksburg, and Some Personal Experiences Connected Therewith," p. 1, Ida Barlow Papers, MDAH.

26. "Recollections of Eliza Ann Lanier," 1911, Old Courthouse Museum, Vicksburg, Miss.

27. Trotter, "Story of the Siege of Vicksburg," p. 4.

28. Quotation in Groom, *Vicksburg*, p. 367.

29. Shelby Foote, *The Civil War, A Narrative* (New York: Random House, 1958), pp. 384–387.

30. *New York Herald*, June 19, 1863.

31. Foote, *The Civil War*, pp. 410–413; Groom, *Vicksburg*, p. 364.

32. Gregory, "Vicksburg," p. 103.

33. Trotter, "Story of the Siege of Vicksburg," p. 3.

34. [Dora Richards Miller], "A Woman's Diary at the Siege of Vicksburg," edited by George W. Cable, *Century Magazine* (September 1885), pp. 767, 768.

35. [Mary Ann Webster Loughborough], *My Cave Life in Vicksburg. With Letters of Trial and Travel* (New York: D. Appleton, 1864; repr., Bedford, Mass.: Applewood Books, n.d.), pp. 56, 72.

36. [Miller], "A Woman's Diary," p. 768.

37. *Charleston Mercury*, June 27, 1863.

38. Gregory, "Vicksburg," p. 104; [Loughborough], *My Cave Life in Vicksburg*, p. 60.

39. Quotations, in order: Trotter, "Story of the Siege of Vicksburg," p. 4; [Miller], "A Woman's Diary," p. 768.

40. Alison (Joseph Dill) Diary of Camp Life, Siege at Vicksburg, June 10, pp. 15–16, MDAH; [Miller], "A Woman's Diary," p. 772; Groom, *Vicksburg*, p. 355.

41. [Loughborough], *My Cave Life in Vicksburg*, pp. 106–107.

42. Gregory, "Vicksburg," p. 103.

43. [Miller], "A Woman's Diary," pp. 771, 772.

44. Emma Balfour Diary, May 25, 1863, p. 12, MDAH.

45. [Miller], "A Woman's Diary," p. 768.

46. [Miller], "A Woman's Diary," p. 771.

47. Gregory, "Vicksburg," p. 104.

48. [Miller], "A Woman's Diary," p. 767. See, too, [Loughborough], *My Cave Life in Vicksburg*, pp. 58, 72.

49. [Miller], "A Woman's Diary," pp. 771–772.

50. [Loughborough], *My Cave Life in Vicksburg*, pp. 63–64, 67, 68.

51. Ballard, *Vicksburg*, pp. 360–369; quotation on p. 365.

52. Gregory, "Vicksburg," pp. 104, 105.

53. [Loughborough], *My Cave Life in Vicksburg*, pp. 17, 56–57, 61; Groom, *Vicksburg*, pp. 364–365.

54. [Miller], "A Woman's Diary," p. 768.

55. Quoted in [Miller], "A Woman's Diary," p. 768.

56. [Loughborough], *My Cave Life in Vicksburg*, p. 96.

57. Ballard, *Vicksburg*, p. 160. See also pp. 197, 223, 247, 333. Quotation from Hoehling, *Vicksburg*, p. 11.

58. *New York Herald*, March 17 and 22, 1863. Food riots in the Confederacy were more common than is often realized. Richmond's were the most famous, but there were also ones in Atlanta, Georgia; Salisbury, North Carolina; Mobile, Alabama; and Petersburg, Virginia. See Stephanie McCurry, *Confederate Reckoning: Power and Politics in the Civil War South* (Cambridge, Mass.: Harvard University Press, 2010), pp. 180–187 esp.

59. Ballard, *Vicksburg*, p. 22.

60. Grabau, *Ninety-Eight Days*, p. 19.

61. [Miller], "A Woman's Diary," p. 767.

62. As reported in the *New York Herald*, March 4, 1863. It should be noted that Pemberton did attempt to procure food in anticipation of the siege for residents. See Ballard, *Vicksburg*, p. 251.

63. [Miller], "A Woman's Diary," p. 768.

64. [Miller], "A Woman's Diary," p. 768.

65. *Charleston Mercury*, May 25, 1863.

66. *Charleston Mercury*, June 4, 1863.

67. Balfour Diary, May 17, 1863, pp. 3–4.

68. Balfour Diary, May 23, 1863, pp. 8–9.

69. Groom, *Vicksburg*, p. 363; Balfour Diary, May 17, 1863, p. 3.

70. [Miller], "A Woman's Diary," p. 768.

71. [Miller], "A Woman's Diary," p. 771.

72. [Miller], "A Woman's Diary," p. 771.

73. [Loughborough], *My Cave Life in Vicksburg*, pp. 60–61, 100.

74. Alexander St. Clair Abrams, *A Full and Detailed History of the Siege of Vicksburg* (Atlanta: Intelligencer Steam Power Presses, 1863), p. 47. Groom, *Vicksburg*, p. 385.

75. See Ballard, *Vicksburg*, p. 382.

76. [Loughborough], *My Cave Life in Vicksburg*, p. 137.

77. Trotter, "Story of the Siege," p. 3; Alison Diary, June 10, p. 16. "Drought continues. Spring oats destroyed. Vegetables cut short. Corn crop seriously threatened." Such was the news from Vicksburg, where a correspondent

said, "I can give you no comfort" on June 22. *Charleston Mercury*, June 22, 1863.

78. *New York Herald*, July 8, 1863.

79. Trotter, "Story of the Siege of Vicksburg," p. 3.

80. Gregory, "Vicksburg," pp. 97–108. The quotation is from the table of contents.

81. Quotation in Ballard, *Vicksburg*, p. 387.

82. [Loughborough], *My Cave Life in Vicksburg*, p. 118.

83. [Miller], "A Woman's Diary," p. 771.

84. [Loughborough], *My Cave Life in Vicksburg*, p. 105.

85. See, for example, Myrtle Ellison Smith, *A Civil War Cook Book* (Harrogate, Tenn.: Lincoln Memorial University, 1961), p. 29.

86. [Miller], "A Woman's Diary," p. 771.

87. [Miller], "A Woman's Diary," p. 771.

88. Alison Diary, June 10, p. 16. Reports differ on this issue. Union men learned from Confederate deserters as early as late May that provisions in the city were scarce; one "says his heart is as strong in the cause of the Confederacy as ever, but that he was not going to stay in there to be starved to death." Quoted in Ballard, *Vicksburg*, p. 381. The mood in mid-June was jaunty. "A gentleman just from Vicksburg," reported the *Charleston Mercury* (June 18, 1863), "says that the garrison there is in the best spirits, with plenty to eat and an abundance of ammunition." Private letters from the besieged city dated June 17 concurred, insisting "the garrison is bountifully supplied with provisions. Full rations are still issued." Reported in *Charleston Mercury*, June 25, 1863.

89. Joel Shew, M.D., *Tobacco: Its History, Nature, and Effects on the Body and Mind. With the opinions of Rev. Dr. Nott, L. N. Fowler, Rev. Henry Ward Beecher, Hon. Horace Greeley, Dr. Jennings, O. S. Fowler, Dr. R. T. Trall, and Others* (Cowen Tracts, 1860), pp. 22, 25. On the effect of tobacco on the senses, see *A Dissertation on the Use and Abuse of Tobacco. In Relation to Smoaking, Chewing, and Taking of Snuff, Humbly Inscrib'd To the Ladies and Gentlemen, who use it in any of the above-mention'd Ways* (London: Printed for J. Roberts, 1720), p. 21. On chewing, Eyre Crowe, *With Thackeray in America* (New York: C. Scribner's, 1893), pp. 129–130; E[yre] C[rowe], "Sketches in the Free and Slave States of America," *Illustrated London News*, September 27, 1856, p. 314. On tobacco in Confederate rations at Vicksburg,

see Andrew F. Smith, "May 18, 1863: Start of the Siege—And Starving— of Vicksburg," May 18, 2011, http:www.commandposts.com/2011/05/ may-18-1863-start-of-the-siege%E2%80%94and-starving%E2%80%9 4of-vicksburg/. Confederate and Union soldiers on picket duty were known to exchange food and tobacco. Ballard, *Vicksburg*, pp. 373–374.

90. [Miller], "A Woman's Diary," p. 771.

91. Alison Diary, June 10, p. 16.

92. Trotter, "Story of the Siege," p. 3. See, too, Groom, *Vicksburg*, p. 392.

93. [Loughborough], *My Cave Life in Vicksburg*, p. 116.

94. Alison Diary, June 23, July 4, p. 17. Some Confederate regiments were certainly reduced to rat and mule meat by the end of June. See Allan C. Richard Jr. and Mary Margaret Higginbotham Richard, eds., *The Defense of Vicksburg: A Louisiana Chronicle* (College Station: Texas A&M University Press, 2004), pp. 217–220.

95. Alison Diary, June 10, p. 16.

96. Quoted in Ballard, *Vicksburg*, p. 381.

97. Alison Diary, June 10, p. 16; [Miller], "A Woman's Diary," p. 772.

98. [Loughborough], *My Cave Life in Vicksburg*, p. 104. Ballard, *Vicksburg*, p. 382.

99. [Miller], "A Woman's Diary," p. 772.

100. Ballard, *Vicksburg*, pp. 375–376.

101. Ballard, *Vicksburg*, p. 379.

102. *Charleston Mercury*, September 5, 1863.

103. [Miller], "A Woman's Diary," p. 774.

104. *New York Herald*, July 9, 1863; July 10, 1863; July 12, 1863.

105. Quotations, in order, *New York Herald*, July 12, 1863; July 8, 1863.

106. *Chicago Tribune*, July 25, 1863.

107. *New York Herald*, July 15, 1863.

108. [Miller], "A Woman's Diary," p. 774.

109. *New York Herald*, July 15, 1863.

110. Gregory, "Vicksburg," p. 106.

111. "Letter of Grant to His Father, on the Capture of Vicksburg, 1863," *American Historical Review*, 12 (October 1906), p. 109. See also *Christian Recorder* (Philadelphia), May 2, 1889.

112. *Charleston Mercury*, March 22, 1864.

113. *Charleston Mercury*, August 18, 1863. By June 1865, gustatory normalcy had returned to the city. Food, good food, tasty food, was now available in Vicksburg's stores. Coffee, rice, tea, salt, whiskey, tobacco, and flour: these staples were now on the shelves. But so, too, were mustard, sugar-cured hams, and dried apples. And as was pointed out, this food was "fresh." And for all intents and purposes, Yankee. John J. Robacher to "Cap. Hall," Rodney, June 29, 1865, John J. Robacher and family correspondence, MDAH.

114. Gregory, "Vicksburg," quotation on pp. 107–108. See also [Loughborough], *My Cave Life in Vicksburg*, pp. 12, 22, 60.

115. Quoted in Ballard, *Vicksburg*, p. 349.

116. [Loughborough], *My Cave Life in Vicksburg*, p. 114.

117. [Loughborough], *My Cave Life in Vicksburg*, p. 82.

118. Quoted in Ballard, *Vicksburg*, p. 399.

119. Ballard, *Vicksburg*, p. 384; [Loughborough], *My Cave Life in Vicksburg*, p. 138.

Chapter Five

1. Report of Lieutenant Higginson, US Navy, of the U.S.S. *Canandaigua*, February 18, 1864, *Official Records of the Union and Confederate Navies in the War of Rebellion*, ser. 1, vol. 15, South Atlantic Blockading Squadron from October 1, 1863, to September 30, 1864 (Washington, D.C.: Government Printing Office, 1902), p. 328 (hereafter *OFCUN*). On water conditions, see, too, Order of Rear-Admiral Dahlgren, U.S. Navy, Flag-Steamer *Philadelphia*, Port Royal Harbor, S.C., February 19, 1864, *OFCUN*, ser. 1, vol. 15, p. 331.

2. On Union knowledge of the *Hunley*, see Tom Chaffin, *The H. L. Hunley: The Secret Hope of the Confederacy* (New York: Hill & Wang, 2008), p. 172.

3. Order of Rear-Admiral Dahlgren, U.S. Navy, February 19, 1864, *OFUCN*, ser. 1, vol. 15, p. 330; Report of Lieutenant Higginson, U.S. Navy, of the U.S.S. *Canandaigua*, February 18, 1864, *OFUCN*, ser. 1, vol. 15, p. 328; Report of Rear-Admiral Dahlgren, U.S. Navy, February 19, 1864, *OFUCN*, ser. 1, vol. 15, p. 329; Proceedings of a court of enquiry convened on board the U.S.S. *Wabash*, February 26, 1864, *OFUCN*, ser. 1, vol. 15, p. 333; extract from the *Charleston Daily Courier*, February 29, 1864, *OFUCN*, ser. 1, vol. 15, pp. 336–337.

4. On the design of the boat, see Chaffin, *The H. L. Hunley*, pp. 232–233.

5. On the ports and paint, see Chaffin, *The H. L. Hunley*, pp. 167, 233.

6. Chaffin, *The H. L. Hunley*, p. 172.

7. Chaffin, *The H. L. Hunley*, p. 168.

8. Chaffin, *The H. L. Hunley*, pp. 233–234; author's interview with Johanna Rivera, Conservator, Archaeological Materials, Collections Manager, Warren Lasch Conservation Center, Clemson University Restoration Institute, June 28, 2013.

9. Letter from captain [M. M.] Gray [Captain in Charge of Torpedoes], C. S. Army, to Major-General Maury, C.S. Army, regarding the loss of the *H. L. Hunley* and its crew, Office Submarine Defenses, Charleston, S.C., April 29, 1864, *OFUCN*, ser. 1, vol. 15, p. 337.

10. Information on the crew is located at the Warren Lasch Conservation Center, Charleston, S.C.

11. G. T. Beauregard, Charleston, S.C., February 21, 1864, *OFUCN*, ser. 1, vol. 15, p. 336.

12. Author's interview with Johanna Rivera, June 28, 2013. Whether the handles were encased with a wooden or leather sheath is unclear simply because, as of this writing, the *Hunley* conservators have not yet removed the concrete-like sediment that built up on the crankshaft over the years.

13. J. H. Tomb, Notes from the First Assistant Engineer Tomb, C. S. Navy, regarding the submarine torpedo boat, Charleston, S.C., January, 1864[5], *OFUCN*, ser. 1, vol. 15, pp. 334–335.

14. Report of Lieutenant Higginson, U.S. Navy, of the U.S.S. *Canandaigua*, February 18, 1864, *OFUCN*, ser. 1, vol. 15, p. 328; proceedings of a court of enquiry convened on board the U.S.S. *Wabash*, February 26, 1864, *OFUCN*, ser. 1, vol. 15, p. 333; extract from the *Charleston Daily Courier*, February 29, 1864, *OFUCN*, ser. 1, vol. 15, pp. 336–337. For a different estimate of the timing—but still suggestive of the speed at which the object was closing in—see Report of Rear-Admiral Dahlgren, U.S. Navy, February 19, 1864, *OFUCN*, ser. 1, vol. 15, p. 329.

15. On British perceptions of submarines as unseemly and ungentlemanly because they were visually sneaky, note Michael Kozlowski, *The Long Patrol: The H. L. Hunley, Charleston and the Civil War* (n.c.: Lion, 2013), p. 11. On submarines and disguised explosives as "infernal" because they were visually dishonest, see Chaffin, *The H. L. Hunley*, pp. 32–33, 46–49.

16. Report of Rear-Admiral Dahlgren, U.S. Navy, Flag-Steamer Philadelphia, Port Royal Harbor, S.C., February 19, 1864, *OFCUN*, ser. 1, vol. 15, pp. 328–329; Order of Rear-Admiral Dahlgren, U.S. Navy, Flag-Steamer

Philadelphia, Port Royal Harbor, S.C., February 19, 1864, *OFCUN*, ser. 1, vol. 15, p. 331. On Dahlgren's worries about submerged craft and their threat to the blockade, see Kozlowski, *The Long Patrol*, p. 82.

17. E.S., On the Field near Sharpsburg, September 17, 1862, *New York Times*, Tuesday, September 23, 1862. On the greater incidence of wounds caused by bullets and artillery rather than bayonets at the Battle of the Wilderness, for example, see Brent Nosworthy, *The Bloody Crucible of Courage: Fighting Methods and Combat Experience of the Civil War* (New York: Basic Books, 2005).

18. "The Fight as Seen from Cummings' Point (from a special correspondent on Morris Island)," in *The Battle of Fort Sumter and First Victory of Southern Troops, April 13, 1861* . . . (Charleston, S.C.: Evans & Cogswell, 1861), p. 12.

19. Chester Barney, *Recollections of Field Service with the Twentieth Iowa Volunteers* (Davenport, Iowa: privately printed, 1865), p. 173.

20. "Notes of the War," *Charleston Mercury*, August 27, 1861.

21. Quoted in David A. Mindell, *Iron Coffin: War, Technology, and Experience aboard the USS Monitor* (Baltimore, Md.: Johns Hopkins University Press, 2012), p. 63.

22. Quoted in Mindell, *Iron Coffin*, p. 62.

23. Quotations in Mindell, *Iron Coffin*, pp. 63–64.

24. No sense has been more slighted than touch, even by historians of the sensate. See *Sensing the Past: Seeing, Hearing, Smelling, Tasting, and Touching in History* (Berkeley: University of California Press, 2008); David Chidester, "The American Touch: Tactile Imagery in American Religion and Politics," in *The Book of Touch*, ed. Constance Classen (New York: Berg, 2005), p. 61. Compared with literary, theoretical, sociological, and philosophical treatments of hapticity, historical work on the haptic generally is relatively rare, virtually all of it on European history, and a good deal of it indebted to literary scholars and historians of medicine. See Sander Gilman, "Touch, Sexuality, and Disease," in *Medicine and the Five Senses*, eds. W. F. Bynum and Roy Porter (Cambridge, England: Cambridge University Press, 1993), pp. 198–225; Sander L. Gilman, *Goethe's Touch: Touching, Seeing, and Sexuality* (New Orleans, La.: Graduate School of Tulane University, 1988); Marjorie O'Rourke Boyle, *Senses of Touch: Human Dignity and Deformity from Michelangelo to Calvin* (Boston: Brill, 1998); Laura Gowing, *Common Bodies: Women, Touch, and Power in Seventeenth-Century England* (New Haven, Conn.: Yale University Press, 2003); Elizabeth D. Harvey, ed.,

Sensible Flesh: On Touch in Early Modern Culture (Philadelphia: University of Pennsylvania Press, 2003). For literary and theoretical treatments, see, most obviously, Steven Connor, *The Book of Skin* (Ithaca, N.Y.: Cornell University Press, 2004); Santanu Das, *Touch and Intimacy in First World War Literature* (New York: Cambridge University Press, 2005). Note, too, Joy Parr, "Notes for a More Sensuous History of Twentieth-Century Canada: The Timely, the Tacit, and the Material Body," *Canadian Historical Review*, 82 (December 2001), p. 742. Thankfully, an excellent, recent study has done much to expand our understanding of the sense of touch. See Constance Classen, *The Deepest Sense: A Cultural History of Touch* (Urbana: University of Illinois Press, 2012).

25. On eating, see Jean-Louis Flandrin, "Distinctions through Taste," in *A History of Private Life*, vol. 3: *Passions of the Renaissance*, Roger Chartier, ed., trans. Arthur Goldhammer (Cambridge, Mass.: Belknap Press of Harvard University), p. 266.

26. John E. Crowley, *The Invention of Comfort: Sensibilities and Design in Early Modern Britain and Early America* (Baltimore, Md.: Johns Hopkins University Press, 2001), pp. 141, 142–143, 166–168, quotation on 142; "The Senses. II—Touch," *Harper's New Monthly Magazine*, 12, no. 68 (January 1856), pp. 179–185.

27. Mark M. Smith, *Sensing the Past: Seeing, Hearing, Smelling, Tasting, and Touching in History* (Berkeley: University of California Press, 2008). p. 107; Michael Zakim, *Ready-Made Democracy: A History of Men's Dress in the American Republic, 1760–1860* (Chicago: University of Chicago Press, 2003).

28. Ruth Finnegan, "Tactile Communication," in *The Book of Touch*, ed. Constance Classen (New York: Berg, 2005), pp. 20–21; Richard Bauman, *Let Your Words Be Few: Symbolism of Speaking and Silence among Seventeenth-Century Quakers* (Cambridge, England: Cambridge University Press, 1983), p. 47. Touch was deployed by presidents in the twentieth century, none more obviously than Bill Clinton. In the early 1990s, he offered America the "New Covenant" as his slogan, one aiming to repair "the damaged bond" between the people and their government. Clinton was so haptically inclined that he derided openly "the vision thing" of George H. W. Bush as somehow unreliable and inauthentic. And then there was touching of another kind, that of a White House intern. See the superb analysis offered by Chidester, "The American Touch," pp. 52–53.

29. "Table-Talk," *Appleton's Journal: A Magazine of General Literature*, vol. 4, no. 81 (October 15, 1870), p. 473; "Hand-Shaking," *Harper's Weekly*, May 21, 1870, no pagination, online at Harpweek, http://app.harpweek.com; Alain Corbin, *Time, Desire, and Horror: Towards a History of the Senses*, trans. Jean Birrell (Cambridge, England: Polity, 1995), pp. 191–192. Shaking hands incorrectly within American culture betrayed inner character traits, flaws, and weaknesses, and, as such, the practice was politically risky. Refusing to shake hands was the greatest offense, a "declaration of hostility," no less. But pressing the flesh had to be done with care. Too tight a grip indicated "tyranny," a product of either unwitting strength or malicious intent. More "odious" was "he who offers you his hand, but will not permit you to get fair hold of it," reflecting "cool contempt or supercilious scorn." "Hand-Shaking," *Harper's Weekly*, May 21, 1870, no pagination, online at HarpWeek, http://app.harpweek.com.

30. Quotations, in order: William Jackson Palmer, "Underground Walks in England: The Black Country,' No. 7," *Miner's Journal* (Pottsville, Pa.), November 10, 1855, pp. 24–25; William Jackson Palmer, "Underground Walks in England: The Black Country,' No. 2," *Miner's Journal* (Pottsville, Pa.), August 18, 1855. See also Thomas G. Andrews, *Killing for Coal: America's Deadliest Labor War* (Cambridge, Mass.: Harvard University Press, 2008).

31. Alexander Falconbridge, *Late Surgeon in the African Trade, an Account of the Slave Trade on the Coast of Africa* (London: J. Phillips, 1788), pp. 20, 24, 25, 28.

32. Description of clothing based on author's interview with Johanna Rivera, June 28, 2013.

33. On the "primitive" technology of the hand-powered gin in the 1860s, see Angela Lakwete, *Inventing the Cotton Gin: Machine and Myth in Antebellum America* (Baltimore, Md.: Johns Hopkins University Press, 2003), pp. 182–183 esp. On early gin technology in the Old South and the use of the hand-powered crank, see Karen G. Britton, *Bale o' Cotton: The Mechanical Art of Cotton Ginning* (College Station: Texas A&M University Press, 1992), pp. 13–15.

34. Report of Lieutenant Higginson, U.S. Navy, of the U.S.S. *Canandaigua*, February 18, 1864, *OFUCN*, ser. 1, vol. 15, p. 328; extract from the *Charleston Daily Courier*, February 29, 1864, *OFUCN*, ser. 1, vol. 15, pp. 336–337.

35. Chaffin, *The H. L. Hunley*, p. 233; Friends of the Hunley, "The Spar," www.hunley.org/main_index.asp?CONTENT=THESPAR.

36. See Kozlowski, *The Long Patrol*, pp. 82–83.

37. Report of Lieutenant Higginson, U.S. Navy, of the U.S.S. *Canandaigua*, February 18, 1864, *OFUCN*, ser. 1, vol. 15, p. 328; Report of Rear-Admiral Dahlgren, U.S. Navy, February 19, 1864, *OFUCN*, ser. 1, vol. 15, p. 329; Proceedings of a court of enquiry convened on board the U.S.S. *Wabash*, February 26, 1864, *OFUCN*, ser. 1, vol. 15, p. 333. A later report suggests that the *Housatonic*, in trying to back away, succeeded merely in colliding with the *Hunley*. Extract from the *Charleston Daily Courier*, February 29, 1864, *OFUCN*, ser. 1, vol. 15, p. 336.

38. According to Captain Green, U.S. Navy, commanding U.S.S. *Canandaigua*, February 18, 1864, *OFUCN*, ser. 1, vol. 15, p. 327. Other reports say "about" 9 P.M. See Report of Rear-Admiral Dahlgren, U.S. Navy, February 19, 1864, *OFUCN*, ser. 1, vol. 15, p. 329.

39. Report of Captain Green, U.S. Navy, commanding U.S.S. *Canandaigua*, February 18, 1864, *OFUCN*, ser. 1, vol. 15, p. 328; Report of Lieutenant Higginson, U.S. Navy, of the U.S.S. *Canandaigua*, February 18, 1864, *OFUCN*, ser. 1, vol. 15, p. 328.

40. Extract from the *Charleston Daily Courier*, February 29, 1864, OFUCN, ser. 1, vol. 15, p. 337.

41. C. C. Fulton, [Telegram], Baltimore, March 2, 1864, OFUCN, ser. 1, vol. 15, p. 332.

42. J. H. Tomb, Notes from the First Assistant Engineer Tomb, C.S. Navy, regarding the submarine torpedo boat, Charleston, S.C., January, 1864[5], *OFUCN*, ser. 1, vol. 15, pp. 334–335.

43. Brian Hicks and Schuyler Kropf, *Raising the Hunley: The Remarkable History and Recovery of the Lost Confederate Submarine* (New York: Random House, 2002), pp. 60–61.

44. J. H. Tomb, Notes from the First Assistant Engineer Tomb, C.S. Navy, regarding the submarine torpedo boat, Charleston, S.C., January, 1864[5], *OFUCN*, ser. 1, vol. 15, pp. 334–335. See, too, Craig L. Symonds, *The Civil War at Sea* (New York: Oxford University Press, 2012), p. 50. Regarding the positions of the crew members: Dixon was found at his station because his body was the first to become silted. The skeletons of the other crew are slightly mingled because their bodies were not covered with silt as quickly and became waterlogged. Their bodies floated, and their bones then settled on the floor of the sub. But the small extent of the intermingling suggests that each man remained at his post. Author's interview with Johanna Rivera, June 28, 2013.

Epilogue

1. An exceptional treatment of Sherman's army and march, one wholly attuned to the experience of it, is Joseph T. Glatthaar, *The March to the Sea and Beyond: Sherman's Troops in the Savannah and Carolinas Campaigns* (Baton Rouge: Louisiana State University Press, 1985), pp. xii–xiii esp.

2. Grant to Sherman, April 4, 1865, *War of the Rebellion: Official Records of the Union and Confederate Armies* (70 vols. in 128; Washington, D.C., 1880–1901) ser. 1, vol. 32, pt. 3, pp. 245–246. While present throughout the war, as Mark Grimsley and, more recently, Megan Kate Nelson, have brilliantly shown, the determination to ruin Southern whites took on pronounced intensity during the march. Mark Grimsley, *The Hard Hand of War: Union Military Policy toward Southern Civilians 1861–1865* (New York: Cambridge University Press, 1995); Megan Kate Nelson, *Destruction and the American Civil War* (Athens: University of Georgia Press, 2012), pp. 61–97 esp.

3. Glatthaar, *March to the Sea*, p. 7.

4. Glatthaar, *March to the Sea*, pp. 8–11.

5. Glatthaar, *March to the Sea*, pp. 12–13.

6. Quotations from Glatthaar, *March to the Sea*, pp. 6–7.

7. Glatthaar, *March to the Sea*, p. 17.

8. Glatthaar, *March to the Sea*, pp. 41–42.

9. Quoted in Glatthaar, *March to the Sea*, p. 82.

10. Burke Davis, *Sherman's March* (New York: Vintage, 1988), quotation on p. 147.

11. Quoted in Glatthaar, *March to the Sea*, pp. 67, 71.

12. Glatthaar, *March to the Sea*, p. 62.

13. Glatthaar, *March to the Sea*, p. 108.

14. Glatthaar, *March to the Sea*, pp. 32–33.

15. E. C. Dawes Diary, Box 2, Folder 76, July 21, 1864, Newberry Library, Chicago [hereafter NL].

16. Glatthaar, *March to the Sea*, pp. 35–38.

17. Glatthaar, *March to the Sea*, p. 114 (first quotation), p. 117 (second quotation), and also p. 115.

18. Glatthaar, *March to the Sea*, pp. 22, 25, 27.

19. Glatthaar, *March to the Sea*, pp. 82–83, 108–109.

20. Glatthaar, *March to the Sea*, p. 19.

21. Glatthaar, *March to the Sea,* quotations, in order, pp. 6–7, 92, 38. See, too, p. 102.

22. Glatthaar, *March to the Sea,* pp. 27–28, 71–72.

23. Glatthaar, *March to the Sea,* pp. 7, 12.

24. E. C. Dawes Diary, July [19?], 1864, NL.

25. Quotations in Glatthaar, *March to the Sea,* pp. 78–79.

26. Davis, *Sherman's March,* p. 97, p. 149 (first quotation), p. 107 (second quotation).

27. Because most men of fighting age were away at war and because lots of people fled long before Sherman's army descended on their town, the troops had relatively little to do with Southern whites on the march. When they did, they tended to encounter mostly women. The most protracted encounters took place in the larger Southern cities. See Glatthaar, *March to the Sea,* pp. 66–67.

28. Glatthaar, *March to the Sea,* p. 70.

29. Glatthaar, *March to the Sea,* p. 71.

30. Quotation in Glatthaar, *March to the Sea,* p. 71.

31. Quoted in Davis, *Sherman's March,* p. 60. On the altered soundscape of Savannah, see the magisterial treatment offered in Jacqueline Jones, *Saving Savannah: The City and the Civil War* (New York: Alfred A. Knopf, 2008).

32. Davis, *Sherman's March,* p. 95; John G. Barrett, *Sherman's March through the Carolinas* (Chapel Hill: University of North Carolina Press, 1956), p. 96.

33. Davis, *Sherman's March,* p. 96. On the sound of axes in Americans' taming of the howling wilderness, see Mark M. Smith, *Listening to Nineteenth-Century America* (Chapel Hill: University of North Carolina Press, 2001).

34. Glatthaar, *March to the Sea,* p. 37.

35. Glatthaar, *March to the Sea,* quotations, in order, pp. 112, 150.

36. David Power Conyngham, *Sherman's March through the South with Sketches and Incidents of the Campaign* (New York: Sheldon, 1865), p. 328; Davis, *Sherman's March,* pp. 62, 166.

37. Davis, *Sherman's March,* pp. 145–146, quotations on p. 146.

38. Quotation in Davis, *Sherman's March,* p. 63.

39. Emma LeConte, Diary, 1864–1865, pp. 28, 35, http://docsouth.unc.edu/fpn/leconteemma/leconte.html.

40. Davis, *Sherman's March*, p. 79; LeConte, Diary, 1864–1865, pp. 70, 43.

41. Quotation in Davis, *Sherman's March*, p. 67.

42. The debate over whether we might reasonably characterize the Civil War as a "total war" is, of course, complicated and hardly resolved. I remain sympathetic to the position argued by James McPherson in his chapter "From Limited War to Total War," where he stresses the importance of Sherman's war on civilians in realizing total war. See McPherson, *Drawn with the Sword: Reflections on the American Civil War* (New York: Oxford University Press, 1996). Understood from a sensory perspective, the march certainly has a "total" feel to it.

43. Glatthaar, *March to the Sea*, p. 139. Sherman's men literally carried the smell of war on their bodies. The smell of burnt pine infused their blankets and uniforms. Smoky blankets helped contain lice; burnt cities helped contain rebels; both must have lent the Union troops a burned air, almost sulfurous to the noses of Confederate civilians. Glatthaar, *March to the Sea*, p. 83.

44. Glatthaar, *March to the Sea*, p. 142; Smith, *Listening to Nineteenth-Century America*; Lisa M. Brady, *War upon the Land: Military Strategy and the Transformation of Southern Landscapes during the American Civil War* (Athens: University of Georgia Press, 2012), pp. 130–131 esp.

45. Quotation in Glatthaar, *March to the Sea*, p. 136. See also p. 149.

46. Quoted in Glatthaar, *March to the Sea*, p. 145.

47. Elizabeth Waties Allston Pringle, *The Chronicles of Chicora Wood* (New York: Charles Scribner's Sons, 1922), p. 241; Davis, *Sherman's March*, pp. 77, 79.

48. Quoted in Glatthaar, *March to the Sea*, p. 133. To be sure, no process, not even as one as focused as total war, sweeps clean. Instances of Union troops sharing food with Southern whites can be found. Human dignity and mutual respect sometimes trumped war, and army rations were sometimes shared with rebel enemies. This was all the more remarkable since Union troops sometimes encountered, as they did in Columbia, South Carolina, Union prisoners of war who told Sherman's men how they had been virtually starved and maltreated in the Confederate prison there. Civility was not entirely eclipsed by this brutal war. See Glatthaar, *March to the Sea*, p. 74.

49. Daniel Heyward Trezevant, *The Burning of Columbia, South Carolina. A Review of Northern Assertions and Southern Facts* (Columbia: South Carolinian Power Press, 1866), p. 10; Davis, *Sherman's March*, p. 59; Glatthaar, *March to the Sea*, pp. 73–74, 87.

50. Quotation in Glatthaar, *March to the Sea,* p. 53. Sherman himself was not unsympathetic to the slaves, but he certainly saw their numbers as problematic from a purely military, not racial, standpoint. When approaching Savannah, he wrote that he "had at least 20,000 negroes, clogging my roads, and eating up our subsistence." He added: "The same number of white refugees would have been a military weakness." Quoted in Noah Andre Trudeau, *Southern Storm: Sherman's March to the Sea* (New York: HarperCollins, 2008), p. 519.

51. Glatthaar, *March to the Sea,* pp. 54–59.

52. Glatthaar, *March to the Sea,* pp. 60–61, 63.

53. Davis, *Sherman's March,* pp. 91–93.

54. Quotations, in order: Davis, *Sherman's March,* p. 170; LeConte, Diary, pp. 31–32. See also p. 48.

55. Quoted in Davis, *Sherman's March,* pp. 62, 162, 168. See also Sewell S. Farwell, "Letter of Major S. S. Farwell to His Home Paper from the Field," *The Annals of Iowa, a Historical Quarterly,* 15 (July 1925), p. 63.

INDEX

Page numbers followed by *f* indicate figures. Numbers followed by n indicate notes. Numbers in *italics* indicate maps.

abuse, 143–144
acoustic shadows, 3–4
aesthetic taste, 2
Africans, 45
Alabama, Fourth, 57
Alabama Fourth, 64–65
Alabama Sixth, 54
Alexander, E. Porter, 43–44
Alison, Joseph Dill, 108–109
American Hotel (Richmond, V.A.), 86–87
Anaconda, 115, 117
Anderson, Robert, 9–10, 25–30, 32, 34, 36–38, 40
Antietam, 123
Army of Georgia, 134–135
Army of Northern Virginia, 70
Army of the Potomac, 69–71
Asians, 45
Atlanta, Georgia, 134, 142
auditory revolution, 18
Australians, 45

Balfour, Emma, 87, 103–104
Barlow, Ida, 106
Barry, William F., 59, 61
Bartow, Francis S., 58
battle lines, 43
Battle of Gettysburg, 2, 7, 66–83, 76*f*, 82*f*
Battle of Iuka, 82–83
Bayley, Harrie Hamilton, 73
bayonets, 42
Beaufort, South Carolina, 135, 140
Beauregard, P. G. T., 31–32, 39–43, 52, 54–55
Becker, Arnold, 119, 132–133
Bee, Barnard E., 57–59
bees, 48
bells, 15–17, 23–24, 96–97, 144
Bigelow's (Ninth Massachusetts) Battery, 82*f*
Big Round Top, 69
birds, 34
blackberries, 94, 163n28

blacks, free, 11, 188n50

black voices, 145–146, 146*f*

blindness, 63

blue coats, 50, 53–55, 165n56

body odor, 2–3, 78, 117

bombs, 33–34, 49; mines, 136–137; stink bombs, 83

bonfires, 23–24

Bonham, 39

Bonner, William G., 45

brass bands, 19

Broadhead, Susan, 81

Brown & Kuhn, 88

buck fever, 53

Buell, Don Carlos, 27–28

bullets, 97

Bull Run: First Battle of, 7, 39–65, *41, 64f, 65f*

burials, 75–77, 76*f*, 82–83, 113, 170n34

Bush, George H. W., 182n28

buttons, 53

cadet gray, 165n54

Cameron, Simon, 165n56

Camp Beauregard, 51

Camp Pickens, 40

candles, 31

cannons, 48–49, 72

Carlsen, C. F., 120, 132–133

Carruth, Capt., 56–57

Cassler, John O., 53

Castle Pinckney, 24–26

casualties, 73

Catton, Bruce, 4–5

caves, 98–100, 123

Cemetery Ridge, 69, 74

Charleston, South Carolina, 9, 11–15, 154n1, 157n27;

evacuation of, 19; sounds of politics in, 21–22, 22*f*; sounds of secession in, 9–38, 20*f*; at war's end, 144–145, 145*f*

Charleston Courier, 10

Charleston Harbor, 11, *12,* 24–25, 37, 115

Charleston Mercury, 44, 63–64, 103, 110

cheering, 23–24, 30

Chesnut, James, 31–32

Chester, James, 51

chewing tobacco, 108

Chicago Tribune, 110–111

Child, Henry T., 71, 77

Chisholm, James A., 31–32

chloride of lime, 80

Clinton, Bill, 182n28

clocks, 15, 32

clothing, 126–128. *See also* uniforms

Cocke, 39

Collins, Frank, 119, 132–133

colors, 19, 50, 57–58, 61, 65; company, 53; flag, 50; uniform, 47, 53–56, 60–61, 63–65, 165n54, 165n56; Zouaves, 52, 54, 59–61

Columbia, South Carolina, 135, 139, 142, 143*f*

concealed batteries, 52–53

Confederate States Army: cadet gray, 165n54; uniforms, 50, 53–57, 60, 65, 165n54, 165n56, 165n60. *See also specific divisions*

Confederate States Navy, 31; *H. L. Hunley,* 7, 115–133, 118*f,* 121*f*

confusion, 60–63

cotton gins, 128, 129*f*

cotton swatches or strips, 58, 60

coup d'œil, 43, 46
Crawford, Samuel Wylie, 23–24, 27
Crosby, J. K., 115–116, 122,
    129–130
CSS *Virginia*, 124
Culp's Hill, 69, 73
Cummings, Arthur C., 60–62
Cummings Point, 33–35, 123

Dahlgren, John A., 122
dances, 14
darkness, 31, 55, 63, 98–100
Davidson, N., 79–80
Davis, Jefferson, 32, 69, 102
Dawes, Ephraim Cutler, 138
deaths, 70, 74; at Battle of
    Gettysburg, 75, 76*f*, 81, 82*f*;
    at First Battle of Bull Run,
    63, 64*f*
deception: feints, 59; female spies,
    164n46; visual, 52–53
Democratic convention, 19
demonstrations, 19
Devil's Den, 69
diet, 89–90, 110–111
digging, 98–99
Dixon, George, 118–119, 130–133,
    184n44
Doubleday, Abner, 19, 24, 28–29, 38
drums, 17, 30
dust, 48, 50, 53, 58

Early, Jubal, 39, 63
ear men, 45
East Cemetery Hill, 69
Emancipation Day, 145–146, 146*f*
Enlightenment, 43, 125
Europeans, 45
Evans, Nathan G., 39, 58

Ewell, Richard S., 39, 69
excitability, 26–27
explosions, 34
eye men, 45

Fairfax Station, Virginia, 39
famine, 101–102, 174n23
Faust, Drew Gilpin, 170n34
feints, 59
female spies, 164n46
field glasses, 45
field hospitals, 80, 170n35
fifers, 30
fire, 23–24, 142
fire-bells, 163n25
fireworks, 81
First Battle of Bull Run, 7, 39–65,
    41, 64*f*, 65*f*
Fisher, C. P., 164n41
flag colors, 50
flags, 19, 30, 56, 60–61, 63; Stars
    and Stripes, 36; Union, 141
flag signals, 25–26, 43–44, 63
Florida, Spanish, 16
food, 162n18, 163n28; mule meat,
    108–112, 178n94; peace for,
    105–106; rations, 105–108,
    117, 138, 177n88; rat meat,
    178n94; during siege of
    Vicksburg, 86–94, 101, 104–106;
    soldiers' rations, 117; Southern
    cuisine, 86–88, 91, 110–111, 138
food exchanges, 177–178n89
food riots, 176n58
food shortages, 101–102, 105,
    174n19
Foote, Shelby, 4–5
Fort Johnson, 28
Fort Moultrie, 9–10, 19–20, 24–30

Fort Sumter, 7, 10, 24–26; bombardment of, 31–38, 35*f*; occupation of, 28–29
Fourth Alabama, 57
Fourth of July celebrations, 19
free blacks, 11, 188n50
freedom: sensory signatures of, 144; sounds of, 145–146, 146*f*
friendly fire, 61, 63

Gardner, Alexander, 75, 76*f*
gaslights, 23–24, 154n1
General Clinch, 29
German migrant workers, 11
Germantown, Georgia, 138
Gettysburg, Pennsylvania, 69; Battle of Gettysburg, 2, 7, 66–83, 76*f*, 82*f*; population, 70
Gist, William Henry, 18
Gorman, Willis, 61–62
Grant, Ulysses S., 91–105, 110, 112, 134
graves, 170n34
gray uniforms, 50, 53–57, 60, 65, 165n56, 165n60; cadet gray, 165n54; "Napoleon in Gray," 40
Gregg, John C., 48
Griffin, Charles, 59, 61–62
gunfire, 97; friendly fire, 61, 63; night firing, 51
guns, 97
gustatory taste, 2, 89, 101, 107, 179, n113

H. L. Hunley, 7, 115–133, 118*f*, 121*f*, 184n37
Hagood, Johnson, 34
"Hail, Columbia," 145–146
Hampton, Wade III, 58

Hancock, Cornelia, 66–67, 68*f*, 71, 77–79, 81, 167n2
handshaking, 126, 183n29
Hardeeville, South Carolina, 141
Harper's New Monthly Magazine, 1, 14, 45–46, 66–67, 89
hats, 19
Hawthorne, Nathaniel, 125
hearing. *See* sounds
heat, 47
height, average, 169n24
Heintzelman, Samuel P., 61–62
Henry House Hill, 57–58, 61–62
Hill, A. P., 69
Hilliard, Miriam Brannin, 88
history, sensory, 5, 8, 150, 151, 152
Hôtel de Vicksburg, 111
Hudson, Edward, 165n60
human contact, 125–126
hunger, 102–103, 106–107, 113, 139
Hunley, Horace, 117–118
Hunter, Alexander, 47, 56
hush arbors, 17
hygiene, personal, 2, 78, 171n36

Inglis, Chancellor, 22–23
Institute Hall (Secession Hall) (Charleston, S.C.), 20–23, 22*f*
intelligence, 32, 47
intimacy, 123, 125–127
Irish migrant workers, 11
Iuka: Battle of, 82–83

Jackson, Stonewall, 43, 58–60
James Island, 34
Jamison, D. F., 23
John, Samuel D., 64–65
Johnston, Joseph E., 59, 110
Jomini, Antoine Henri, 43, 160n6

Jones, D. R., 39

Kemble, Fanny, 16–17
Kershaw, J. B., 52, 55–56
Keyes, Erasmus D., 62

lamplight, 125
Lanier, Eliza Ann, 94
LeConte, Emma, 141
Lee, Robert E., 135; at Battle of
    Gettysburg, 69–70, 73, 75;
    at First Battle of Bull Run,
    39–40
Lee, Stephen Dill, 32–33
Lexington, South Carolina, 135
lighting: candles, 31; gaslights,
    23–24, 154n1; lamplight, 125;
    streetlights, 154n1
lime: chloride of, 80
Lincoln, Abraham, 18–19, 43
Little Round Top, 69
Longstreet, James, 39, 69
lookouts, 43–44, 47
Loughborough, Mary Ann
    Webster, 113
Louisiana, First, 54
Lumpkin, 119, 132–133

Macon, Georgia, 135
Magrath, A. G., 21
Manigault, Margaret Izard, 16
martial sounds, 30–31
masked batteries, 52–53
Massachusetts, First, 56–57
Massachusetts, Ninth, 82*f*
mass graves, 170n34
mass rallies, 19
Matthews Hill, 59, 63, 64*f*
Mayo, Perry, 164n47

McDowell, Irvin, 39, 42–43, 54–55,
    57, 63
McKay, Charlotte, 70–71
Meade, George G., 69
Michigan, First, 56–57
military batteries: Bigelow's (Ninth
    Massachusetts) Battery, 82*f*;
    masked, 52–53
military drills, 19, 27
Milledgeville, Georgia, 135
Miller, 120, 132–133
Miller, Dora Richards, 96, 98,
    102–103, 107, 109–111
Miller, George, 48
mines, 136–137
Mitchell's Ford, 44
Mobile, Alabama, 102
modernization, 167n6
morale effects, 31
Morris Island, 33, 123
mortar shells, 33
mule meat, 108–112, 178n94
music, 19, 30, 33–34, 47

Natchez, Mississippi, 86
Native Americans, 45
"New Covenant," 182n28
New Jersey, Twelfth, 78–79
New Orleans, Louisiana, 87
New York Eleventh, 59
New York Fourteenth, 60
New York Herald, 79–80, 110,
    176n62
New York Seventeenth, 162n18
New York Sixty-Ninth, 55, 57
night, 31
night firing, 51
noise, 15, 19, 21–23, 29, 96
noiseless movement, 17

nose men, 45
noses, 66–68, 68*f*

odors, 65–83, 170n30; body odor,
2–3, 78, 117; stenches, 82–83,
113, 116, 142; stink bombs, 83
Oken, Lorenz, 45
Old Sherman's Smokehouse
Rangers, 142
opera glasses, 45
oratory, 18–19, 27
Ordinance of Secession (South
Carolina), 23–24
O'Sullivan, Timothy H., 75, 81, 82*f*
"Our Homes," 58

pastoral sounds, 49
peace for food, 105–106
Peach Orchard, 69
Pemberton, John C., 95, 102, 110,
112, 176n62
Pennsylvania College Hospital, 80
personal hygiene, 2, 78, 171n36
Pickens, Francis W., 23
Pickett, George, 69–70, 74
Pioneer, 117
Pitts, Thomas, 47
police, 16
Porter, J.L., 76
postmortems: Battle of Gettysburg,
75, 76*f*, 81, 82*f*; First Battle of
Bull Run, 63, 64*f*
Potter, W. W., 71–72
prisoners of war, 4, 55, 137,
187n48

Quakers, 126
quick look, 43
quiet, 17, 24, 28–29, 33

Quigg's Bakery (Vicksburg,
Miss.), 88

railroad, 47
rallies, 19
rape, 143–144
rations, 105–108, 117, 138, 177n88
rat meat, 178n94
reconnoiter, 43
re-enactments, 2–4
retreat, 103–104
Revolutionary War, 19
revolutions, 18–19
Richmond, Virginia, 101
Ridgaway, Joseph, 120–121,
132–133
riots, 176n58
rockets, 23–24
Ruffin, Edmund, 18

sanitation, 169n30
Savannah, Georgia, 135
scents, protective, 80–81. *See also*
odors; smells
Scott, Winfield, 26
secession: Ordinance of Secession
(South Carolina), 23–24; sounds
of, 9–38, 20*f*; South Carolina
Secession Convention, 20–23,
22*f*, 23–24
Secession Hall (Institute Hall)
(Charleston, S.C.), 20–23, 22*f*
Seminary Ridge, 69, 74
sensory experience: 1852
knowledge and understanding of,
1–2; re-enactments, 3–4
sensory historians, 5, 152
sensory overload, 48
shadows, acoustic, 3–4

Sharpsburg, 123
shells, 31, 34, 49, 72, 96
Sherman, Ambrose, 55, 57
Sherman, William Tecumseh, 49, 134–137, 188n50
Sherman's bummers, 143
Sherman's march, 134–144, 143f, 185n2, 187nn42–43, 188n50
shouting, 18–19, 23–24
Shute's Folly, 24–25
Sibley tents, 51
sightlines, 42
sights: blindness, 63; *coup d'œil*, 43, 46; of First Battle of Bull Run, 39–65; importance of, 136–137; visual confusion, 60; visual deception, 52–53, 59, 164n46; visual signals, 58–59
signals, 43–44, 60
silence, 28–29, 144; quiet, 17, 24, 28–29, 33; of surrender, 37, 111
Simms, William Gilmore, 14
Singer torpedo, 130
singing, 47, 96–97
skin men, 45
slavery, 14–15, 17–18, 24, 86, 128, 129f
slaves, 11, 144
slave ships, 127
sloganeering, 19
"smelling the powder," 73–74, 168n18
smells, 65–83, 170n30; body odor, 2–3, 78, 117; control of, 77–78; protective, 80–81; stenches, 82–83, 113, 116, 142; stink bombs, 83
Smith, William, 56–57
smoke, 37–38, 47, 50, 53, 58, 141

songs, 47, 96–97; "Yankee Doodle," 38, 50, 140, 145–146
sounds: auditory revolution, 18; of cannon, 72; of coming army, 140; of freedom, 145–146, 146f; martial, 30–31; pastoral, 49; of politics, 21–22, 22f; of reinforcements, 47; of revolution, 18; of secession, 9–38, 20f; of siege, 96–97; of slavery, 17–18, 24; of war, 34, 35f, 38, 47–48, 50, 74, 136; of war preparations, 30–31
South Carolina, 138; Emancipation Day, 145–146, 146f; Ordinance of Secession, 23–24; Secession Convention, 20–23, 22f, 23–24
Southern cuisine, 86–88, 91, 110–111, 138
Southern Episcopalian, 14
Southern women, 136, 139–140, 143, 186n27
Spanish Florida, 16
spectators, 45, 161n12
speeches, 18–19, 27
spies, 164n46
St. Andrew's Hall (Charleston, S.C.), 21
St. Michael's (Charleston, S.C.), 15
St. Philip's (Charleston, S.C.), 15, 20–21
Stars and Stripes, 36
"Star-Spangled Banner," 30
starvation, 94–95, 101–106, 139, 174n19
stealth, 28–29
stench, 82–83, 113, 116, 142
Stevens, Major, 38
stink bombs, 83

Stirling, James, 157n27
Stone (Union surgeon), 55–56
Stono Insurrection, 16
streetlights, 154n1
streets, 157n27
Stuart, J.E.B., 60–61, 70
submarines: *H. L. Hunley*, 7,
    115–133, 118*f*, 121*f*
Sullivan's Island, 9, 24–25
"Sumter," 60
surrender, 37, 111
Surtees, William, 13
sweat, 47, 116

tactile force, 3
tastes, 88–89, 108; aesthetic, 2;
    gustatory, 2; judgment of, 3;
    meanings of, 89; of Southern
    cuisine, 86–88, 91, 110–111, 138;
    tongue men, 45
tattoos, 33–34, 47
tents, 51
Thompson, John, 28–29
tobacco, 107–108, 177–178n89
Tomb, J. H., 131
tongue, 89–90
tongue men, 45
torching, 142
torpedoes, 136–137
torpedos, 130
total war, 7, 134–146, 187n42
touch, 2–3, 125–127, 181n24,
    182n28, 183n29
towers, 43–44
trains, 47
"Trans-Mississippi West," 112–113
trenches, 98–99, 99*f*, 109, 123, 135
Trotter, Ida Barlow, 94
Tyler, Daniel, 47

uniforms, 47, 60–61, 63–65; blue
    coats, 50, 53–55, 165n56; grays,
    50, 53–57, 60, 65, 165n54,
    165n56, 165n60; Zouaves, 52,
    54, 59–61
Union Army. *See* United States
    Army
Union flag, 141
Unionists, 19
United States Army, 136; uniforms,
    54–55, 165n56. *See also specific
    divisions*
United States Artillery, Fifth, 59
USS *Canandaigua*, 131
USS *Housatonic*, 115–116, 122,
    129–131, 184n37
USS *Monitor*, 124–125

Vesey, Denmark, 16
Vicksburg, Mississippi, 84–87,
    113–114, 172n1; siege of, 7,
    83–114, 85, 93*f*, 99*f*, 123
Vicksburg Daily Citizen, 97
Virginia Forty-Ninth, 56
Virginia Thirty-Third, 60–61
visual confusion, 60–65
visual deception, 52, 59, 164n46;
    concealed batteries, 52–53; *coup
    d'œil*, 43, 46; photographic,
    63, 64*f*
visual signals, 58–59
visual technology, 6–7

war: colors of, 65; Enlightenment
    approach to, 43; "smelling the
    powder," 73–74, 168n18; sounds
    of, 34, 35*f*, 36–38, 47–48; total, 7,
    134–146, 187n42
war policy, 93–94

war preparations, 30–31
Warren, Robert Penn, vii
Washington Hotel (Vicksburg, Miss.), 88
Washington Light Infantry, 20*f*
watchwords, 58
water, 109
Welles, Gideon, 91
West Point, 160n6
Wheatfield, 69
white Southern women, 136, 139–140, 143, 186n27
Wicks, James A., 120, 132–133

Wiley, Bell Irvin, 4–5, 165n56
Winnsboro, South Carolina, 135, 140
Wisconsin, Second, 56
women: spies, 164n46; white Southern, 136, 139–140, 143, 186n27. *See also individual women by name*

"Yankee Doodle," 38, 50, 140, 145–146

Zouaves, 52, 54, 59–61

9 780190 658526